Advance Praise for
From Richard Wright to Toni Morrison

"Jeffrey J. Folks's perspective on American fiction, especially Southern, has developed over the past two decades into a multifaceted view that with this book achieves that high seriousness one must demand of any book on ethics. He joins those valiant few, whose vanguard was led by the novelist and critic John Gardner, who insist neither aesthetics nor linguistics should dominate our perception of fiction. His case is made all the more powerful and useful by his choice of writers who are fine artists and by representing an unusually balanced mingling of male and female, African American and white writers. The desire of these writers to deal with those ethical issues that are grounded rather in our human nature and predicament than in transitory issues finds expression in works of art, even when the art is, as in the case of Agee's *Let Us Now Praise Famous Men,* generally considered to be flawed."

David Madden, Donald and Velvia Crumbley Professor
of Creative Writing, Louisiana State University

"Jeffrey J. Folks's *From Richard Wright to Toni Morrison: Ethics in Modern and Postmodern American Narrative* traces the return of literary criticism to the realities of human existence and survival. As a whole the essays communicate the fashion in which symbolic language from literature to music embodies the shared experience of the finite human community. Experiencing the shared suffering, we transcend the shackles of stasis and isolation to the joy of community and ethical realization."

Robert Reid, Professor and Chair,
Division of English and Applied Linguistics, University of Guam

From Richard Wright
to Toni Morrison

Modern American Literature
New Approaches

Yoshinobu Hakutani
General Editor

Vol. 25

PETER LANG
New York • Washington, D.C./Baltimore • Bern
Frankfurt am Main • Berlin • Brussels • Vienna • Oxford

Jeffrey J. Folks

From Richard Wright
to Toni Morrison

Ethics in Modern
& Postmodern
American Narrative

PETER LANG
New York • Washington, D.C./Baltimore • Bern
Frankfurt am Main • Berlin • Brussels • Vienna • Oxford

Library of Congress Cataloging-in-Publication Data

Folks, Jeffrey J. (Jeffrey Jay).
From Richard Wright to Toni Morrison: ethics in modern
and postmodern American narrative / Jeffrey J. Folks.
p. cm. — (Modern American literature; vol. 25)
Includes bibliographical references and index.
1. American fiction—20th century—History and criticism. 2. Ethics in
literature. 3. American fiction—Afro-American authors—History and criticism.
4. American fiction—Southern States—History and criticism. 5. Postmodernism
(Literature)—United States. 6. Modernism (Literature)—United States.
7. Southern States—In literature. 8. Afro-Americans in literature.
9. Narration (Rhetoric). 10. Race in literature. I. Title. II. Modern
American literature (New York, N.Y.); vol. 25.
PS374.E86 F65   813'.509353—dc21   00-041253
ISBN 0-8204-5105-3
ISSN 1078-0521

Die Deutsche Bibliothek-CIP-Einheitsaufnahme

Folks, Jeffrey J.:
From Richard Wright to Toni Morrison: ethics in modern
and postmodern American narrative / Jeffrey J. Folks.
–New York; Washington, D.C./Baltimore; Bern;
Frankfurt am Main; Berlin; Brussels; Vienna; Oxford: Lang.
(Modern American literature; Vol. 25)
ISBN 0-8204-5105-3

Cover design by Joni Holst

The paper in this book meets the guidelines for permanence and durability
of the Committee on Production Guidelines for Book Longevity
of the Council of Library Resources.

Printed in the United States of America

To Nance,

"infinitely loving,

and infinitely beloved"

Contents

Acknowledgments

I would like to express my appreciation to the many scholars who have contributed to my thinking on ethics and American narrative. These include my dissertation director, Professor James H. Justus, now retired from Indiana University; Professor Lewis P. Simpson, Boyd Professor Emeritus at Louisiana State University, whom I first met during a National Endowment for the Humanities Summer Seminar in 1979; and Professor Lucinda MacKethan, Professor of English at North Carolina State University, with whom I studied during a National Endowment for the Humanities Summer Institute in 1990. I have had the pleasure of working with many other colleagues on various projects and seminars, including Professors Martha E. Cook, James Grove, Sue Laslie Kimball, David Madden, Richard Marius, James A. Perkins, Robert Reid, Frank Shelton, and others too numerous to list. I am also grateful for the advice and insight of the editors of those journals in which a number of the chapters in this book first appeared: I would especially thank Professors Fred Hobson, Kimball King, Robert L. Phillips, Jr., and Stephen Flinn Young. Most of all, I am grateful, as always, for the wise counsel and loving support of my wife, Nancy Summers Folks.

A number of the chapters in this book first appeared in academic journals. I would like to acknowledge permission to reprint the following essays:

"'Last Call to the West': Richard Wright's *The Color Curtain*." Originally published in *South Atlantic Review* 59.4 (1994).

"James Agee's Quest for Forgiveness in *Let Us Now Praise Famous Men*." Originally published in *Southern Quarterly* 34.4 (1996).

"James Agee's Fashioning of Guilt: *The Morning Watch*." Originally published in *Southern Literary Journal* 29.1 (1996). Reprinted with the permission of the *Southern Literary Journal*.

"The Ideal of Community in Ernest J. Gaines's *A Gathering of Old Men*." Originally published in *South Carolina Review* 28.2 (1996).

Introduction

C. S. Lewis's description in *Surprised by Joy: The Shape of My Early Life* of his as a generation of "lapsed Protestants" (and of his own role as a "lapsed atheist" within this generation) is apt for this study, although with hindsight we might rather categorize the twentieth century as a whole, not merely Lewis's generation, as one of lapsed faith, at least among the intelligentsia if not among the public at large. In American culture, the century's landmark events—the Scopes "Monkey Trial" of 1925, the Dust Bowl and the Great Depression, World War II and the Holocaust, the civil rights movement, the war in Vietnam and the anti-war protests that accompanied it, the passage of and controversy surrounding the Supreme Court ruling in *Roe vs. Wade* in 1973, the public disillusionment following Watergate—may all be seen in hindsight as trials of the nation's shared values and beliefs.

As Lewis's discussion implies, Western intellectuals entered the century ill-prepared for the ordeals that were to come. In America, the lapse of common belief took the form, quite often, of a short-sighted anticlericalism, accompanied by a smug self-assurance in a future utopia based on technological progress and social freedom. In the post-World War I era, traditional ethical distinctions were undermined by a large number of writers, critics, and artists. Critics such as H. L. Mencken and George Jean Nathan derided conventional morality as "puritanical" and old-fashioned. In a trilogy of works on ethics (*Notes on Democracy*, 1926; *Treatise on the Gods*, 1930; *Treatise on Right and Wrong*, 1934), Mencken argued that democracy was a failed political system, that religion was an illusion, and that conventional notions of morality based on concepts of virtue or sin were unscientific and thus useless. As co-editor (with Nathan) of *The Smart Set* and *American Mercury*, Mencken urged public opinion toward a posture of moral skepticism, anticlericalism, and scientific rationalism. Both Mencken and Nathan brought to their writing a cosmopolitan "European" outlook as well as an elitist disdain for American democratic culture.

Among American novelists and playwrights, Sinclair Lewis, Theodore Dreiser, F. Scott Fitzgerald, and Eugene O'Neill were important figures in the reaction against Victorian standards of morality. In his best-known works, *Main Street* (1920) and *Babbitt* (1922), Lewis often satirized the moral restrictiveness of provincial American society. Unfortunately, the consequence for the postwar generation was a sweeping rejection of conventional sources of ethical understanding and a disdain for those institutions and communities that might support individuals in ethical decision making. The legacy of Mencken and Lewis has been generations of ethical confusion in which both questionable practices (the severe moral restrictions on personal freedom characteristic of Victorian morality) and valid sources of ethical identity (religious faith, regional and national identity, and conventional standards of respectability and conduct) have been discredited. As John Gardner wrote, "sophisticated modern free society tends to be embarrassed by the whole idea of morality and by all its antique, Platonic, or scholastic-sounding manifestations—Beauty, Goodness, Truth" (19). This posture of disdain for traditional sources of belief accompanied by naive self-assurance in modern science and technology arose forcefully in the decades after World War II. It could be said that as it faced each new national crisis, the American public was less well equipped in terms of ethical understanding: there was only the legacy of a now lapsed religious culture and the uncertain promise of a modern secularism.

Among most literary critics working in the period after World War II, ethical issues were avoided for similar reasons. The familiar New Critical dictum against authorial intrusion in narrative dates back to the criticism and practice of Henry James, Gustave Flaubert, and Joseph Conrad, yet this ideal of authorial distance and objectivity forecloses many forms of narrative that might address ethical issues in a direct way. The neglect of ethics as an approach to literature since the 1950s is attributable in part to a misapprehension that ethical readings are a violation of "art" (the almost sacred value of the text itself) or that they constitute an outdated and illiberal form of reading. In the place of ethical reading, most literary criticism in the past half-century has not departed from methodologies based on formalist, linguistic, and structuralist assumptions that largely exclude a consideration of moral principles. The formalism of the New Critics was succeeded by structuralist and myth criticism such as that of Northrop Frye—approaches that, however insightful, limited critical debate to overly determined frameworks of thinking that tended to avoid direct discussion of the re-lation of literature to particular historical communities. During the late 1960s and 1970s, poststructuralist critics such as Paul de Man and Hay-den White moved further away from humanistic modes of interpretation, asserting the absence of referentiality as they stressed the purely linguis-tic textuality of narrative discourse. During this period, to suggest that literature spoke to issues of virtue and conscience was to risk being taken as impossibly old-fashioned or critically naive.

Fortunately, during the 1990s many critics began to reconsider the nature of literature's relationship to human experience and to develop more contextualized and historicized approaches to reading texts. As a result significant new resources now exist for reading ethics in literature and in the humanities generally, a fact that was underscored by the ap-pearance of a special issue of *PMLA* (January 1999) devoted to "Ethics and Literary Study." Edited and introduced by Lawrence Buell, this worthwhile issue demonstrated the urgency of contemporary efforts to reinsert ethical discussion into literary interpretation. As Buell writes in his "Introduction": "Ethics has gained new resonance in literary studies during the past dozen years, even if it has not—at least yet—become the paradigm-defining concept that textuality was for the 1970s and histori-cism for the 1980s" (7). As Buell goes on to show, current thinking about ethical reading is "pluriform," deriving from many theoretical ori-gins and interests including: an "approach to literature as ethical reflection" in the tradition of Arnold and Leavis; "a moral or social-value approach to literary studies" as employed by Richard Rorty or Martha C. Nussbaum; "a defense [within deconstructionist criticism] of 'rigorous unreliability' in critical reading as itself an ethics" (including the "ethical turn" of Jacques Derrida's late writing); a new emphasis in Michel Foucault's later writing on "the care of the self conceived as an ethical project," accompanied by a reevaluation of the purported "cogni-tive skepticism" of earlier poststructuralism; a number of approaches to postcoloniality and subalternity; the influence of "increased self-consciousness about professional ethics" within the academy; and the ethical implications of the discussion of canon formation (Buell 7–16). Employing the resources of these various methodologies and approaches, and exhibiting the influence of such theorists as Derrida, Foucault, Em-manuel Levinas, Nussbaum, Paul Ricoeur, Rorty, and Gayatri Spivak, among others, the essays in this *PMLA* issue illustrate the possibilities of a new critical endeavor focused on ethics.

Among recent theorists of literature and ethics, the names of a number of other critics might be added to those listed above. In his many
books addressing, directly or indirectly, the effects of the Holocaust and
the ambiguities of modern political ethics, George Steiner has provided a
model for ethical criticism of a sort that is both eloquent and morally
responsible. Geoffrey Galt Harpham's articulate analysis of the ethics of
reading, *Getting It Right: Language, Literature, and Ethics* (1992), attempted a rigorous analytic study of the relation of textual interpretation
and ethics. More recently, Andrew Delbanco has studied the changing
conception of "evil" within American society in *The Death of Satan:
How Americans Have Lost the Sense of Evil* (1995). Perhaps the most
influential of recent books, however, have been Wayne C. Booth's *The
Company We Keep: An Ethics of Fiction* (1988) and Martha C. Nussbaum's *Love's Knowledge: Essays on Philosophy and Literature* (1990).
In these works, Booth and Nussbaum have presented insightful critiques
of previous theory and critical practice, and they have advanced a valuable analysis focusing especially on the relationship of form and content
in literary ethics. Nussbaum provides an incisive analysis of the neglect
of ethics in New Critical and poststructuralist literary theory: "one rarely
found anything but contempt for ethical criticism in literature," she notes
of the academic culture of that time (12–13). In particular, the influence
of poststructuralist theory was to repress interest in ethics, for "the views
that were then reigning [during the late 1960s and early 1970s]—as the
New Criticism waned and Deconstruction took over—continued to be
largely hostile to the idea of bringing a broad range of human concerns
into connection with literary analysis" (Nussbaum 21).

Booth's *The Company We Keep* also intends to supply an ethics of
narrative which has been ignored by a generation of formalists (a period
that included his own seminal work, *The Rhetoric of Fiction*). Actually,
Booth's book, at its crucial points of argument, appears to support the
formalist position—the idea that the "value" inherent in a literary work
rests in the "craft" or skill of its author. In sketching the process of
reading a literary work, such as a poem by Yeats, Booth notes that "we
are implicitly engaged in an act of ethical criticism inseparable from our
judgment of craft. As we stretch our own poetic character to meet the
implied character of the maker, we do not say that his craft is one thing
and his character another; instead we feel that we are meeting the character we take in the craft" (107). In its welding of ethics to formalist
concerns, Booth's theory continues to rely on the very formalist assump-

tions that have comprised a substantial portion of the resistance to ethics in criticism over the past sixty years. In this view, the author's dedication to craft is evidence of ethical devotion that must claim our admiration and influence our own reading.

The contributions of Booth and Nussbaum—in altering the cultural climate in which literary ethics is received and in offering thoughtful models of ethics-based interpretations—are significant. However, to a greater extent than Booth and Nussbaum, who view relationships between content and form as inseparable from any reading of ethics, I am more concerned with narrative content in itself and with its representation in terms of ethical meaning. Behind my concern lies, of course, a particular conception of the role of literature within society, of the ways in which literature affects readers, and of the nature of a just society—or in Nussbaum's terms, a conception of "how one should live" (23). My interests in southern literature and history, and in African American, immigrant, and postcolonial writing, have influenced my aesthetic assumptions, for in my reading of these cultures, each of them with legacies of long periods of struggle and deprivation, I find an urgent need to assign priority to narrative content itself—the versions of history that are represented in various ways in the lives of particular characters or communities. Because I am focused to a greater extent on populist and mass cultural aspects of literary culture, I am less convinced than are Booth and Nussbaum that the refinement of perception based on reading novels is an effective form of moral training.

In some important respects, the readings of Booth and Nussbaum open literary ethics to charges of elitism, for their ethics is not tied to the inherited moral traditions of a particular social community. The texts that they choose to examine (Henry James, Proust, Austen, and Woolf, among others) and the manner in which these texts are read (Booth's moral critique of Rabelais as offensive to women and of Twain's *Adventures of Huckleberry Finn* as racially tasteless) distance their criticism from mass consciousness, not so much in what they include (the controversial aspects of *Huckleberry Finn* are by now a critical commonplace) as in what they ignore. From the point of view of the general reader, Nussbaum's characterization of the pursuit of ethical knowledge as a search involving "mystery and indeterminacy" (47) would seem to avoid the inescapable needs of human beings for moral guidelines if not for actual "rules" of conduct. By stressing the "nonrepeatability" of ethical situations, especially those involved in relations of love and friendship, Nussbaum makes it difficult to validate the sort of "general rules" that may be necessary for a just and orderly existence in actual human communities. In everyday life one suspects that friendships are immured in circumstances that make their nature less nonrepeatable, and indeed it may be the common aspects of our existence that make for the possibility of meaningful forms of moral choice within a shared human community.

The basis for an ethics of literature is the recognition that a shared knowledge of moral conduct exists, that this ethical knowledge is necessary to the survival of human societies, and that the function of literature is to hold this knowledge clearly before our sight. To admit the priority of ethics does not diminish but enlarges the significance of literature, for within all civilizations literature has been the most important means of communicating shared ethical beliefs. Narrative literature, in particular, has been the means by which people have understood the shape of their lives and the nature of the human condition. Through storytelling, as Alasdair MacIntyre explains in *After Virtue: A Study in Moral Theory*, humans have gained a consciousness of their humanity and a recognition of the purposes of their cultural traditions. As the teacher of ethical tradition, literature has performed a function far greater than that imagined in formalist criticism.

It is possible of course to read literature as if it is not a representation of actual lived existence, as if the cold and wind of *Lear* had never chilled actual human beings, as if the poverty and bigotry of *Light in August* never existed in the American South (or elsewhere). In my view, however, it is only through what we, as particular human beings, have experienced and observed that we can comprehend the joys or hardships of others. Every impression that we gain from reading is understood as if it has happened or could happen to us, in the course of our lives, or to particular human beings whom we know or can imagine as actually living in the way that we live. The ethical value of literature lies in its ability to help us think about and feel, more than we otherwise might, the consequences of choices within our own lives and those of others. This ethical function allows readers to contemplate the effects of actions within the context of imagined lives and to understand aspects of our lives that may be overlooked or misunderstood. Most importantly, ethical reading focuses our attention on the particular shape of our lives; it requires us to concede the bounded potential of human existence, and in doing so, it impels us to respect the value of particular moments of life.

The difficulty with Booth's ethics of narrative in this respect is that, in its embrace of "pluralism" and the corollary that pluratic reading must be an unrestricted engagement with a wide range of disparate visions, it undermines the basis of an ethics rooted in the particularity of human existence. In place of meditation on mortality, Booth's theory substitutes a potentially endless series of encounters with new "friends" (the "implied authors" that Booth values as forming a Bakhtinian heteroglossic narrative). As Booth writes, "the serious ethical disasters produced by narratives occur when people sink themselves into an unrelieved hot bath of one kind of narrative.... [A] steady immersion at any age in any one author's norms is likely to be stultifying—even if they happen to be as broad and conventional as those of a Shakespeare or Tolstoy" (282). To this, one might ask whether the "steady immersion" of classical Greek civilization in Homer produced a "serious ethical disaster"? Or whether the immersion of Protestant Anglo-American culture in Miltonic thought was really so catastrophic? Even more serious, Booth's characterization of great authors within Western tradition as disparate "voices" occludes the fact that, to a great extent, these authors were in fact writing within a single tradition and that the "implied authors" in their works are not merely a collection of voices but part of a cultural tradition with shared assumptions and values. To read Shakespeare and Tolstoy, Austen and Twain, as distinct and separate ethical voices is a peculiarly modern project and one that judges the worth of literary works according to whether they meet the standards of our own taste while it strips the Western tradition, of which they are meaningful parts, of its authority.

While there may be a good deal of value in encountering different cultural perspectives in the way that Booth suggests, there is also danger in a theory that obscures those most crucial questions of ethics: what is the purpose of my life? What direction should my life take, given the limits of time and conditions that I take on with my birth? What should I honor and respect outside myself? In contrast with MacIntyre's profound reading of Aristotelian tradition, Booth's explication of Aristotle's conception of virtue is perfunctory, and it is revealing that Booth construes Aristotle's key conception of friendship in terms of "personal" relationship to the self, a valuing of the friend for his or her "own" qualities, for his or her own "self." As Booth writes, "we seek [friendship] *for the sake of the friendly company itself—the living in friendship.* Hours spent with this best kind of friend are seen as the way life should be lived" (173). In Booth's reading of Aristotle, friendship in itself, not its relation to the performance of moral duties or judgments, seems to be the ultimate value. More accurately, Aristotle's philosophy, as MacIntyre argues, values the friend as one engaged in a shared ethical quest: a common pursuit of the "good," a mutual affiliation with what are recognized as ethical purposes.

A key concept in Booth's ethics of reading is "coduction"—his term for the manner in which ethical judgments are produced by communities of readers over time (73). Booth conceives of ethical reading practice as a dialogue akin in some respects to Bakhtin's concept of heteroglossy, for in Booth's view ethical perceptions are the result of a discussion of ethics carried out by a multiplicity of voices. The difficulty with Booth's conception of coduction is that, in practice, it is hardly distinguishable from a short-term practice of literary politics. If ethics is whatever the majority agree it is, shifting within each period and culture to accommodate local preferences, there is no safeguard against the condoning of the most heinous moral acts by the literary establishment of a particular era: indeed, this is precisely George Steiner's reading of what took place within the academic and literary culture of Nazi Germany. Certainly the "coduction" of most German academics during the 1930s would not have extended much sympathy to Jewish citizens, as the expulsion of Jewish intellectuals from German universities early in the Nazi period demonstrated. In the same way, the coductions of our own cultural period afford no safeguards against distortions of ethics that, in the broader scheme of civilization, might be recognized as such. Booth's own model readings—of gender issues in Rabelais and of racial issues in Twain—are in themselves evidence of the limitations of an ethics of reading that adopts whatever current correctness prevails as the measure of "ethical truth." For many of the authors whom I choose to consider, the utility of Booth's (and Nussbaum's) emphasis on an ethics of "perception"—the basis of ethical action in the absence of general rules—is mitigated by a menacing social environment and by the burden of historical legacies. For authors such as Richard Wright, Flannery O'Connor, Ernest J. Gaines, and Kaye Gibbons, among others treated in this book, the force of history threatens to deprive their communities of a workable consensus as to even the most fundamental sorts of social identity and shared ethical assumptions. It is as a consequence of this deprivation that modern and postmodern American writing, particularly that of southern, African American, and immigrant authors, is engaged in a project of recovery of collective identity and ethical knowledge.

Within the context of American history and society, ethical writing is localized within particular social environments, develops out of a particular history, and addresses certain shared issues. Nowhere are these facts more pertinent than in the literature of the American South. As Edward C. Ayers has shown in *The Promise of the New South: Life After Reconstruction*, the modern South is shaped by the historical forces of Reconstruction, whose legacy is one of conflicting motives and interests. As Ayers demonstrates, nearly every aspect of southern history has been influenced to a large degree by the conflicting economic and cultural interests that were set into motion by the South's defeat and its gradual recovery after the Civil War. The legacy of conflicting interests was not limited to economics and politics, however, for in terms of social mores the modern South is equally a field of contestation in which it has become necessary to recover and perhaps to reinvent ethical practices from whatever resources may be available.

The multiracial nature of southern society requires that its literature deal centrally with issues of race, and yet because of the political and social stresses associated with a racially mixed (and for most of its history, inequitable and repressive) society, a strong pressure was exerted on southern narrative and southern criticism to repress the very moral issues that were obviously of greatest significance. To a large extent, Richard Wright must be considered a seminal figure in modern southern and American writing, for his influence on the national dialogue concerning race, and on the issue of the role of the imaginative writer within this dialogue, was so profound that for at least a generation his work, especially *Native Son*, stood as a defining literary event. For subsequent writers such as James Baldwin, as for the later generation that included Alice Walker and Ernest J. Gaines, it was necessary to come to terms with Wright's powerful ethical formulation. Wright's conception of the "protest novel" in *Native Son* elicited an extensive revisionary project on the part of later American writers, especially those like Baldwin whose historical proximity to Wright necessitated a deliberate break from his influence. In essays such as "Notes of a Native Son" and "Everybody's Protest Novel," Baldwin distanced his own aesthetic from that of Wright in terms of Wright's singular emphasis on race as the defining feature of African American existence. While admitting the legacies of slavery and Jim Crow, Baldwin sought to expand his artistic canvas beyond the single-minded emphasis on racial victimization that seemed to occupy Wright's thinking. As Baldwin wrote (clearly directing his critique at

Richard Wright) in "Everybody's Protest Novel": "The failure of the protest novel lies in its rejection of life, the human being, the denial of his beauty, dread, power, in its insistence that it is his categorization alone which is real and which cannot be transcended" (17). Wright's work might well be said (to employ Baldwin's phrase) to insist on the power of "categorization" in its exploration of the ethical failings of American society, but his legacy remains intact in the form of his highly realistic narratives of racial repression in and out of the South and in his probing analysis of the psychological and ethical consequences of this injustice for African Americans and for Americans as a whole.

As indicated in the chapter "Race, Class, and Redemption in Walker Percy's *The Last Gentleman*," the moral crucible of racial politics in the South (and in the nation as a whole) during the 1950s and 1960s was manifested in the narrative emplotments of race and class in Percy's fiction. As a writer who appeared to distance his work from parochial ethical concerns—indeed as one who repeatedly denied that his work was "southern" in any crucial sense—Percy is an intriguing example of a modern southern writer whose narrative reflects continuing pressures to confront moral truths and to an equal degree to repress moral failings that may not have been apparent to the author himself. In psychologically complex ways, Percy's fiction would seem to be a continuation of those strategies of symbolic repression and recovery in the psychopolitics of race and class in the South that Lesley Ginsberg has termed the "political uncanny" (123). As a cultural critic, Walker Percy voiced often conflicting opinions concerning contemporary ethical issues, including civil rights, sexual freedom, women's liberation, and gay rights. The nation's apparent shift following the 1950s toward greater democratization and social integration and the conflict of this shift in values with traditional southern practices of noblesse oblige and social hierarchy occupy much of his cultural criticism. Percy's response to these public issues was manifold and unpredictable since it reflected a genuine agonizing of conscience in response to complex moral dilemmas.

Like other critics of his time, however, Percy was at least in part motivated by the need to defend the South in a period of continuing regional bias. If the South's record of progress in civil rights had been greatly inadequate, those who attacked the South on this score did so often for partisan reasons. A criticism that is focused only on social ills may well be termed, as Percy wrote in "A Southern View" (1957), "gratuitously offensive," for it may be grounded in a cultural bias against the

South as a region and against the values of a cultural tradition based, as Percy describes it, on "a stable family life, sensitivity and good manners between men, chivalry toward women, an honor code, and individual integrity" (*Signposts* 90–91). Percy's review of the South's moral record in essays such as "A Southern View" reflected a defensive response to the pressure of northern liberals for immediate change in southern policies toward integration and voting rights. Percy's views on civil rights were characteristic of those of southern moderates of his day, but by the 1960s the nation as a whole had progressed toward a more egalitarian posture. The changing climate of civil rights was itself reflected in Percy's evolving perspective on race relations, particularly following the disgrace of the September, 1962, riots after the admission of James Meredith into the University of Mississippi (which Percy discussed in "Mississippi: The Fallen Paradise" and which he rendered imaginatively in a climactic scene in *The Last Gentleman*). Nonetheless, despite the shameful failings of what he saw as racism localized among the lower- and middle-class in the South, Percy consistently credited the South's valuable heritage and cultural accomplishments, and he asserted the region's *potential* for moral guidance of the entire nation. A common theme, in fact, of much southern cultural criticism from Faulkner to Percy was that very notion that the South, having already worked through ethical dilemmas that the nation as a whole had yet to encounter, possessed resources for moral leadership.

Few would defend the South's record in civil rights to the extent that Percy attempted in "A Southern View," and few today would seek to preserve all of the traditional aspects of southern gender codes or class hierarchies in the manner that Percy suggested in speaking of "good manners between men, chivalry toward women, an honor code, and individual integrity"—terms that summon up antebellum images of aristocratic manners and noblesse oblige. Among recent scholars, there is quite a different focus on the "marginalized" and outcast elements of southern society, and an interest in those writers who appear to ground their work in the historical facts of racism, classism, and sexism within southern society. Among some, there is an increasing understanding of the South's position within a system of "internal colonialism" in which the South after the Civil War was relegated to an inferior status within the national economy and culture. Interpreted in the terms of postcolonial theory, southern literary culture can be seen to have developed through the three classic stages of colonization, resistance, and equality.

Passing through these stages in the Reconstruction and modern periods, the South evolved from an initial posture as a defeated and pariah culture, to an intermediate stage of defense of southern identity, and lastly to a more mature stage of cultural independence. Contemporary southern writers have begun to work from the posture of "worldliness" that Edward Said identifies as the mature condition of an independent and confident postcolonial people—attitudes not unlike those postures of self-creation and independence suggested in the African American fiction of Toni Morrison or in the immigrant writing of Henry Roth. Along the road to this more independent identity, however, there has been a great deal of anxiety and uncertainty in formulating the South's cultural relationship to the national culture.

As recent studies of the narrative indirection and symbolic ambiguity of Edgar Allan Poe's Gothic fiction have demonstrated, the avoidance of ethical specification is a feature of early southern writing—coterminous, in fact, with the increasing social and political stresses involved in the maintenance of the institution of southern slavery from the late eighteenth century on. The tendency toward moral obfuscation, coupled with or "shadowed by" an intense pressure to confront repressed moral facts, remained a crux of southern writing well into the twentieth century, and remains a feature of southern and American writing today.

During the 1950s in particular, a period in which the southern canon first came to occupy a significant place within academic curricula, there was an effort on the part of literacy scholars to ensure the "respectability" of the southern literary subject. While those early scholars were far from ideologically monolithic, their effort to establish an academic southern canon necessitated an emphasis on culturally prestigious subjects: Faulkner made respectable by the awarding of the Nobel Prize, Welty linked to the discourse of artistic craft, Warren figured as a philosophical novelist. Even such relatively moderate political subjects as Katharine Anne Porter's liberal humanism or Richard Wright's fiction of racial protest received little emphasis in comparison with writing that was amenable to formalist analysis or aesthetic interpretation. In the effort to establish southern writing within the academy, however important this effort may have been, the emphasis on the conception of narrative as self-contained works of art displaced attempts to address issues of social ethics. As co-editor [with Robert D. Jacobs] of *Southern Renascence: The Literature of the Modern South*, Louis D. Rubin, Jr., had much to do with the creation of an early "canon" of southern letters. As elaborated by Rubin, Jacobs, and the other contributors to *Southern Renascence,* this early canon reflected the temper of criticism in the late 1940s and early 1950s. It is not surprising that of the twenty-nine essays in *Southern Renascence,* few addressed women and African American writers. Likewise, except for a diffident treatment of Erskine Caldwell and an ambivalent chapter on Thomas Wolfe, there was little discussion of the southern poor white and working class.

In such major critical works as *Tell About the South: The Southern Rage to Explain* and *The Southern Writer in the Postmodern World,* Fred Hobson has studied regional identity and social community in southern fiction. In his analysis, Hobson considers the problematic relationship of moral "self-consciousness" and artistic creativity in regard to the literature of regional or other identity groups. Addressing Donald Davidson's concept of the "autochthonous ideal," Hobson focuses on the danger of self-consciousness in the manner in which the southern writer presents his or her subject. The "autochthonous ideal" is, in Hobson's words, "a condition in which the writer was in a certain harmony with his social and cultural environment, was nearly unconscious of it as a 'special' environment, quaint or rustic or backward, and thus was not motivated by any urge to interpret or explain" (*Southern Writer* 80). In Davidson's view, "the urge to interpret or explain" led the writer away from artistic creativity and into "sociological" (and inartistic) approaches to the subject. Hobson claims that, among contemporaries, "few southern writers today are out to reform the South" (*Southern Writer* 81), but he fears that, with an increasing national interest in southern culture and with the success of its literature, an excessive regional self-consciousness may eventually result in a new version of "local color" writing.

Hobson is drawing an important distinction and one especially pertinent for any attempt to interpret the ethical dimensions of a regional or ethnic literature. While the distinction between social reportage and imaginative fiction is problematic, most readers would assent, I believe, that fiction and journalism are separate genres. The difficulty with Davidson's thesis lies not in the distinction it draws between art and reportage, but in the degree to which it opposes these genres and in its unwillingness to credit the extent to which fiction may draw from social observation and contribute to our understanding of social issues. The critic need not look far afield for models of narrative art explicitly ethical: among southern writers, a strong social emphasis and a measure of "editorializing" are apparent in classic works such as Wright's *Native*

Son and Faulkner's *Go Down, Moses*. These are dramatic novels evincing the formal qualities of high art, but they also contain morally explicit passages such as Boris Max's defense of Bigger Thomas or Issac McCaslin's discussion of Carothers Edmonds's moral responsibility toward his African American mistress and child. In Faulkner's case most of his fiction after *The Sound and the Fury* contains "editorials" about social change, patriotism, and individual responsibility—issues that he addressed as well in his public speeches and lectures. By Davidson's standard, we might conclude that Faulkner's art declined after his early novels, and, indeed, many readers have reached this conclusion. It may be, however, that as readers we have not possessed the critical tools to analyze and discuss Faulkner's shift toward a more self-conscious ethical narrative.

The essays in this book cover a number of important southern, African American, and immigrant writers from the 1930s to the present with the intention of understanding the representation of ethical issues in their works. Among the most original American authors, in ethical as well as aesthetic terms, was James Agee. It could be argued that, among socially conscious writers of his time, Agee in *Let Us Now Praise Famous Men* displayed the most profound response to the "sharecropper problem" of the 1930s, if not to the entire matter of the ethical dilemma of class divisions within a democratic nation that professed ideals of equal opportunity and the right to the pursuit of happiness. Agee approached the sharecropper problem with a profoundly uneasy sense of his own position of social privilege, yet he was impelled to confront his own ambivalent class origins as well as the class conflicts evident in the South and the nation as a whole. To a great extent it was Agee's work in *Let Us Now Praise Famous Men*, and in his *Fortune* articles and *Time* reviews and editorials (including an extraordinary piece on the ethics of the Hiroshima bombing written just after the event), that set the standard for what American narrative in the following decades would accomplish in addressing contemporary ethical issues.

One of the more important narrative resources for American writers interested in the moral ambiguities of American traditional culture has been the Gothic narrative—a genre that Wright adapted to racial narrative in *Native Son*. As Eric Savoy argues in "The Face of the Tenant: A Theory of American Gothic," Gothic writing in America stands in relation to "a poetics of terror" that originates in the repression of Otherness within American social history. As Louis S. Gross stresses, "what the dominant culture cannot incorporate within itself, it must project out-ward onto this hated/desired figure" (quoted in Savoy 5), and yet, despite the ceaseless motive of repression connected with the Gothic site, Gothic writing inescapably follows "a psychic imperative—the impossibility of forgetting" (Savoy 9). The repressed "recurs" always, and as signifier of this reiteration the Gothic narrative "generates an allegorical sign ... that returns the repressed Other to the vitally performative" (10). The unset-tling discoveries and revelations of Gothic narrative are elements in a tropics centered on disturbed (and disturbing) ethical zones of exclusion and authority.

In their own ways, Flannery O'Connor, William Styron, and Kaye Gibbons employed elements of Gothic romance to confront the aliena-tion and terror of human disability, racial strife, and class control, yet the "otherness" that these writers summon up and that American society has conventionally striven to repress extends well beyond differences of race, class, and disability. Equally important, these writers involve the reader in encounters with repressed elements in the reader's own psyche: universal terrors of human isolation, dependence, and death that are too easily displaced onto the fantasized landscape of social relationships. Clearly, writers such as Flannery O'Connor engaged in the creation of serious art that can serve as a tool for comprehending social injustice and human corruption. They embrace, in John Gardner's phrase, "the tradi-tional view ... that true art is moral: it seeks to improve life, not debase it" (5).

However flawed the result, William Styron's *The Confessions of Nat Turner* might well be read as a novel that originates with the same moral intention. In this controversial novel, Styron depicted a "heroic" rebel who organized a murderous revolt against the slave owners of southeast-ern Virginia and subsequently, before his execution, dictated his own "confessions" culminating in (as we are to imagine) an ecstatic religious conversion and partial repentance. The subject and perspective of Sty-ron's novel suggest a revealing comparison with a similar narrative by the Australian novelist Thomas Keneally: *The Chant of Jimmie Black-smith*. By comparing the figures of Nat Turner and Jimmy Blacksmith—subaltern revolutionaries as imagined by white middle-class authors—I investigate the ethical difficulties of fictionalized autobiography as it purports to represent, or to achieve what Gayatri Spivak terms the con-dition of "ethical singularity" with, a very different consciousness from that of the author.

Kaye Gibbons's *Ellen Foster* and *A Virtuous Woman* involve a quite different approach to fictionalized autobiography. Clearly, the social landscape that Gibbons imagines for her seemingly helpless child and adolescent narrators is one of "terror"—not the supernatural fright of classic Gothic romance but the social terror of severe family neglect and abuse, of class and regional prejudice, and of the psychological consequences of this exclusion and victimization. Despite its social limitations, the human society that Gibbons records is in possession of a coherent and functional culture that is more complex than most narrative reportage has suggested. To counter the stereotypical assumptions based on region, class, and other factors, Gibbons's novels provide convincing accounts of the humanity of her subjects and the worth of their inherited cultural traditions. The terror of the abused subject is balanced by the knowledge that the southern rural poor, unlike the stereotypical poor white of popular American imagination, do not exist in a cultural or moral wasteland. Rather they are the inheritors of valuable and workable systems of mores and values—a cultural inheritance that in the writing of Erskine Caldwell's *Tobacco Road* or James Dickey's *Deliverance* was almost entirely obscured. To Gibbons's credit, her fiction has recorded the dimensions of lives that lie beyond class or regional categorization.

The Gothic site of displacement in southern narrative is equally evident beneath the quotidian surface of Richard Ford's novels and stories, either as the "uncanny" terror of suburban isolation or the more overt violence in the American West, Mexico, or the working-class South. In response to the dislocating stresses and marginalizing politics of American life, Ford explores a fictional ethics of communal association and institutional responsibility: even his aesthetic impulses toward a "consoling" fiction and toward narrative coherence are markers of the terrifying disruption and loss that he locates in the American subject. In Ford's fiction, the most convincing—because the most mundane and universal—site of this terror is middle-class suburbia, with its inescapable burden of heedless individualism and mistrustful privacy. In a subtle emplotment of Gothic agony in *The Sportswriter* and *Independence Day*, Ford shifts the location of the unspeakable to the ever more familiar site of commonplace suburban existence.

If the Gothic mode is employed in many of the southern and African American narratives discussed in this book, the conditions for terror are also amply present in American immigrant narrative. The writing of Henry Roth, a Jewish writer who lived in New York and later in New

England and New Mexico, reveals the writer's conflict between loyalty to the values and customs and his historical heritage—the immigrant culture of his parents and extended family—and the writer's sense of the necessity of assimilation within mainstream American culture. Out of this wrenching conflict, Roth develops an understanding of the extent to which immigrant communities experience pressures to repress their traditional identity. In Roth's case the conflict between his identity as a writer of eastern European Jewish heritage and his aspiration to join the national literary culture resulted in a period of silence that amounted, as Roth quipped, to "the longest writer's block in history." The ultimate cause of Roth's lengthy silence was the ethical dilemma inherent in the writer's abandonment of his ancestral culture and the coherent moral systems it embodied. Like so many southern and African American writers, Roth's writing emerged from a painful crucible of colonizing forces threatening the writer's loyalty to his traditional culture.

In a complex narrative emplotment of similar thematic issues, Toni Morrison's novel *Jazz* traces the lives of immigrants from the rural South to New York's Harlem at the turn of the twentieth century. As the novel uncovers the harrowing legacies of slavery and racism in characters such as Violet and Joe Trace, it focuses on the difficulties faced by these characters in engaging in authentic ethical choices beyond the colonizing control of their cultural environment. Morrison investigates strategies of "re-memory" and retracing by means of which her characters gain freedom from the legacies of their history. Rather than seeking to restore traditional structures or institutions as a basis for order, however, Morrison's fiction points toward the possibilities of "improvising" ethical behavior from the fragmented remainders of collective experience.

In this book, I explore a wide range of texts from modern and postmodern American narrative. These diverse texts are, however, closely connected to a core group of ethical questions focusing on social exclusion and cultural hegemony. In the works included for study, I wish to suggest the conflicting interests that underlie the social history of any region or people but that are particularly apparent in the American South and in racial and immigrant communities in which the legacies of many forms of conflict and repression are evident. In the writing of Richard Wright, James Agee, Ernest J. Gaines, Toni Morrison, and Henry Roth, and others treated in this book, I trace an effort to revise the legacies of historical repression and to imagine a future in which the potential exists for a fruitful ethical discourse.

As John Gardner wrote in *On Moral Fiction*, narrative that embodies an ethical vision "is civilization's most significant device for learning what must be affirmed and what must be denied" (146). The narratives that I have chosen to discuss are important examples of ethical art; in reading these works, we would do well to heed Gardner's advice concerning the role of the "true critic," whose function "is to show what is healthy, in other words, sane, in human seeing, thinking, and feeling, and to point out what is not" (180). There are, of course, many critical approaches that lead to this end, but it is, I believe, crucial that interpretive theory again address ethical matters of the sort that Gardner, MacIntyre, Nussbaum, and others have enunciated. In the chapters that follow, I study a number of examples of American narrative art that center on just such questions of "what must be affirmed and what must be denied."

1

"Last Call to the West": Richard Wright's The Color Curtain

As the record of Richard Wright's travel to Indonesia in 1955 to attend the Bandung Conference of African and Asian nations, *The Color Curtain: A Report on the Bandung Conference* (1956) reveals Wright's effort to understand his own identity in relation to non-Western cultures. In his capacity as a freelance observer rather than delegate, Wright was perhaps more independent ideologically than others, although his indirect State Department funding (through the Congress for Cultural Freedom) "was [without Wright's knowledge] actually financed in part by the CIA" (Cobb 233). Without overestimating Wright's understanding of his non-Western subject, I believe that *The Color Curtain*, in addition to telling much about Wright's independence as a thinker and his autobiographical predilections, says much that is still worth considering about the relationship of the West to the non-Western world. As Michel Fabre notes after considering Wright's relationship to America and to the developing world, "[Y]ou have probably noticed how modern his attitude is and how relevant to our present concerns with freedom, the cultural revolution, and the making of a world civilization" ("Wright's" 139). In contrast to the personal isolation that James Baldwin theorizes in his essay "More Notes of a Native Son"—a critique of Wright's individualistic personality as well as of his limitations as a political theorist—Wright's impulse in *The Color Curtain*, in *Black Power*, and perhaps in *Pagan Spain* and *The Outsider* as well, is toward a broadening of community and a search for cultural connection.

Most significant, perhaps, is the fact that Wright did travel to Bandung—on an arduous flight to Indonesia from Madrid, via Rome, Cairo, Baghdad, Calcutta, and Bangkok. It may well be that Wright's decision to travel to Africa in 1953 and to Indonesia in 1955 was related to his repressed hope of finding a satisfying "connection" with humanity, a desire for shared closeness despite what others read as his air of defensive superiority. Wright's very decision to undertake the arduous journey to

Jakarta to attend the Bandung Conference implied an interest in the psychological identification with the largest possible groups—to counter the anxiety that Russell Brignano terms his "disquietude about his own figurative survival" (103) as one who, at least in his literary education, felt himself to be the "product" of Western civilization. The ambivalence of Wright's position at the Bandung Conference as a person of color who was also an American, with all that America's world position in the 1950s implied, is figured into his own record of the trip and into his stance as an independent and somewhat reserved observer.

At the same time, for Wright the Bandung Conference was a significant step in a lifelong journey of self-definition and articulation. Similar to the "sense of freedom and independence" (Hakutani 193) that Wright imagines for his protagonist at the conclusion of *Native Son*, in *The Color Curtain*, Wright seeks for himself an "articulation" of his own relationship to human society in the broadest sense. To adopt the terms in which Valerie Smith reads Wright's other works, "learning to tell his own story gives [Wright] a measure of control over his life and releases him from his feelings of isolation" (143). Telling his own version of the Bandung Conference, however, not only offered a sense of control and release but also served to articulate a social ethics as Wright sought to express his view of the urgent need for global cooperation.

The essential conclusion to be drawn from *The Color Curtain* is that Wright, envisaging a non-Western cultural and political course distinct from Western as well as from communist models, is searching for identity beyond himself and his own cultural limitations. The crucial point is that, even as Wright often parroted assumptions of Western scientific superiority, he identified with the colonized peoples who had been the victims of this technology. His attitude toward African and Asian cultures often reflected the deepest divisions in his own psyche, based on his bitter struggle to achieve his own position in a Western society. It is no wonder that he was drawn to Africa and Asia, for through their colonized histories, Wright was conducting an exploration of his own most profound psychological and ethical divisions. As M. Lynn Weiss notes, Wright "emphasizes those features of Western culture he most admires: the separation of church and state, individual rights to free thought and speech, the autonomy of artistic expression and scientific inquiry" (126). Nonetheless, all of Wright's assumptions concerning the West, and concerning his relationship as an African American to American culture, had to be tested in his "report" on Bandung, just as they had been repeatedly tested and revised in his earlier writing. All of Wright's "private" ambivalence—over Western technological dominance, over secularism versus religious fundamentalism, over the destructiveness of colonialism toward indigenous cultures—keenly reflects his enormous sensitivity to the major human problems that can be traced to the devastating effects of colonialism.

As Jack B. Moore notes, Wright was by temperament "a prickly thinker who seemed to go out of his way to express his feelings and ideas even when these were not popular" (*"Black Power* Revisited" 162). In *The Color Curtain* Wright records the background of the Bandung Conference and dutifully notes its major speakers, but his interest centers on what one might term the novelistic, on the agency of character and psychology, rather than on the political forum. Clearly Wright is impressed by the collective aspects of the conference: the gathering of leaders from twenty-nine nations, a "conglomeration of the world's underdogs" (*Color Curtain* 135) representing over a billion people, which Wright describes as "the human race speaking," yet his emphasis on masses and on the gathering of different cultures uncovers ambivalent possibilities either for apocalyptic conflict or unprecedented unity. As he had in *Black Power*, in *The Color Curtain* Wright recognizes that the social environment under colonialism had created structures of dependence that were not easily removed in newly independent countries. "There is a nervous kind of dependence bred by imperialism," he wrote of neocolonial paternalism (*Color Curtain* 112). As Nina Kressner Cobb notes, "[a]ccording to Wright, the greatest crime that took place under the aegis of imperialism was not economic exploitation, but the creation of a servile personality structure in the native population" (231).

In Wright's view, the neocolonial ambitions of leaders such as Chinese Premier Zhou Enlai threatened the independence of other newly independent peoples (Wright's opinion of the Chinese leader was much less admiring on the whole than is suggested in a recent article by Chinese journalist Zhang Yan). Wright also foresaw the danger of civil anarchy and unrest represented by "millions of restless and demanding people" with unrealistic expectations brought about by the newly achieved freedom of Asian and African nations. Wright predicted the unleashing of old hatreds and ethnic divisions, and he believed in the West's obligation to "interfere": "civilization itself is built upon the right to interfere" (*Color Curtain* 211). As the proclaimed champion of human freedom and secular, scientific culture, America should "educate people in how to build a nation" (212). The positive value of the West lay in its "secular outlook grounded in the disciplines of science" and industrial knowledge (218). In his controversial paper "Tradition and Industrialization" presented at the first world conference of black writers, meeting in September 1956 in Paris, Wright announced that his position is a split one, "that is, Western and black." For Wright, Western political thought was the source for important ideals of political freedom, justice, and equality, but as an African American of his generation, he also felt deeply alienated from Western institutions.

Because his political thought was based on his own ideals and not on any systematic approach to politics, Wright has been criticized for his political naiveté, and indeed he seems to have been unaware of or simply uninterested in the subtle behind-the-scenes maneuvering at Bandung. For example, Wright interpreted Nehru's abstention from the opening remarks as a sign of his "neutrality," a wise strategy of the "great man." According to Carlos Romulo, the pro-Western representative from the Philippines, Nehru in fact abstained because of his anger at being out-voted after he had adamantly opposed permitting opening statements by all nations. Zhou Enlai's stance of compromise, which Wright interpreted as a shrewd gesture of "good will," should be attributed, according to Romulo, to his lacking the diplomatic skill to steer the meeting his own way (14). Zhou's "conciliatory posture," noted by George Kahin, was also a deliberate attempt to defuse the mounting tension between mainland China and the United States over Taiwan. Certainly Zhou could not have fully supported the statement in the conference's final communiqué "that the cultures of Asia and Africa rest on spiritual foundations." Nor could Zhou have been pleased with the communiqué decision to oppose "all forms of colonialism" (Romulo 15), including implicitly communist expansion in eastern Europe and Asia. Only insofar as Zhou was able to use the issue of nuclear arms control was he successful diplomatically, according to Romulo.

For whatever reasons, Wright showed little interest in the diplomatic subtleties of negotiation underlying the final communiqué. While many representatives privately expressed their bitter memories of colonial domination, the focus of public statements was the necessity of economic cooperation. The final communiqué stresses, as its first point, the need for economic cooperation with the West based on the employment of foreign capital, stabilization of commodity trade, elimination of mercantilist practices, and the like. A section on the problems of dependent people does appear, but it is focused narrowly on the struggle of French colonies in North Africa. The material superiority and arrogance of America, coupled with its unequal foreign aid for Africa and Asia relative to Europe and its assumption that American-style democracy was right for Asia, were other points of criticism.

As a consequence of his disinterest in politics per se, the essentially individualistic gestures that Wright saw as the focus of the conference—its "call to the West" and the role of the "Westernized Asian" in its deliberations—correspond little with what political scientists have stressed. According to Kahin, the difficult work of the conference was "defining the kind of colonialism the Conference was to condemn or the principles it would recommend for promotion of peace" (30), especially "the principle that freedom and peace are interdependent" (31). The results of the conference, Kahin notes, included the expression of a new Asian "dignity" and independence vis-à-vis the West: in this respect, Zhou Enlai's participation also promoted China's break with the Soviet Union by expanding its ties with the rest of Asia. Looking back from 1965, the Indonesian Executive Command saw the significance of Bandung as strengthening nationalist movements in Africa and Asia, encouraging governmental cooperation among African and Asian states, and promoting nongovernmental cooperation, as in the 1958 African-Asian Writers' Conference that "urged all African-Asian writers to develop national literature" and to spurn "modern civilization" (*Revolutionary Flame* 31).

Thus, from the perspective of many political observers, Wright's report on the Bandung Conference might well be termed subjective or idiosyncratic (Zhang Yan described Wright's "in-depth observations" as involving "a historical and very special personal perspective" [278]). If Moore's statement that "Wright sometimes creates his own Africa" in *Black Power* is accurate ("*Black Power* Revisited" 185), is the same true for his "creation" of Asia in *The Color Curtain*? Did Wright assume too readily that, as an African American, he could identify with the African and Asian peoples represented at Bandung? As Robert Felgar notes, such an attempt is the "essential Wrightian theme" that appears in *White Man, Listen!* (1957) and other books: "[Wright] had an obsession for seeing that the position of blacks in the Deep South is only the situation of all the dark races, of all the oppressed, on a global scale" (150). Wright may also have felt that his association with African writers and his earlier visit to the Gold Coast, out of which he published *Black Power*, had prepared him for Bandung. He had long shared a friendship with the Afro-

Caribbean writer George Padmore (who had arranged his visit to the Gold Coast in 1953), with C. L. R. James, and with other Pan-Africanists living in London. His knowledge of the writings of Franz Fanon offered some theoretical framework for his understanding. After 1948, with his move to Paris, he was associated with the influential journal *Presénce Africaine* and developed friendships with French-speaking adherents of négritude and black power, including Alionne Diop, Aimé Cesaire, and Leopold Senghor. In a general sense, at least, Wright's background did in fact prepare him to interpret the issues of class, race, religion, and colonialism underlying the conference. Certainly Wright had experienced poverty and racial oppression; he had also suffered from an intensely fundamentalist religious upbringing, and he understood from personal experience the economic and cultural restrictions of colonialism.

Indeed, the sympathies that Richard Wright brought to Bandung had been formed very early in his life. Margaret Walker goes so far as to single out Wright's early experiences in the South as the primary determinants of his personality. As Walker writes: "He reflects almost in totality the mirror image of racism in the South as it is seen in both black and white men" (181). As elsewhere in his writing, Wright both analyzes and reacts passionately to the racial issues he encounters at Bandung. Whether he suffered from a "flawed personality" as a result of "the psychic wound of racism" (Walker 295) is a question of interpretation; certainly, he struggled with and against his psychological ambivalence all his life. In both *Black Power* and *The Color Curtain*, Wright in fact assumes a close analogy between his southern experience and the colonial experience of Africa and Asia. In certain passages of *Black Power*, it is difficult to determine whether he is writing about Africa or the American South, for Wright's views on Africa, and Asia as well, are often reminiscent of what he wrote concerning African American experience in *12 Million Black Voices* (1941), where in his foreword he stressed the movement toward urbanization of twentieth-century African Americans. Socially conditioned by "what we see before our eyes each day," African Americans inevitably become Westernized (*12 Million* 48), yet they have at the same time "never been allowed to be a part of western, industrial civilization" (127).

The psychological alienation resulting from colonization was shared by Wright and by many of the representatives of formerly colonized peoples attending the conference. Following the African Diaspora, Wright states, American life is "the only life we remember or have ever known"

(*12 Million* 146), yet tragically Wright himself felt alienated from both Africa and white America. As he wrote in *Black Boy*: "In all my life—though surrounded by many people—I had not had a single satisfying, sustained relationship with another human being" (249). He wrote in *The Outsider* (projecting his autobiographical feelings into the character of Damon Cross) that "he needed these people and could become human only with them" (509). The intensity of Wright's desire to establish connection with others—and its relationship to Wright's situation as an African American living in exile—is underlined in *The Outsider* when he analyzes Cross: "What really obsessed him was his nonidentity which negated his ability to relate himself to others" (525). Clearly, much of his life, Wright experienced the same "opposition" that Trudier Harris identifies in the protagonist of *Native Son*: "between Bigger as a representative of something larger and freer, indeed more American" (63) and the representatives of more "limited" cultures, whether that of the African American working class or of the non-Westernized postcolonial. This very alienation and self-division, however, as Craig Werner points out in his analysis of Bigger Thomas, make Wright's protagonist "a truly representative figure" (147).

Because of his own sensitivity as an outsider to much of postwar African American culture and to American culture in general, Wright fixes on an apparently minor aspect of the Bandung Conference: the "Westernized Asian" also alienated from his own culture. It should be no surprise, given the focus on such a character throughout his fiction and travel writing, that a major theme of *The Color Curtain* becomes the plight of the alienated intellectual, separated from his traditional roots but not accepted by modern Western culture. One example of the Westernized Asian is the educated Indonesian whom Wright meets who feels that the influence of the West has a positive effect in terms of its ability to moderate the excesses of traditional practices. Wright notes the constant self-consciousness of the cultural hybrid who, like Wright himself (a lifelong sufferer from gastrointestinal disorders and associated ailments) experiences chronic anxiety resulting from cultural insecurity. Wright finds that "the classical conception of the East is dead even for the Easterner" and that "the Asian elite was, in many ways, more Western than the West" (*Color Curtain* 70–71), yet cultural leadership has passed from the West to a future that non-Western culture will shape. Without considering the possibilities for new forms of exploitation, Wright predicts that cheap non-Western labor will break Western economic power.

In his consideration of the economic potential of formerly colonized nations, Wright showed a great deal more perception and independence than did the Western journalistic media, yet he shared the fear of "racism in reverse" expressed in the Western press. The pervasive sense in the American and European press was that the Bandung Conference, at which whites were excluded, was a "planning stage" for an African-Asian "combination" impelled by bitterness toward the West, a perspective that is also reflected in contemporary reviews of *The Color Curtain* (see Reilly 273–85). The very numbers that arouse Wright's interest also contain the potential for a misuse of power. When Wright receives his press card ahead of a white journalist, he experiences the disturbing power of racism—a racism in reverse to which Wright objected as vehemently as he had to that directed against African Americans or colonized Africans or Asians. Interestingly, the official representatives at Bandung did not stress their numbers in the same way that Wright and the Western press did. Rather, as Carlos Romulo stated in the conclusion of his opening speech at the conference (from which he quotes in his 1956 book), "[o]ur strength flows not out of our number though the numbers we represent are great. It flows out of our perception of history and out of vital purpose for tomorrow" (58).

What Wright most feared was not the newfound power of the formerly colonized nations—a changing order that he accepted and celebrated—but the potential misuse of power through an irrational combination of ethnic and religious emotionalism. In the postcolonial world, Wright observed that "a racial consciousness, evoked by the attitudes and practices of the West, had slowly blended with a defensive religious feeling: here, in Bandung, the two had combined into one: *a racial and religious system of identification manifesting itself in emotional nationalism which was now leaping state boundaries and melting and merging, one into the other*" (*Color Curtain* 140; Wright's emphasis). In *Black Power* and in *The Color Curtain*, he "demonstrate[s] his suspicions of political leaders whose control of the masses seemed based on religious fervor and mysterious impulses" (Moore, "Dream of Africa" 235).

The characterization of passionate religion as non-Western indicates that Wright believed that in his own fundamentalist upbringing he had been victimized by the proselytizing force of Christianity. As Cobb points out, Wright applied the same lesson to non-Westerners dominated by custom and mysticism that he had drawn from his own rebellion: "The rural, religious milieu that he rejected spelled poverty and degradation"

(238), and only secular humanism could secure progress. Margaret Walker notes that Wright "was adamant against *all* religious faiths," including African religion (231). Felgar may be correct in noticing that Wright saw that Moslems "could use their strict life-pervading religion to help themselves" (145), but Islam was especially troubling to Wright, in part because of his close personal associations with Jewish radicals in Chicago, and in part owing to his marriage to a Jewish woman. In Moslem belief he saw "the firm rejection by the Asian mind of a division between the secular and the sacred" (Felgar 124). Wright's distaste for all forms of religious fervor is captured in his scornful characterization of "the men of the East" as "religious animals" (*Color Curtain* 80).

It is curious, given his friendship with a number of African writers and his interest in African and Asian cultures, including the culture of Japan, that Wright should be so often seen as wanting to impose Western culture on non-Western societies. Yet the idea that Wright believed "the culturally subjugated country's vacuum can be filled in some way by such Western values as individualism, rationality, technology, science" (Felgar 143) can certainly be supported by passages in Wright's writing, if not by his work as a whole. Felgar states the "paradox" in Wright's attitude toward Africa: "[T]hey should throw the West out and then become as Western as possible" (155). The idea of the irrevocable "triumph" of Western over Pakistani culture (*Color Curtain* 70, quoted in Felgar 143) is representative of Wright's view of the lack of cultural vitality in Africa and Asia, at least outside of India, China, and Japan. In *Black Power*, to cite another example, Wright repeats a common misconception that the products of material culture cannot survive long in the hot, humid climate of West Africa. After five hundred years of colonialism, much of Africa and Asia were, in Wright's opinion, left without a vital indigenous culture. The same traumatizing process had, in Wright's view, affected African Americans, so that in *Native Son*, despite Bigger Thomas's relationship to family and to a few others, "Wright intended [him] to be a man without a culture" (Ochshorn 387).

Despite Wright's belief that the process of colonization has destroyed much of non-Western culture, it is not accurate to say that he believed that Western culture could, or should, fill the vacuum left by this destruction. Wright obviously admired many aspects of Western culture, particularly its technological prowess and its tradition of secular humanism. Nonetheless, he recognized the need for self-determination as the first requirement of developing countries, and he looked toward a future in which Africa and Asia would take the lead in economic and political terms. Given Wright's tendency toward dramatic generalizations, however, it is difficult to achieve a balanced and fair view of his writing in relationship to the developing world. First of all, Wright's psychology was itself that of a complicated genius projecting into the minds of characters his own inner divisions. His most vivid responses to Bandung were to human situations rather than to political arguments. (One should note that he imagines a world "without ideology" in ideal terms, as he says that "maybe ideology was a weapon that suited only certain hostile conditions of life" [*Color Curtain* 176].) Wright was rarely inaccurate in capturing the human motives and fears of the characters he created, but these created personae could hardly correspond to the objective observations of less creative correspondents. Furthermore, Wright did not have the advantage of recent cultural studies discrediting Western hegemony; he wrote at the very moment in history when Western power and wealth, especially American power and wealth, appeared most imposing.

Perhaps, however, even given his limitations, Wright saw more clearly than many of his contemporary critics. He may have intuitively understood that cultural nationalism of the kind that romanticizes the past simply promotes further colonial domination. As Wimal Dissanayake writes, Wright prodded non-Westerners "to scrutinize and reject those aspects of their culture and personality which conformed to the terms defined by the regnant discourse and thereby pave the way for the assertion of their own identity" (484). Wright did not ascribe to the simplistic notion that modernization was inimical to non-Western cultural identity. Industrialization, in Wright's view, presented formerly colonized nations with an opportunity for creative endeavor that would be meaningful in a modern context and would thereby help those peoples regain belief in themselves (Dissanayake 486).

Wright's analysis is perhaps even more controversial today than when he published his conclusions in *Black Power* and *The Color Curtain*, for Wright clearly had little patience with the kind of interest in mystical and irrational forces that is now asserted as an alternative to Western "linear" thinking. Clyde Taylor effectively summarizes a certain direction in non-Western writing toward a "transrational consciousness" with emphasis on oral culture, ritual, sacred symbology, nonlinear organization of time and space, and magic (795). This conception of the non-Western, which Taylor traces in recent postcolonial fiction and which John Edgar Wideman invokes in speaking of "a powerful, indigenous vernacular tradition" (vii) in African American culture, is certainly very far from the future Wright envisaged.

To the extent that he does feel hopeful, Wright places his faith in the interrelationship of cultures. The West must learn from and respect non-Western cultures, but Africa and Asia must also learn from the West. Wright's appreciation for American science and technology was matched by his personal discomfort with disorder and squalor of any sort, yet one should not dismiss the sincerity of Wright's belief in the potential of non-Western societies. The future, as Wright envisages it, involves a new leadership on the part of African, Asian, and African American cultures. Admittedly Wright's knowledge of these cultures, even (as Baldwin charges) of postwar African American society, was at times superficial and his pronouncements tactless, yet his fundamental vision of the relationship of Western and non-Western cultures should not be dismissed out of hand.

Indeed, Wright's very first publication, a poem appearing in *Left Front*, had, in his own words, "linked white life with black, merged two streams of common experience," and he had discovered his ambition to "make these lives merge with the lives of the mass of mankind" (*Black Boy* 303, 316). As Andrew Delbanco stresses, the same intention—"a plea that racial identity be submerged in the colorless fact of being human" ("American Hunger" 146)—underlies all of Wright's work. The effort to find a common humanity, to "bind men together in a common unity" (*Color Curtain* 24) reflects Wright's overriding fear of a primal violence that he sees rooted in racism and religious extremism. In literary terms, Wright promotes a "broadening" of postcolonial writing toward "the common themes and burdens of literary expression which are the heritage of all men" (*White Man, Listen!* quoted in Brignano 111). As Margaret Walker noted perceptively, "[m]ind and body he wandered over the earth seeking always a common ground of humanity" (212). She sees Wright's dream as moderate, not radical; it is "to have an ordered, rational world in which we all can share" (202). Underlining his entreaty with capitalization, Wright characterizes Bandung as "THE LAST CALL OF WESTERNIZED ASIANS TO THE MORAL CONSCIENCE OF THE WEST!" (*Color Curtain* 202). A "de-Occidentalized world" in which non-Western societies will develop autonomously need not reject the humanistic political tradition of human dignity and individual freedom that Wright valued so highly. It is significant that Wright's last public speech, delivered on November 8, 1960, at the American Church in Paris, dealt with the policies of the West toward developing nations. To the very end of his life, Wright retained his dream of a world governed by ideals of reason and individual dignity in which all cultures would contribute and from which all would benefit. Standing almost alone against the reigning climate of bitterness and global distrust in which he lived, Wright continued to uphold those values of reason, progress, and humanity he believed could be shared by all.

2

James Agee's Quest for Forgiveness in Let Us Now Praise Famous Men

In the opening pages of *Let Us Now Praise Famous Men*, James Agee announces that the book will be structured along the lines of a quest, to begin with a search for the "average" white tenant family. Meeting with the first such "clients of Rehabilitation," Agee awkwardly communicated his purposes, then followed the valley down the road to "where we did not find what we sought" (37). Like Dante's pilgrimage, to which Agee often alludes, his journey involves the reader as a collaborator, so that at the end of Part One, as author and reader stand together "at the peak," like Pilgrim and Virgil before their descent into Lower Hell, Agee asks the reader to bear in mind this panorama of the entire scene so that "when we descend among its windings and blockages, into examination of slender particulars, this its wholeness and simultaneous living map may not be neglected" (111). From early on, Agee understands that the inferno he is entering is peopled by "living" souls who are only dead to the visiting middle-class reader who may observe "slender particulars" too closely and forget life's wholeness.

Agee and co-author Walker Evans are constantly in pursuit of a moral and holistic understanding of their subject, yet this understanding repeatedly eludes them. Coming across the photographically "perfect" country church, the journalists encounter a passing Negro couple and are "ashamed and insecure in our wish to break into and possess their church" (40). Wishing to explain his motives, Agee follows the black couple in what turns into an absurd "chase scene," with Agee, hoping to express his friendship and to be understood, only causing them further anxiety. In its sad absurdity, the chase encapsulates in miniature the two-month quest that Agee and Evans have undertaken. Filled with "self-hatred" for intruding on the lives of the couple, Agee then feels an impulse to kiss their feet as an expiation for his insensitivity. Agee returns often to this ethical point: investigative reporting and photography are by definition "intrusive," but unlike the approach of social reformers such as Margaret Bourke-White, whose "purposeful rearrangement" of her subjects resulted in "making the poor seem consistently worn, repugnant, alien, and stupid" (Shloss 602–3), Agee and Evans attempted to record the sharecroppers in their own terms. As Shloss demonstrates, Agee associated Bourke-White's "photographic interference with larger, more diffuse forms of social control. Through her he understood that institutions around him were involved in creating self-serving concepts of poverty" for their own interests (Shloss 603).

Contrary to Alan Holder's assertion that Agee fails to "present any significant politics at all" (200), Agee's "politics" may be seen as comprising a passionate defense of the rights of the disadvantaged to an existence in their own terms. Warren Eyster recognizes that *Famous Men* "uplifts the poor and uneducated and reveals them to have as much pride, as deep a moral sense of guilt and sin, and as complex an emotional awareness of life as any statesman or artist or high churchman" (349). Quite explicitly Agee analyzed the motives of those—from reactionary landlords to reform-minded New Dealers—who wished to control the tenants through one patronizing means or another. As Joseph Wydeven flatly states, "Agee is disgusted with the flaccid liberalism of Depression documentary" (109). Agee wisely saw that no "client" relationship would alleviate the sharecroppers' condition since all institutions purporting to relieve their suffering served the interests of those in power. This realization helps to explain Agee's general sense of unworthiness before all those less privileged than he, those "poor lives I have already so betrayed" (*Famous Men* 439); his quest is for self-forgiveness that would confirm his own right to exist in a world of suffering.

Certainly one of the guiding values of Agee's life was his sense of personal responsibility toward others. Linked to his strong sense of responsibility—a sense that, as we shall see, is coupled with his having "failed" his own father—is Agee's imagined or actual unworthiness, the "subtle dialectics of sin and guilt [that] pervade his life and work" (Madden 34). Agee's self-destructive personal habits were real enough—his excessive use of alcohol and tobacco, his punishing schedule, his frequent marital infidelity, his artistic blockages and "apathy"—but perhaps these failings were psychologically inescapable. Keeping faith with his father somehow meant that Agee must continue to be responsible for his father's death, and for this to be, he must be punished. Toward the end of his life, on February 12, 1953, he could write to Father Flye: "I am by now much more deeply addicted to alcohol than at any time before"

(*Letters* 210). Agee never came to terms with his personal sense of guilt for very long, although he found temporary solace in many friendships and pursuits.

In *Let Us Now Praise Famous Men*, the young James Agee had already sketched the outlines of his life-drama with its futile search for forgiveness and for a reconstituted sense of identity. Agee, as Durant da Ponte writes, "became emotionally involved in everything he undertook" (28), and thus he transformed a journalistic assignment into a search for knowledge of his father's world. At its farthest reaches, this endeavor involved not only a quest for connection but for the father's revivification by means of the sympathies that his son would bring to his memory. Richard H. King makes an illuminating connection between Agee's lifelong fascination with photography and his quest to recover a lost place, for in photographs, which for Agee become "icons that both imply and negate time," he found a way to "stop time": the camera "returned an absence to presence, and this was what he was seeking in Alabama" (King 218).

The artistic and human task that Agee undertakes is monumental. In his essay "A Real Bohemian" Louis Kronenberger claimed to find "something weak" in Agee: "it perhaps derived from a kind of scorn of something so middle class as willpower" (111). Perhaps Agee's limitations, however, were not so much the result of weakness as of an uncompromising ambition and honesty that demanded too much. Admitting from the start the impossibility of his *Fortune* assignment—to write a succinct report on the lives of "average" tenant farmers—the more daunting task that he defines for himself runs up against the ethical difficulty of ever "knowing" another human being, and beyond this lies the aesthetic problem of expressing all that is "beyond designation of words" (*Famous Men* 100). Practically all that is most important for Agee is beyond expression: the subtlest feelings, atmospheres, particular lives in particular settings, and the author's and reader's understanding of them. What Agee seeks is for words to "embody" life itself, what he calls the "particular existence" (*Famous Men* 409) of life in one place, but he simultaneously declares this embodiment an impossibility. In trying to convey the full sensuous reality of the Gudgers's house and storeroom, Agee encounters this hopeless task: it is impossible to convey the actual physical quality of existence; Agee can only hint at the enormity of what he has observed. The very "plainness and iterativeness of work ... make it so extraordinarily difficult to write of," Agee explains (320), so that he draws from the physical objects ("overalls" stained with sweat, for example) a way of communicating the harsh, plain, functional existence of the southern farmer. In poetic and impassioned sections, such as the description of "the beds" (174–76), Agee intends to embody the filth, poverty, unromantic sexuality, and overwhelming exhaustion of tenant life.

To a great degree Agee finds the answer to his artistic quest in the example of what the tenant families are able to create out of their impoverishment, under which their material culture evolves a restrained, functional aesthetic that Agee describes as "innocent" and "classical." The tenants live an elemental existence inextricable from the natural world. William J. Rewak shows that the overall structure of *Famous Men*, following the central narrator's investigation of the sharecroppers' living conditions, "is the organic process of birth, life, and death" (93). Agee compares tenant culture with classical Doric or New England puritan aesthetics, and in his writing he aspires to the same purposeful simplicity that he finds in their "hand-made" houses (although, if this is so, Agee's prose style is often the opposite of his intention). Evocative and poetic, by turns sentimental and moralistic, the language that Agee has at his disposal seems middle class in origin, much closer to his mother's rhetoric of "Christian duty" than his father's earthy directness. Were Agee not aware of this fact, and did he not employ it to reenforce the tension between his questing soul and the desperate condition of the tenants as the object of his quest, the language he employs would seem false.

Instead, Agee consciously explores the paradox that his privileged education and training, his facility with language, evince a "disease of consciousness" (*Famous Men* 229) while the tenant children, inarticulate or even silent, are truer and healthier "artists." What little education the tenant children receive is only "poison" that they may be better off without. The intellectual curiosity that Agee notices in ten-year-old Louise Gudger will, at best, be worn down to mediocrity by the public educational system. In 1934 Agee had in fact written to Father Flye concerning the possibility of his teaching at St. Andrew's and during the months in Alabama he thought further about the abominable conditions, for blacks far worse than whites, of public education in the South. Perhaps his solution of hiring only artists as teachers—"the only fit teachers never teach but are artists" (*Famous Men* 290)—sounds implausible, but Agee did enunciate some worthy educational goals: development of the whole person and of a sense of moral responsibility for others rather than rote learning and the textbook approach. Robert Coles is correct in noting that "we are not given an alternative, any kind of blueprint" (56) for the very reason that Agee wants us to experience the children's misery in its own terms, not to consider an "agenda."

"Nothing can be held untrue," Agee proclaims in Whitmanesque fashion. The lack of symmetry of ramshackle southern farms, reflecting the suffering of human experience, in contrast with the orderliness of midwestern farms on "perfect" land, speaks as eloquently as the greatest works of art. Agee rarely has the tenant farmers speak in their own voices, perhaps, as he claims, out of "respect" for their dialect, which he feels he is incapable of reproducing. As Paul Ashdown writes, the tenants "speak obliquely": "They are especially garrulous in their silences, communicating more by their countenances and their primitive intuitions than by their voices" (70). Instead of transcribing dialect, Agee's method is overwhelmingly to evoke the lives of the tenant farmers through his own poetic or descriptive language. As Michael Staub insightfully notes, the stylized passages in which Agee does record speech directly make the point of reversing "the conviction that 'educated' people can grasp more than others can" (150), but they do so at the expense of empathy and understanding. The limited sociological truth of naturalistic fiction excludes the "beauty" and "poetry" that exist in the lives of the poor, as well as among the middle class. In attempting to create sympathy, the rhetoric of naturalism may dehumanize its subjects and portray the impoverished as "a creature apart, a comic and contemptible sub-species of the human race" (Holder 190). Intent on "listening" not just to speech but to the "wholeness" of others' lives, Agee must mediate and translate their existence into a work of art that would then be comprehensible to a general reader.

As Holder writes, Agee's engagement with his subject pressured the book's form toward "what might be termed an anti-book, an object that departed from or caricatured the usual apparatus of a published volume" (193). Certainly the book's preface matter, the digressions, addresses to the reader, and appendices break with conventional narrative form and have a common purpose of shocking the reader into *listening* intently. "Suspicious of the conservative implications of literary modernism," as King points out, Agee nonetheless used "the techniques of literary modernism" as he "sought to forge a type of sophisticated realism that would in turn avoid the dangers involved in a naive attempt to mirror reality"

(215). To the extent that a literary model existed, Agee perhaps looked to Joyce, in whose fiction the Dublin idiom is rendered artistically through severe methods of selection, stylization, and placement within the structure of the whole work. It seems improbable that, after a sympathetic reading of Joyce's entire canon, Agee would have resorted to a direct transcription of speech in a book, taken by many to be Agee's masterpiece, filled with technical experimentation akin to that of *Ulysses*. As David Madden writes, Agee's "proclaimed antipathy to art was always expressed in the most artistic context, concepts, and diction" (33).

Aware of the danger of sentimentalizing the poor, Agee tempers his view with realism about the hardships of tenant life and about the human failings of the sharecroppers themselves. Fred Ricketts is characterized as "one of the most piteously insecure men I have ever known" (*Famous Men* 271), while Ivy Woods is a "hot and simple nymph, whose eyes go to bed with every man she sees" (372). All three Woods women are said to come from the "sexually 'loose' stock of which most casual country and small-town whoredom comes" (280), a characterization that is surely connected with the confused emotions to which Robert Fitzgerald alludes when he states that Agee himself recognized, at the end of his life, unexamined motivations toward women ("I gather that he got cooler and tougher about everything in his last years, in particular about love" [92]).

The admission that Agee is "in love with" Louise Gudger, that he is physically attracted to Ellen Woods and sees in her daughter Pearl an incipient "looseness," is further instance of Agee's tone of sexual bravado, calculated both to shock the reader and to disclose female characters who are distinct from his "respectable" maternal relations. Linda Wagner-Martin sees Agee's narrator (the created "character of Agee") in a "voyeuristic role" (48) whose relationship toward the sharecropper women involves guilt and ambivalence because of the representation of these tenant women as "sexual prey" and their role in a "love story" with the character of Agee as implicit "rescuer" (51). Agee does indeed suggest just such a narrative, so that Richard H. King finds the narrator's "sexual desire" for Emma Woods to be among the more "powerful" passages in the book (217). Yet the difficulty with this reading is that so many other levels of relationship are opened up as well, a proliferation of ambiguities and oppositions suggesting sexual desire and much more. To acknowledge that the metaphors are at many points "blatantly sexual" or that Agee's exploration of the Gudger house "re-creates sexual excitement" (Wagner-Martin 52) points in the right direction, toward what is in Agee's book an exploration of the varieties and levels of love pervading the entire universe of beings and things. Thus, sexuality as "mechanism," the coarse fantasies of the lonely narrator returning from Birmingham to Centerboro, or of Agee and Evans in imagined intimacy with Emma Woods before her departure to rejoin her unappealing husband, is later balanced with the mystery of Annie Mae Gudger's love for her threatened children. The inevitable suggestion of conventional romance—the affluent urban visitor suddenly appearing and transforming the lives of impoverished rural women—is undermined in part by the narrator's growing sense of helplessness to change the economic or cultural conditions of those he hopes to rescue, although Agee's ultimate purpose in publishing his account is in fact to bring succor to the tenant class.

The more specific role of the tenant women in Agee's imaginative world, however, centers not on sexual attraction but on Agee's identification with and rebellion against his mother, Laura Tyler Agee, whose social superiority diminished his father during his lifetime and whose eventual remarriage to Father Erskine Wright seemed a betrayal. In this reading, Annie Mae's relationship to Agee is an attempt to reconstitute a childhood home in which the gulf between his actual parents would be eased by the presence of a highly maternal, rural female quite different from the educated, urban figure who dominated his childhood after his father's death. Agee repeatedly refers to this maternal mythology in a series of works going back to poems written at Exeter and originally published in *Permit Me Voyage*, poems that connected his mother with social pretension and marital discord. His early poem, "Sunday: Outskirts of Knoxville, Tennessee," imagines "clerks and their choices" on Sunday outings, but for the particular couple in the poem "Theirs are not happy words." The poem's locale, the "outskirts" of a growing city, is the borderline between rural and urban, qualities associated with his father and mother, but in this case the expected merging of differences is rebuffed by the mother's severity masked by a genteel exterior and even her control of elocution. In "Fellow Traveller," Agee describes his turning away from his mother's religious pietism. In the later poem, "Sonnets XIV," he speaks bitterly: "Not of good will my mother's flesh was wrought" (*Collected Poems* 43).

In contrast to this middle-class domination of the family, which is seen to be "strangling" and divisive, Agee is "drawn to" Annie Mae in ways that may include "erotic elements" (Wagner-Martin 54) but that

stems more powerfully from the madonna-like role in which she is protective and nurturing, rather than merely sexual. Agee's description of
the infant at her breast as "ecstatic with love" (*Famous Men* 441), shel-
tered by its mother as the defenseless family huddles with its guest
during a threatening thunderstorm, is the culmination of their visitor's
meditation on all of the various possibilities of human need and concern,
neither exclusive of nor limited to the sexual. As in the early poem
"Epithalamium," Annie Mae's sexuality has elements of divinity that
separate her from ordinary human passion. The bridal bed is filled with
"holy lust," and her groom's desire is purified by Hesperus. What Agee
imagines so vividly in this poem is no ordinary romantic script but a
transformed existence for women and men that is the product of his embittered reaction against his parents' divisive marriage and of his later
reading of romantic literature of a strongly mystical and metaphysical
nature. Without dismissing any of the romantic or erotic qualities of
love, Agee repeatedly focuses on women and men in their marital and
parental relationships. As Victor Kramer points out, Agee at the time
was still "haunted" by his father's death: by 1936 he had already written
"Knoxville: Summer of 1915," his lament for a lost childhood especially
focusing on his father. Centering on the theme of "domestic love," his
1957 novel *A Death in the Family* re-creates "moments that would fade
away with no memorial if he chose not to write of them" (Kramer 116).
Similarly, but from a less balanced perspective, *Let Us Now Praise Famous Men* is a study of the cultural oppositions between Agee's parents,
an analysis of the author's emotions toward them, and a memorial to his
father's memory.

In fact, Agee's "love" for the tenant women alternates between two
scripts: his protective, paternal concern for women and children who are
horribly misused by their society and his agonizing need, both filial and
sexual in nature, to be saved himself. If we recall what Agee insisted at
the beginning of the journey, that "its wholeness and simultaneous living
map may not be neglected," we may understand that the moral and aesthetic challenge of *Famous Men* was to express the existence of each
character as an "entire being." As Agee wrote in another context, his
artistic and human task was "to recognize oneself and others, primarily
as human beings" (*Agee on Film* 278). As such, Annie Mae and the other
tenant women are represented as complex figures, sacred and mysterious
in their creative and life-affirming abilities, and the attitudes of Agee's
narrator toward them are equally complicated.

If the tenant males seem to be represented as less creative and mysterious, it may be in part because of their constraints within the culture of tenant farming, in part because of their association with death connected with Agee's father. Unlike their men-folk, who must at least feign acquiescence to retain their places, the sharecropper women openly express their hostility and bitterness toward their "superiors." For Agee this transparent display of contempt, so wise and exacting a statement of their social dispossession, seems, as he says, "holy"—the silent communication of sacred humanity that is conspicuously lacking in his depiction of Mary Follett in *A Death in the Family* with her opaque rhetoric of religious acceptance. In Walker Evans's photograph, Annie Mae Gudger stares painfully at the lens, her tragic expression concealing nothing of her tired despair and self-knowledge. Agee's emotional intimacy with the tenant women seems understandable as a form of complicity against his mother's cowardly dishonesty in the face of her equally tragic condition. Instead of burying the raw nerve of life and seeking comfort from a life-numbing religiosity, Agee wants from his mother what he would never get: the terrifying, grief-stricken wail at the utter injustice and irredeemable loss of his father. Instead, she withdraws into pious acceptance of "God's will," and her early remarriage to a churchly figure further suppresses the grief that her son requires. No wonder Agee fantasized an intimacy with so many tenant women: tragically cast down, as he had been, but staring into life directly, these women were irresistible to a young man who knew that life at its core is bitter disappointment and whose grief has never found a mate.

If in avoiding a connection with his mother's respectability, the tenant women are sometimes cast as promiscuous, they are more often depicted as angelic or holy. Driving back from Birmingham to Centerboro, Agee resists the siren appearance of a roadside prostitute but soon fantasizes meeting a strange madonna-like girl who assuages his despair at ever doing "one page" of good writing or "one good minute" of film, and his greater despair of hurting people (*Famous Men* 384). Beginning with his own childhood, Agee has experienced enough of the harm that human beings do; without knowing how, he pleas to be exonerated from the guilt of participating in such a world. An unspoken association exists between Agee's continuing to live in the world made unjust by his father's death and the injustice of life for girls such as Louise Gudger: as the innocent victim of the world's injustice, the sharecropper girl could best extend forgiveness to the "guilty" and privileged son of Laura Agee.

Agee's great investment of private emotion makes his task of writing more difficult, but it also accounts for much of his originality, especially so in seeing that the harshness of life at the bottom does not extinguish the humanity of that life. The tenants are fully capable of intelligent irony, humor, pleasure in the moment, and hope for the future. As in Charlie Chaplin's films, which capture both the pathos and vitality of their subjects, Agee seeks a "language of 'reality'" that, trying to combine the "poetic" and "realistic" polarities of his subject, he describes as "beautiful and powerful" but also "the heaviest of all languages" (236). "Forget that this is a book," Agee writes; it is a human being "telling the truth" (246). Recording the crucifixions in each moment of every life, those "generations unceasingly crucified" (100) that Agee eulogizes in a long passage imitative of Hopkins, the artist is mostly a silent listener who gazes in stunned silence into the very heart of another human being. Although he is still striving with only partial success, the task that Agee sets for himself is one of total empathy and understanding. While he "tries on" the poetic style of idolized writers including Whitman, Joyce, Hopkins, and Blake, only in silence and failure, a discourse without and "beyond" words resembling that of Kafka or of Chaplin, would Agee as a true artist find a voice separate from his mother's middle-class rhetoric as well as his father's working-class speech. Still, Agee repeatedly insists on his personal failure in, and even betrayal of, the art that he has attempted. Later, following a brief section on education condensed from twenty-seven pages of notes, he states that "the mere attempt to examine my own confusion would consume volumes" (294). Like Kafka whom he so admires, Agee burrows deeper into his own sense of failure even as he pursues the enormous ambition of finding a true voice.

That Agee characterizes his artistic limitations, understandable enough at age twenty-six, as "betrayals" suggests the very private origin of his inspiration. As David Madden points out, "his lifelong compulsion was to see mirrors face to face, endlessly reflecting each other, himself and others, himself and the tenant families" (38). A recurrent obstacle to success is Agee's sense of his unworthiness to approach the central, grail-like subject of his book, whether we see this as the human suffering of tenant farmers or the cultural origins of his father (which come to be embodied in the Gudger family). As Victor Kramer shows, Hugh James Agee "had come of a mountain family, and he embodied many of the rural qualities of persons who had left farms and become urbanized" (105–6). Having not had to live as the Gudgers do, Agee feels "sin" in witnessing the beauty as well as the "abomination" of the cabin (*Famous Men* 203). This consecrated matter is identified with his paternal ancestry, about which he has been denied knowledge by his mother and her Tyler relations. During the first night at the Gudgers's house, Agee feels hopeful that he is "at the end of a wandering and seeking ... at rest in my own home" (415). He associates George Gudger with his father and finds connection with the tenant culture: "For half my blood is just this" before being "softened" during a childhood spent among Tyler women (415). "These are true tastes of home" (416) he says of dinner, feeling a masochistic pleasure in suffering what the croppers suffer, whether in sleeping on an infested pallet or drinking the foul water.

In contrast with the enormous significance of the sharecroppers' lives, Agee feels his own life to be trivial, as one literally "passing through" and "playing at" suffering, rather than having to live permanently as the sharecroppers must, ten million souls as surely "imprisoned" as were those at Andersonville. He feels insubstantial, with almost the feeling that those literally and figuratively dead so envy his life that he cannot keep hold of it ("[D]o we really exist at all?" he asks early in his quest [53]). Feeling unworthy among the sharecroppers, and distrusting his own potentially exploitative motives as a "journalist," Agee searches for signs of acceptance. Emma Woods, whom Agee has imagined on her wedding day as "such a poem as no human being shall touch" (286), confers a measure of acceptance on Agee in her confession that "it's just like you was our own people" (64), a mark of the connection that emerges between the tenant families and Agee's father. Incapable of acknowledging his middle-class mother's influence, even in New York Agee dressed as a Whitmanesque hybrid of working man and bohemian artist: "unshaved as nearly always, work shirt, workmen's shoes, corduroy trousers, as usual" (Chambers 152).

The "strangeness" of Agee and Evans to the locals results from cultural and class differences, but onto the record of their strained meetings Agee transposes his obsessive quest centered on the need to resurrect a lost childhood home. The author's impulse to save the victimized sharecroppers, especially the women and children, results in part from his own unbearable experience of childhood suffering, the infant's "wrenching" from the womb and the child's abandonment in a brutal world, deluded as he or she is in the strength of parents. Thus, after his first meeting with Emma Woods he wants "to shelter her like a child" (*Famous Men* 65). Significantly, Emma is "a young queen" (59) whose family has been dispossessed, reduced to sharecropping from the better life they had known before the Depression. Like Agee himself, she has been cast out from the paradise of an earlier, better time. In another revealing image, Agee describes the Gudger house, "thin-walled, skeletal, and beautiful," as a boat at sea "whose crew slept while I held needless watch" (421). The odd usage of "needless" may imply either the strength of the tenant families or Agee's own helplessness to change things for them, for even their deaths can be spoken of as a precarious voyage, with their new graves "the shape exactly of an inverted boat" (437).

Agee's relationship to the tenant farmers is intimately connected with his rebellion against his mother's God-centered religion, already displaced by his sense of the greater "holiness of human beings" and of "whatever exists." Agee connects the lives of the tenant families with Christian motifs of the nativity, Madonna, and crucifixion, but in the strained application of sacred iconography to the humblest facts of sharecropper life, all bourgeois religious assumptions are undermined. As Rewak points out, "he uses sacramental images to illuminate his idea that the farmers were holy because of the death they had to endure at the hands of a venal society" (101). In the process, Laura Agee's "high-minded" moral idealism and her conception of self-sacrificing "duty" and "nobility" inextricably connected with the assumption of social superiority are exposed, yet the author is painfully aware of how often his relation to the tenants replicates this patronizing model. Against his own middle-class upbringing, Agee sets the more holy lives of the sharecroppers, whose sacredness as human beings is implied in his speaking of the contents of the table drawer in the Gudger front bedroom as a "tabernacle," or the wall in the same room as an "altar" against which are set a table and mantel with the photograph of the Gudger women. Having ransacked their bedroom drawers to understand his subjects better, Agee replaces the "garments" handling them "so reverently as cerements" (*Famous Men* 188), just as the Gudgers return from work in the fields.

The connection of the tenants with his father's family is not always explicit, but it is an important reason for the "sanctity" of the subject. The near-identification, in Agee's mind, of Christ with his father, who died at thirty-six, impels Agee to portray the "father-like" George Gudger, a thirty-two-year-old man, as a struggling but doomed figure approaching the age of Christ's and his father's deaths. The role of Annie Mae Gudger as a madonna-figure is also understandable, for in her perfect devotion and self-sacrifice she contrasts with Agee's sense of his

mother's betrayal. The special weight that Agee places on the consequences of human sexuality is tied to his own childhood betrayal. The
sexual act, "that battling and brutality upon a bed" (109), perpetuates the
cycle of suffering, as the infant is "wrenched" from the sheltering womb
into the monster world, only to grow into a helpless and brutalized child:
already by the time of early childhood (the same point at which Agee
lost his father), the child has experienced the destructive potential of life
and grows up without assurance of happiness.

Even more difficult to comprehend is Agee's representation of himself within the Christ family. He is at once the meek, faithful believer,
whose early breakfast with the Gudgers inspires memories of serving as
an altar boy at St. Andrew's School in Sewanee or whose Sunday afternoon in Centerboro releases unpleasant memories of monotonous
Sunday afternoons in Knoxville, and the skeptical, urban cynic whose
every word is knowing and ironic. In his own phrase, he is "a reverent
and cold-laboring spy" (134), a peculiar hybrid of devout believer and
cold skeptic.

The very vulnerability of these sacred human beings implies the necessity of taking responsibility for others. The "utter tiredness" of Annie
Mae Gudger (88) touches Agee's deepest pity. Those who have grown
up in the middle class, such as Agee himself, must learn how brutal life
can be for those who live at the margins of society; they must also learn
to recognize their ethical responsibility to act on behalf of all others.
Consciousness is "this monster world's one enemy" (108), and only consciousness will awaken social responsibility. The writer's role parallels
that of the analyst, bringing repressed guilt to the surface. Having moved
beyond his artistic apprenticeship with his arrival in Alabama, Agee aspires to the sharecroppers' degree of estrangement, living as they do
"outside society" in almost every respect, partly as a condition of the
great art he wishes to produce, partly in expiation for his privileged and
continuing life in relation to his father's deprivation and early death. In
his view, the literary influences that Agee discusses (Blake, Dostoevsky,
Whitman, Stephen Crane, Kafka, Joyce) similarly require absolute moral
responsibility toward others as a condition for art and thus imply a
priest-like role for the artist. (Agee's lifelong correspondence with Father James Flye has been interpreted as a "father-son" relationship, but
perhaps it is equally the collaboration of two "priests," working at their
common vocation.) So profoundly is his writing enmeshed with psychological survival, the only existence Agee can hope for necessitates this

sacred devotion to his art, yet nearly to the end he is haunted by his own "betrayal" even of art.

Agee looks beyond his own life, which he invariably connects with a historical era of suffering, toward a future paradise, his "anarchist" world of "free human beings" (355). The beauty and nobility that Agee finds in the Gudger household is the product of human suffering, but following Blake and the romantic visionary tradition, Agee looks to a future Jerusalem that words alone can barely communicate. Appropriately, conjoining the ethical and psychological themes of his book, the quest concludes with recitation of the Lord's Prayer, with its focus on forgiveness, and with a page from the apocryphal book of *Ecclesiastes* that begins "Let us now praise famous men, and our fathers that begat us" and that ends in peace and resurrection: "Their bodies are buried in peace; but their name liveth for evermore."

Beyond the superficial purposes of mere art, Agee learns from his journey to Alabama that ethical responsibility is exacted because of the extreme fragility of human lives in the "monster world." Probing his subject further, the young author finds that his quest requires self-analysis and expiation, for his own childhood "in the years of his extremest malleability" (109) seems inextricable from the childhood of deprivation he witnesses in Alabama, or that which he imagines for his father. His obstacles include his own unworthiness, his unworthiness even to witness the human suffering before him, and his artistic failure to fully express what he sees. Summoning up every resource of his moral integrity and his art, in *Let Us Now Praise Famous Men* James Agee approached the grail of forgiveness as closely as he ever would.

3

James Agee's Fashioning of Guilt: The Morning Watch

A Death in the Family has been frequently read as James Agee's most revealing fiction concerning his relationship to his father, Hugh James Agee, who died in an automobile accident on May 18, 1916. While Agee's posthumous novel indeed discloses much about his painful childhood, *The Morning Watch*, the largely ignored short novel that deals with a nearly identical persona at a point six years after his father's death, uncovers considerably more about the lasting effects of the family tragedy. Many details indicate that *The Morning Watch* is in fact a sequel to *A Death in the Family*, and that the character of Richard represents Rufus Follett six years later. *The Morning Watch* (1950) replicates exactly many details of character and plot from *A Death in the Family* (first published in 1957 but, according to Alfred Barson, largely completed in 1947 and 1948). Richard's father has died in exactly the manner as Rufus's, and Richard recalls the brief but unforgettable sight of his father's body: "he saw as freshly as six years before his father's prostrate head and, through the efforts to hide it, the mortal blue dent in the impatient chin" (*Morning Watch* 28).

Along with the early poems that Agee collected in his 1934 volume *Permit Me Voyage*, *The Morning Watch* is Agee's most direct representation of the continuing symptoms of anger and self-punishment that he experiences following his father's death. According to Mark A. Doty, Agee is "exhibiting the classic symptoms of what Freud called melancholia," that is, an excessive tendency toward self-reproach accompanied by delusional expectations of punishment (28). Relying on studies of childhood bereavement by Felix Brown and John Bowlby, Doty speculates that in addition to creating pathological symptoms of depression and suicidal tendency, Agee's grief may have made him a "compulsive worker," one who finds escape from a haunting bereavement only in compelling labor (30). Focusing on *A Death in the Family*, Robert Coles also connects the child's anger with the sense of rejection or absence of his parents, but for Coles, Rufus's symptoms are not pathological: Agee's tensions merely exaggerate the inherent conflicts and complications of development present in any child. Moreover, Coles sees a danger in trying to eliminate such conflicts in the lives of children.

While all children may experience significant conflicts, those that Agee describes in *The Morning Watch* are so overwhelming as to control Richard's inner thoughts and threaten his very survival. Richard's mental identification with his dead father permeates every moment of his life at school and isolates him from his peers to the point that they label him "crazy." Richard's addressing the priests as "Father" from his bed at 4:15 a.m. before his watch inevitably brings to mind a similar bedside visit, Agee's final contact with his actual father, as described in *A Death in the Family*. Richard's transgressions of rules and subsequent punishments (and his own excessive self-punishments beyond the cognizance of school authorities) are, paradoxically, a comforting version of family routine.

Richard's relationships to all older and larger males stir a peculiar excitement in him, for the attention of any adult male suggests an inviting contact with a father's world that has been denied him. The smell of strong coffee taken before his watch is "almost as enviably masculine as white lightning" (*Morning Watch* 20). Richard's description of the "great athlete" Willard Rivensburg includes a lengthy speculation about Willard's motives in joining the watch. Inspired by the fact that Willard speaks a few words of German, learned from his Swiss immigrant family, Richard also decides to study German, which now strikes him as a "more virile language than French" (23). Agee uses words such as "warm" and "comforting" to describe Richard's feelings in Willard's company: "he began to feel a sense of honor and privilege in having this surprising chance to be so near him and to watch him so closely, to really see him" (22). "To really see him" is a phrase applicable to ghosts visiting from beyond the grave, and it suggests that Richard may be confounding Willard with his dead father.

Accompanying Richard's curiosity about and attraction to the masculine is his repugnance at the feminine, traceable to his disgust with himself, a boy not yet very masculine, and to his mother's presumed betrayal of the father. His own body strikes him as inadequately masculine. When Richard and two younger boys strip at the sand pit, Richard immediately compares his sexual organs and body hair with those of Hobe and Jimmy, and he fears that his masculine development is deficient. Even the familiar sentimentalized images of Christ on the Cross upset Richard because they suggest an effeminate mythologizing rather than the muscular agony that he identifies with his father.

Not only is Richard fascinated by his father's memory, but he also sees his own life in relationship to his entire paternal ancestry. In a similar manner, Agee himself had repeatedly compared his own experience at numerous points in his life with the experiences that his father would presumably have undergone. In the "Sonnets" originally published in *Permit Me Voyage*, composed in Agee's early twenties, many aspects of the poet's early psychological development are clarified. Indeed, Agee's early poetry, too often dismissed or ignored by critics as imitative and florid, speaks more bluntly of the emotional conflicts traceable to his childhood than does much of his prose. In the first line of "Sonnet II," Agee writes that "Our doom is in our being," a clear statement of the degree to which he felt controlled by a progression of events that had come to seem inevitable, given his father's fondness for alcohol and his parents' marital differences at the time of his father's death. His father drove off to his death in the speeding automobile by means of which he attempted to escape a failing marriage, its failure seemingly inevitable given the parents' dissimilar births and convictions.

"Sonnet IV" analyzes Agee's central dilemma with great precision: "I have been fashioned on a chain of flesh," Agee begins, "[w]hose ancient lengths are immolate in dust." Agee feels a sense of duty, especially in light of his relative advantages of education and culture (which his father in particular never enjoyed), yet he ends the poem with the assertion that he will eventually "join" the father whom he has "betray[ed]" (*Collected Poems* 38). Agee's famous "Dedication" to *Permit Me Voyage* identifies the volume's central concern, dedicating the poems to the dead and to those "soon to die" who have sought truth. In a tone of modernist despair, Agee also dedicates the poems to those "[w]ho are fooled into the hope that it [the human condition] may be essentially changed," those who believe that political change or scientific progress will change anything, when in fact such "transient matters" only blind mankind and worsen the inevitable reckoning "before his God, where no knowledge nor ease of earth may help him" (*Collected Poems* 13). Change will only come with the arrival of a new race fashioned, perhaps after the imminent apocalypse, in "concord" and "humility."

"Sonnet IX" is painfully revealing of Agee's "cruel love" for Olivia Saunders, whom he had married in January 1933, and demonstrates that in his first marriage Agee was consciously duplicating his parents' conflicts. Agee's persona feels enslaved by his mate's "delight" in him. They are "mismatched victims," and he vows to destroy her smile with "its covert meaning and its patent charm." He wants her to awaken from her sentimental illusion of married love to the truth of "love's surprising hell." Such anxiety regarding woman's love masking control is connected specifically with his mother in "Sonnet XIV." Ironically reversing the class identities of his lower-class father and bourgeois mother, Agee writes of their love's "sullen harvest": "Poor wrath and rich humility, these met" (*Collected Poems* 43). Presumably the "rich humility" was his father.

As in "Sonnet XVII," love is repeatedly figured as "pretense" that deludes the lovers. Beginning with the lines "I nothing saw in you that was not common/ In some degree to any other friend," this sonnet is especially discourteous to the beloved. Love is a dream that only death or the lovers' separation may dispel. "Epithalamium," also originally published in *Permit Me Voyage*, is likewise a very peculiar "celebration" of married love, for it carries an unmistakable undertone of accusation and warning to the "queenly" bride who awaits the groom "in rich humility" (oddly enough, the same phrase he applied to his father in "Sonnet XIV"). In Byronic fashion, the "guilty" groom has pursued "his endless quest/ And gathered every beauty to his breast" (*Collected Poems* 31) but found all women lacking. The poet warns the bride to be careful not to harm him even with a "sigh," an injunction that sets an impossible burden on the bride to begin with. The wedding night itself is not merely passion but *immolation*, with flesh "melting" and becoming "dust," so that the "wall" that flesh imposes between souls is burned away leaving the lovers "one in nothingness." (This is the condition recognized by David Wyatt as voiceless communion. Wyatt points out that in *A Death in the Family* only in silence do father and son experience communion: at the silent film, though accompanied by music, or pausing silently on their walk home.) Yet following this somewhat dubious tryst, day comes "merciless" and stormy, ending the union of souls. Only some version of death, with the lovers united beyond quotidian society, can preserve an untroubled marriage. What is suggested in "Epithalamium," however, is not merely a marriage between man and woman but the union in death of the poet with his dead father.

It is important to realize that the poet's despair of human love is only a secondary motif supporting the dominant theme of ancestral obligation that opens and closes the "Sonnets." The relationship between the poet's inability to accept woman's love and his sense of duty to male ancestors is never spelled out, but it is implied as the final sonnets return abruptly from troubled human love to the comforts of paternal ancestry. Agee finds it more difficult to communicate his central meaning, for it is an existential anxiety that can only be suggested. In "Sonnet XXII," he describes a way of seeing "all things in one" as his goal. His search for stable truth and for security is obviously connected with an attempt to enter into the father's presence, as in "Sonnet XXIII" where the poet's task is "to recall/ What wisdom was before I was this ghost" (*Collected Poems* 48). The final sonnets vacillate, recognizing the danger of an obsequious dependence on "Those men I worship and would stand among" (XXIV) and admitting the need to establish a separate identity, yet in the end he remains faithful, with the simple pledge: "In which respect I shall follow you" (XXV), punning on the word "respect."

The identical question of how far to follow his father's ghost dominates *The Morning Watch*. As a means of analyzing his own feelings, Richard examines the behavior of a boy named Claude who has lost his mother "a long time ago." What is uppermost in Richard's mind is the imperative that Claude's actions be sincere and not "for show" or merely imitative of conventional grieving—the "picture" of grief that Claude may have learned "from some picture of some saint or other" (*Morning Watch* 53)—but even Richard realizes that his criticisms of Claude are an attempt to shift off "something that was wrong with himself" (55), or worse, that in "speculating" on the quality of another boy's prayers, he has "lost his own moment of contrition" (56).

Is it simply the guilty knowledge that he cannot grieve for his father forever and during every moment that troubles him? In fact, Richard's grief displays symptoms of a more pathological nature. In comparing himself to his classmates, Richard invariably finds himself unworthy, lacking in some crucial respect, and he compensates by the performance of grandiose feats, more often imaginative than actual, designed to win respect from others and approval from himself. After the grotesque crucifixion that he imagines for himself, he thinks, "he would never be last again, when they chose up sides" (50). Unfortunately, no feat, however grand, will assuage his feelings of guilt and anger for very long. Agee's childhood grief was unusual not in the forms it took but in its intensity and in the fact that it tormented him unceasingly throughout his adult life. Typically, Richard ends his watch with a sense of self-disgust, for he has failed, even for the period of his brief watch, to concentrate on its meaning or to pray.

Potentially, analysis might illuminate his feelings and ease some of Richard's pain, but precisely because it might alleviate some of his "deserved" punishment, Richard identifies "mind" as the "betrayer" of faith, not only in the sense of religious belief but in his more important commitment to remain under the emotional control of his father. "Mind," which could analyze and assuage his grief and expound its limits, might serve as the means of escape from his father's ghost, and in this sense mind is his enemy. Thus, at the conclusion of his half-hour watch, Richard's heart was "filled to overflowing with a reverent and marveling peace and thankfulness," for the watch has brought him into the presence of his crucified father, "yet what he saw in his mind's eye was a dry chalice, an empty Grail" (87). Opposed to his heart, Richard's mind understands the ritual enactment of the father's death as a step backward toward further dependence.

Richard's complex double reading of the Crucifixion has unlikely consequences, such as his compassion for Judas. In the same way that Richard imagines himself responsible for his father's absence, Judas has betrayed Christ and caused his death. In the same role as Judas, Richard therefore can imagine that the betrayer's soul is far more complex than that represented by Father Weiler, who claims that Judas felt "remorse" rather than "contrition" but cannot explain the difference to Richard's satisfaction. Richard may be thinking that Judas is actually experiencing a great deal of contrition, but that, like himself, Judas is a failure even in his guilty grieving.

Clearly, Richard has been living a shadow existence since his father's death, one designed to preserve his relationship to his father at the cost of his own self-love, and one that he desperately needs to transcend. The central action of this essentially "plotless" novel is the highly dramatic question of whether the boy will ever escape the control of his father's ghost and establish a mature identity. Enacted on Holy Thursday to commemorate the hours before the Crucifixion, Richard's watch suggests to him the hours just before his father's death, which occurred in mid-May a few weeks after Easter. Another connection between the watch and his father is the phrase "Blood of Christ inebriate me," which the boy knows meant "to make drunk, to intoxicate" or, in a coarser definition, "meant just plain drunk" (32). Richard (and presumably Agee) explicitly connects the word "inebriate" with memories of early childhood when older boys played drunk while guzzling soda pop but where his father's reputation for drinking was a more serious matter, and where the connection between alcohol and his father's accident lingers. Richard's mind "sticks" on the word in the service, as it does on other words such as "blood" and "wounds," because the words recall his father's death.

In a manner typical of that of child survivors, the anger originating in his father's death is largely directed at himself. Richard's response to his loss is a classic case of childhood grieving, which in many survivors creates lasting consequences of depression and anger. Richard believes that he has failed his father and that he shares responsibility for his accident. Also, he fears that his father was never really proud of him, since as a son he was not athletic and seemed to take after his mother. Because Richard is obsessed with the sense of having failed his father, his future life will continue to seem a failure no matter how much he is able to accomplish in later life. The slightest mistake, such as his arrival at Lady Chapel a few minutes late, is construed as a betrayal of his father. During the watch Richard prays "with deep self-loathing," and his request to remain with the divine father ("Suffer me not to be separated from Thee") is voiced with uncertainty. Beginning as early as age eleven, Richard practices self-mortification as a psychological punishment. He avoids the "cookies and cocoa" at Father Fish's cottage and relishes his mother's rejection when he attempts to visit her too often. He takes pleasure in punishment for bed-wetting or for failing at lessons, and he has even brought on punishment deliberately. Alone he practices further self-mortification, tasting worms, attempting to taste his own excrement, and imagining his own crucifixion or hanging.

As a child survivor of his father, Richard appears to be doomed to a future of profound uncertainty and even self-hatred. No matter what he attempts, the result will never placate his controlling self-loathing as one who, unfairly it seems, continues to survive in the world that his father has deserted. Consequently, the only future available to Richard may be one of abnegation—withdrawal from the world even as his father had withdrawn—or actual death. A clue to Richard's future, after he leaves the mountain school, is supplied in Agee's own experience at Phillips-Exeter Academy and at Harvard, where he informed his roommate, Bernard Schoenfeld, that "he craved a monk's discipline but not a monk's celibacy" (Schoenfeld 306). Much later, in the last years of his life, he reminded Schoenfeld of the remark "comparing the agonies of any serious writer to the spiritual conflicts of a lecherous monk" (Schoenfeld 308). Richard's mother is not entirely wrong in saying that "there might be a kind of vanity mixed up in his extreme piety" (*Morning Watch* 43). The twelve-year-old Richard realizes that he might actually attempt to become a saint. In Agee's own pursuit of the holy—for example, his satisfaction in spending two self-mortifying summer months in a bug-ridden and brutally exposed cabin in Alabama in 1936—one senses the same motivation that drove Agee almost to suicide as an adolescent. Like Kafka's hunger artist, Agee is vain, for no one can rival his feats of self-mortification. If strenuous periods of monk-like labor were one aspect of his unresolved grief, another was Agee's fatalism. Agee's abuse of alcohol and neglect of his body seem calculated to bring about an early death, and, as Agee's letter to Father Flye on his thirty-sixth birthday shows, Agee believed he might well die at the same age as his father. At least death would bring an end to his suffering, even if it would not reunite him with his father.

Agee reveals Richard's tangled emotions concerning self-punishment in his thinking about sin, especially the sin of self-abuse, and his excessive pride in confessing sin, itself a sinful act of pride, thus requiring further confession and generating new sin in its very confession. Richard's moral confusion traps him between "good and evil as if they were mirrors laid face to face ... there was no true good and no true safety in any effort he might ever make to realize or repent a wrong but only a new temptation which his very soul itself seemed powerless to resist" (79). This passage suggests an important connection between Agee's guilt over his father's death and his hesitancy to acknowledge conventional moral distinctions. The ability to form deliberate ethical principles is certainly a crucial stage of development into adulthood, and as such was a betrayal of his father's control that Agee was not prepared to risk. Sexual amorality, in particular, was an "obligation" that assured Agee's psychological dependence and thus preserved his "proper" status as a child in relation to his father. Agee was indeed a "lecherous monk."

Alfred Barson finds that late in the novel, when trying to protect the snake from Hobe and Jimmy, Richard has undergone a "rebirth" that brings "increased moral sensitivity which ironically prevents him from making clear distinctions between good and evil" (161). Clearly, this process of ethical conflation is underway well before Richard's dive in the sand pit, but the dive does mark a decisive point of recognition. In fact, an anarchic skepticism regarding moral categories permeates everything that Agee wrote in or about his youth. His earliest writing, including such Harvard *Advocate* stories as "Death in the Desert," explored such areas of negativity as the motiveless enjoyment of violence and the attraction of sexual taboo. Gordon Taylor refers to the same moral ambiguity in pointing to the coincidence of the state of "nothingness" and the condition of vision in Agee's writing, and he compares Agee's metaphysics with Emerson's "I am nothing; I see all" (70).

Agee was of course fully aware of the extent to which negativity had been explored in the writing of Whitman (claimed as his mother's distant relation) and other early moderns. As a late modernist, Agee's bohemian attraction to moral ambiguity was if anything conventional: his imaginative limitation consisted not in an inability to break with Victorian moral rigidity—the familiar modernist attack on the ethical pretensions of a hypocritical materialism that Agee applauded in Chaplin's *Monsieur Verdoux*—but in the possibility of his paralysis within the modernist sensibility itself. If Agee was indeed a "failure," as he believed, his failure was that he was too predictably modern.

In fact, Agee's moral sensibility was more complex than that of many of his modernist contemporaries, for his rebellion against Victorian standards of morality was balanced by an intense commitment to ethical responsibility of a sort that many of his generation found to be unusual, if not embarrassing. Always, Agee's moral assumptions seem intertwined with his personal history. As is well known, Agee exhibited a lifelong compassion for the weak, for the disadvantaged, for children and animals; yet he was far from gentle with himself and with those unfortunate women whom he connected with his mother. As Laurence Bergreen shows, Olivia Saunders, an older woman from a genteel and artistic family, resembled Laura Tyler Agee in several respects, just as Alma Mailman, a younger Jewish woman from an impoverished and troubled household, as the antithesis of his mother, was connected with his father. Thus, as Agee wrote in an unmailed letter to Alma before his death, she was the "only woman" he ever loved. Agee's mental cruelty toward Olivia—which included the open secret of his affair with her friend Alma and his torturous inability to decide between them (there was even the suggestion to Father Flye that he might remain "married" to both)—seems an acting out of his anger toward his mother and a reflection of his own guilt in aligning himself with her before his father's death.

The final episodes of *The Morning Watch* represent Agee's effort to understand the self-destructive nature of his, and Richard's, obsession with his father's death. It is also an effort to envisage a psychological and moral development beyond this immature posture. In Section III of *The Morning Watch*, in the climactic episode of the novel, Richard accompanies Hobe and Jimmy to the sand pit. Emerging from the stifling air of Lady Chapel, the boys find "an air so different from the striving candles and the expiring flowers that they were stopped flat-footed on the gravel" (91). If the chapel atmosphere suggests adolescent futility, reenforcing Richard's immature self-conception as a failed and guilty son, one might think that nature promises freedom and the possibility for human camaraderie. At first, Richard does experience just this sort of release, decisively leading his friends toward the sand pit in flagrant violation of the school rules. Accompanied by Hobe, who is part Indian and who "never concealed his own body or his interest in another" (102), Richard's adventure seems to replicate those many accounts of boyhood freedom in American literature.

However, as Barson writes of Agee's protagonists in general, "nature does not bless them any more than human contact" (161). If anything, the episode suggests a natural freedom available to others but not to him, and Richard is soon assaulted with the same conflicts he strove against inside the chapel. He simply carries his struggle with guilt to the arena of nature. As for human companionship, no doubt Agee enjoyed at times, almost addictively, the company of others. Warren Eyster testifies to Agee's remarkable talent in "his ability to open up other people, to coax them into talking about things of more importance and to make them feel the importance of what they were talking about" (351), and Joseph O. Milner finds the need for communion with others, in conflict with the protagonist's sense of isolation, as the central theme in *A Death in the Family*. Even so, the search for communion and the legendary all-night conversations were always an escape from, never a solution to, Agee's haunting sense of guilt.

Traversing the mountain woods filled with vivid sights, odors, and sounds, Richard discovers a locust shell symbolic of his father's sudden but painful metamorphosis from sensuous life to death. With its "face of a human embryo" and its split back suggesting the pain of his father's broken body, the locust shell claims Richard's protection so that he detaches it "only with great care and gentleness" (*Morning Watch* 98–99). Examining the shell, Richard is amazed at the strength required of the locust in its passage to a new life, and with "veneration" he later replaces it on the tree.

The passage that follows, Richard's dive "as deep as he could go" into the sand pit, is the most important symbolic passage in the novel. The dive is an exploration of death and a futile attempt to know with certainty what lies beyond—a question that, despite his misgivings concerning conventional Christianity, always preoccupied Agee. By approaching death, Richard feels that he has made contact with his lost father, and reaching the bottom, "he wished that he need never come up" (103). He waits until the last moment to struggle to the surface, but even so, he feels he has failed. Agee writes that "he had tried to stay down too long as an act of devotion" (105), as more a devotion to his father than to anything else. With the realization that he has come close to death, Richard wins a moment of "tenderness and thankful wonder" (106), but his comforting moment is cut short by the appearance of an alarming visitor—a snake that complicates the novel's ending and has confounded more than one commentator.

Richard's reverence for the newly molted snake—"dazzling" and "just struggled out of his old skin" (107) and representing "all that is alien in nature and in beauty" (108)—parallels his idolatry for his father. Like his father, "princely" and "to be adored," the snake lays claim to his respect, but in its enthralling magnificence, it may be dangerous as well, a question that Richard never conclusively answers in his later examination of the snake's smashed head. Richard's impulse to spare the snake makes him conscious of new feelings that are difficult to understand and that also make him "uneasy" (109). Is this "something new" not Richard's newfound familiarity with "negativity" and with death itself? Does not the newly molted snake come, dazzling and in the princely figure of his father's memory, to claim him for all time? Even his emerging sexuality, in reality more pronounced than that of Hobe or Jimmy, binds him with the snake's element of time and death. The other boys automatically strike the snake in recognition of the alien forces it represents; only Richard meets the dying snake's eye and realizes his own condition of suffering can only be ended by an identical condition of death. Like the snake, which "would not die until sundown" (111), Richard's wounded life (including, we infer, his emerging sexuality) will seem one long death.

Perhaps in stopping to collect the locust shell and carry it back in his pocket, Richard shows that he has dealt with his father's death, but it seems highly unlikely that Richard will for long escape his father's ghost. True, after the effort of ending the wounded snake's suffering, "the veins stood out on his forearm almost like a man" (112)—a suggestion that Richard has "almost" attained maturity—and returning to the dormitory the boys feed the snake's body to the hogs, thus ridding him of the physical reminder of death. However, even this episode Richard connects with his father as he recalls the phrase "ever any more"—a phrase that was part of his mother's explanation that a merciful God took his suffering father to heaven and he "won't come back to us ever any more" (120). In any case, Richard explicitly connects his future life with that of the dying snake, dying all the day long, like climbing the hill back to school "forever so long as he might be alive." When he asks for God's forgiveness at the end of the book, Richard finds only "heaviness" and "sadness." Whatever note of resolution is contained in the final sentences, in which Richard feels a lessened sense of pain and "diminishing weight in his soul and body" (120), it seems only temporary comfort.

What does it say that the defining moment in Agee's life occurred at age six with the death of his father, and that he never moved conclusively beyond the great anger and self-punishment that this event engendered? Contrary to those who see Agee's obsession with the weak and disadvantaged exclusively as evidence of his "selflessness," I find that the more important fact, Agee's focus on his father's death and his artistic and psychological efforts to "preserve" childhood intact before the awful event, is evidence of an understandably greater priority, and of a priority that contains its own ethical imperatives—the human need for emotional survival in the face of an overwhelming sense of loss and later abandonment. The true center for Agee was indeed "self": witness his preoccupation with Jungian approaches to self-analysis that might connect his isolated soul with a more powerful body of ancestral myth.

Rather than the tragic, saintly figure that many readers discover in his work, James Agee is best seen as a gifted writer who could never put aside the terrible affliction of his childhood, in part because, unlike a similarly disadvantaged child from Dublin's lower middle class, Agee lacked the great shaping imagination that might fully order his raw experience into art and thus remedy his wounds. For all that, James Agee remained "faithful" in more senses than one, and thereby earned our respect as a writer who earnestly attempted to understand his condition of suffering and to fashion his experience, as best it could be fashioned, into serious and enduring fiction.

4

Ernest J. Gaines's Ideal of Community in A Gathering of Old Men

"He who knows only his own house knows little of the community," writes Ernest Gaines in an autobiographical essay ("Order" 250). One's "own house," whether it be one's immediate family or local neighborhood, must in time be broadened by participation in larger and different communities. Among the best examples in Gaines's fiction of this process of redefinition of community is his novel *A Gathering of Old Men*.

By definition the concept of community requires separateness, a sense of belonging within an affiliation that is exclusive or at least identifiable. The virtues of community—the essential human need for the sort of communal support that Jane Pittman finds at the end of Gaines's novel *The Autobiography of Miss Jane Pittman* ("the number of people I saw coming toward me was something I never would 'a' dreamed of" [243])—are realized at the cost of some degree of identity. Gaines's comment that Catherine Carmier could not "exist outside of the South" (O'Brien 86–87) and that she would not be "happier" if she did, reveals a wise recognition of the human need for social identity, as well as an understanding of its costs. Paradoxically, the emotional support provided by any close-knit community makes it possible for some to venture beyond its confines. It is the young men and women who grow up with the secure support of this primary community who are best prepared, and more apt, to establish lives outside their local community. As Thadious Davis writes in reference to Gaines's novel *Catherine Carmier*: "One must understand one's own place in the world and one's relationship to others before being able to go forth into the larger world" (11).

The values learned in "the Quarters"—the former slave quarters and Gaines's preeminent example of a close-knit and supportive community—are no more static than the literal community itself. Change is inherent in all human society, yet, surprisingly perhaps, change is enabled by the stability that the community affords. One young man who benefits from a supportive primary community is Jane Pittman's great-nephew Jimmy, who, in his role as the "leader" in *The Autobiography of Miss Jane Pittman*, "must go through certain steps," as Charles H. Rowell points out, which include absorption of the communal history, performance of good deeds within the community, education and travel outside the community, and return, where "he is tested when the people reject his new ways" (747). Like Jimmy, Jim Kelly in *Of Love and Dust* is one who must stand apart from as well as with the community. Painfully, Jim Kelly must ultimately leave the Quarters, and we are made to empathize with his sense of separation from "the people." Like many of Gaines's protagonists, Kelly is forced into a tragic isolation resulting from racial or social conflict: he is the victim of Marcus's heedlessness, of Cajun prejudice, and to some extent of his own perceptive intelligence and his willingness to become involved. As Alvin Aubert sums it up, Jim Kelly is a reminder to Marcus "of his responsibility for his own predicament" (72), even if "the situation" in which he finds himself was not of his own making. The Jim Kellys of Gaines's fiction fully register the complex web of human weakness and violation; without ever acceding to the system, they are inevitably drawn into and tested by it.

Within Gaines's writing, the transmission of ethical knowledge takes place largely within the localized setting of the family and the immediate community. Such ethical teaching is crucial in any society but particularly within one that has experienced enormous social changes of the sort that have occurred in the modern South. According to Gaines, the first duty of a mother to her children is "to show us how to live, to show us how to survive" (Gaudet and Wooton 65), and clearly, the very survival of Gaines's characters is often at stake. Gaines lovingly depicts the warmth and sheltering identity of "home" in his many stories set in the Quarters, and there is no doubt as to the nurturing value of the primary community, of home and neighbors who share nearly identical experiences and often embrace the same values. Beyond the intimate community of the family, a special sense of community exists among persons of the same generation and background. The old men in *A Gathering of Old Men* claim just such a common generational perspective. It is this community of neighbors that Johnny Paul has in mind when he says to Sheriff Mapes, "You don't see what we don't see"—that is, that Mapes fails to "see" the disappearance of "the people" from the Quarters, the life that once existed that "we don't see" now.

While a supportive community may provide a foundation for moral development, it is also necessary for human beings to develop beyond their limited sense of community, to empathize with and in fact "belong" to other communities. In *A Gathering of Old Men* "the notion of dual consciousness becomes crucial, in part because all the characters have two identities, one for larger society and one for their own intimate community" (Babb 114). Valerie Babb sees this dual consciousness indicated by the two names that each character in *A Gathering of Old Men* carries, the "oral" name in reference to personal identity and the written name in reference to formal society. Chimley, for example, insists that whites call him by his written name, Robert Louis Stevenson, reserving his nickname "Chimley" for a more intimate circle. The written name demands respect, the oral name is a "reflection of character" implying personal knowledge (Babb 114–16).

Gaines's understanding of community centers on the actual and immediate experiences of human beings, not necessarily on more abstract or distant affiliations. By this definition black and white Louisianans share a common history, even if they do not always recognize this fact. In *A Gathering of Old Men*, individuals from different backgrounds are brought together as a result of a shared history and in response to a common crisis. Under the pressure of necessity, they "stand," and their courageous action makes what they share more evident to them. The book's very title, *A Gathering of Old Men*, resonates on many levels of meaning beyond the literal "gathering" of those men with shotguns who join together to support Mathu. During the course of their symbolic journey, the old men themselves come to realize how they are "gathered" inevitably into community with others, as with those ancestors in the cemetery, many of whom they can personally remember and all of whom they recall through stories of "old times." The gathering brings together "black" men who are each individual, differentiated by shadings of color, class, experience, and, most importantly, character; beyond this, it gathers other men and women of various ethnic and social groups who, despite a past of violence and oppression, do come together after the fortitude of the black men has been tested and confirmed.

Every character in the novel faces the same challenge of understanding the present in relation to the past. What Gaines's protagonists initially lack, and what they often come to value most, is the sort of moral knowledge that involves a perception of life as a purposeful and unified movement toward a noble end. As Thadious Davis notes of Jackson Bradley in *Catherine Carmier*, Gaines's hero must satisfy "his need to be a black man with a sense of himself and his place in the world, essentially a man with a knowledge of his future based upon his past experiences" (9).

Having lived through experiences together, individuals gain a sense of affiliation. As Jerry H. Bryant defines it: "History *is* character ... but the character of little people rather than the great movers of events that inhabit formal history books" (861). In the course of their symbolic shared journey, the inevitable underworld journey that leads through death to purgation and rebirth, the old men and women in Gaines's novel articulate shared experience that bonds them in a close community. Miss Merle, for example, tries to remember why Clatoo "hates" Fix Boutan so much: "I knew most of the history of that river and of that parish the past fifty years" (Gaines, *Gathering* 25), she says, remembering that Forest Boutan, Fix's brother, had tried to rape one of Clatoo's sisters, who then defended herself and was sent to the penitentiary for life. Similarly, Gable recalls how his son was executed forty years before in the electric chair for allegedly raping a white woman. Tucker recalls how his brother outworked the mechanized tractor in a race with his two mules, then was beaten to death by the Cajuns while Tucker stood by paralyzed. Just as Tucker watched passively without helping his brother, all the old men share in the guilt of acquiescence. As Rufe comments: "We had all done the same thing sometime or another; we had all seen our brother, sister, mama, daddy insulted once and didn't do a thing about it" (97).

After the publication of his first book, Gaines tells us that he found himself "moving farther and farther back into the past" ("Order" 251). From the perspective of an ethics of fiction, this movement is crucial, for in his exploration of the saga-like history of entire lives, and indeed of the position of individual lives within larger histories, Gaines's storytelling conveys the reality of a *telos* within the pattern of discrete events. For characters like Miss Jane Pittman, storytelling is a crucial means of understanding her own life and the lives of her contemporaries within a history that encompasses periods from slavery times to the civil rights era. Similarly, in *A Gathering of Old Men*, the characters recognize the imperative need not only to understand their relation to the past as individuals but also to articulate and symbolize this moral understanding to their community. For the old men, the unmarked graveyard dating back to slave times is an important site of ethical knowledge, for it is a place in which the saga and *telos* of their history are painfully apparent.

Of course it is not only the black residents who have dead ancestors in the parish cemeteries or who remember their dead. The dead of each ethnic community are assuredly "all mixed together" (Gaines, *Gathering* 44), whether buried in the same plot of ground or not. Valerie Babb comments perceptively on the fact that various communities have always interacted in the historical world that Gaines records, even in the pre–civil rights period of this novel: "in Marshall Quarters forced segregation masks the fact that black and white interact intimately, and the actions of one affect the actions of the other" (123). Candy Marshall, heir to Marshall plantation, looks upon Mathu as a father because Mathu "knew them all" (177), that is, he knew the black and white generations, going back to her grandfather. She wants Mathu to be present for *her* children, to provide an important ancestral continuity. Instinctively, she grasps the value of this teleological knowledge, even as she fails to perceive the needs of her tenants in this regard.

The Quarters, the slave cabins of earlier generations, is no longer viable as an actual community, as Gaines admitted: "When you say 'the future of the land,' I know there is no future for blacks on this place at all" (Gaudet and Wooton 75). Gaines harbors no sentimental attachment to "the land" or to the past, but he does "care very much about the cemetery"—that is, the "people" who are still there, the ancestors buried on the land—and he is intensely concerned with understanding the past and its legacies. In a sense "the land" is already lost, has been lost for a long time, but Rowell is undoubtedly correct in saying that "the old men's stand in *A Gathering of Old Men* is against the whites' violation of the land, which the blacks need for emotional and ancestral attachment as well as a source of survival" (747). The "machines," the Cajuns' tractors that displaced black farmers in an earlier generation, have destroyed Yank's life by ending his profession of horse breaking, but Gaines has no intention of returning to the era of horse and mule. The mechanical world of the present must be confronted and lived in, and a falsely sentimental reversion to agrarianism or a romantic attachment to subsistence farming can only be destructive of people. "I really don't care about the place," Gaines says flatly, speaking of the "old place" where he grew up in rural Louisiana. "I'm not trying to preserve the Old South, for damned sure" (Gaudet and Wooton 75).

The rural setting is important in Gaines's fiction as a site of memory; it is a place of reflection in which his characters gain understanding of the purpose of their lives. There is a ritualized sharing of memories in *A Gathering of Old Men* and other novels by Gaines; there are also ritual acts of bonding. Mat has to borrow a gun and #5 shells to participate in the "gathering": he must also hitch a ride on Clatoo's truck, on which Chimley rides as well. In a symbolic distribution of food, Dirty Red gives Snookum pecans from the cemetery, which Snookum in turn distributes to two other children. Literally, the bodies of the ancestors, in the form of pecans nurtured in the earth of the cemetery, are passed down in communion to the children, who are also part of the "gathering." As Audrey L. Vinson writes: "At the graveyard, Dirty Red, the least auspicious one in the group, conducts a eucharistic ritual by eating and passing out the pecans which had fallen from trees near the graves. His eating these pecans suggest eating the broken bodies of his ancestors (Christ figures in their symbolic, sacrificial lives)" (41). After Miss Merle brings sandwiches, everyone joins in a more inclusive communion that includes both races and all ages: "Not one there was not eating.... We were all hungry," Lou Dimes says (Gaines, *Gathering* 126). Other ritualized scenes suggest universal group affiliation. The climax of the novel involves the ritual crucifixion of Charlie Biggs, who offers his body to the gunfire of the Cajuns as he also shoots Luke Will; afterward men as well as women, of both races, approach Charlie's body and reverently touch it as a gesture of ritual connection intended to affirm their identity, to preserve their memory of the event, and perhaps, in an ancient and instinctive response, to guarantee his soul's safe passage with the support of the living community.

Not least of all is the gathering of "men" in the gender generic sense: the males' action of "standing" draws together persons across gender lines, bringing women and men together in ethical solidarity for the first time as the women extend unstinting respect and the men open their hearts and minds to the women. For each of the elderly black men and women, fear had become normalized behavior, and thus, ashamed of themselves, they have been ashamed to face one another. The gathering of the old men is their last chance to assert both their individuality and their essential identity with others from different communities, but this assertion is based upon a more important development: their common recognition of the moral necessity not only of "standing" in mutual self-defense but also of articulating the shared meaning of their lives. For their part, the women participate in this restoration as much more than spectators, for they offer both emotional support and tangible aid. Beulah contributes her "amen" and wisecracks from the porch steps, while Glo Hebert holds onto Clatoo's hand when he arrives at Mathu's house, so that he felt "she was proud of us all being there now" (51). Miss Merle's act of handing out sandwiches not only satisfies hunger but fosters bonding and a sense of common endeavor, an important stage on the ritual journey to wholeness and life.

As Aubert notes, it is typical of Gaines's fiction that "nothing is absolute, final; all value lies in process, in the potentiality of process to produce viable human options" (71). The degree of racial conflict that Gaines portrays in *A Gathering of Old Men* reflects in a realistic way the experience of a previous generation, but all human experience is continually being reshaped. As in *The Autobiography of Miss Jane Pittman*, in which Gaines "was trying to go back, back, back into our experiences in this country to find some kind of meaning to our present lives" (Gaines, "Miss Jane and I" 34), *A Gathering of Old Men* employs the device of layering the past onto the present by focusing on men and women from the past who have lived on into the present and whose memories keep alive the entire history of their community. Viewed from the present, the reasons why the old men had to confront Beau Boutan do seem "absurd" (Babb 130), what Rowell terms "the struggles of a static world fiercely resistant to change" (736), yet Gaines implies every generation faces a similar condition of moral failure and must break with its own "static world" of resistance. The degree of racial distrust and paternalism portrayed in the novel are out of place in the 1970s and clearly have no future, as is indicated by the context into which the old men are transported, particularly by the existence of Gil Boutan and Cal Harrison, "Salt" and "Pepper" of the LSU football team. As Babb comments, the "racial unity" that Gil and Cal symbolize reflects a dependency "that Gaines, as a literary observer, sees shared by blacks and whites of the South" (128). As Mary Ellen Doyle notes, Gaines insists that he writes for no particular audience though he does speak to "the black youth of the South" of "a sense of proud and free identity" and to "the white youth of the South" of "the essential unity of all human beings" (91). It is important to recognize that Gaines's fiction offers an ethical rather than a racialized message: the significance of the fiction is not bounded by race, gender, or other restrictions.

As Gayle Addison, Jr., notes, in Gaines's view "we are circumscribed by historical patterns and ... those who step outside such patterns are paradigms for future generations" (288). Certainly some individuals are more willing to sacrifice themselves than most in the community, but never is their sacrifice an entirely independent act, in that it is always supported or prepared for, or at least acquiesced in, by many others. As

Gaines noted in an interview, the process of change is itself daunting but inescapable, so daunting that change is never the work of a single individual. In all of his work Gaines is showing "characters [who] make an attempt toward change, and some other character might continue where they left off. But to break away from the past, from one philosophy to another, is a burden that one person cannot endure alone. Someone else must pick up from there and go on" (O'Brien 84).

Particularly in the limited space of the Quarters, even the most individual actions become public events and have a transforming effect on the community. The resilience and creativity of individuals, however, requires the catalyst that often emerges from harsh conditions shared by the group. As Rowell explains, the circumscribed conditions of the Quarters was designed by slave masters to control and break slaves: this purpose was thwarted by slaves who transformed the crowded space of the Quarters into a community that offered "friendship and mutual protection" (737). Conversely, to some extent the loss of a sense of communal values follows upon the physical dislocation of the people and an increasingly private and individualistic lifestyle.

Just as the social conditions of African Americans reflect historical reality, the attitudes of the Cajuns, white Louisianans of French Canadian ancestry, are shown to evolve out of their history. The Cajun locale in *A Gathering of Old Men* is called Bayou Michel, located ten miles from Marshall Plantation. For the older generation of Cajuns, represented by Fix Boutan, Bayou Michel is exclusive, a place where the family is the most important unit and outsiders are suspect. The "liberal" professor from LSU finds much the same atmosphere in a local barroom frequented by defensive Cajuns such as Luke Will. Because of their experiences, the older African American generation deeply distrusted the Cajun population. Gaines commented: "I think that by the time we got there, we did not associate any problems between white and black on False River as a Cajun problem. But I think in the time of my stepfather and his generation, it was" (Gaudet and Wooton 83). Clearly, the Cajuns do not represent to Gaines himself what they did to his stepfather's generation. Although the Cajun people have historically been in competition with, and often in conflict with, the African American tenantry, their portrayal in Gaines's writing demonstrates the author's understanding of the historical limitations under which all human communities have lived. As Thadious Davis acknowledges, despite their Snopes-like qualities, "the Cajuns are [Gaines's] transformational men who slake off the restrictions of their own past deprivations and are hardworking, productive people" (5).

At the end of the novel women and men of all races are transformed in terms of their potential as mature ethical agents, and they return proudly to their communities. The narrative action is symbolic of the possibilities of moral change: the old men at the end are brought to trial but return to their families after sentencing; Mathu rides with Clatoo, whom he now respects as a man; Mat returns to the protective if sometimes domineering love of Ella; Candy leaves the courthouse with the prospect of actually concluding a marriage with her fiancé Lou Dimes. The novel's denouement, returning to an apparently complacent calm, marks the passing of an era of racial distrust and separation. Mathu and others connected with the older generation have survived a ritual journey of death and rebirth and forever surrendered their outdated view of single and separate communities.

The interrelationship between different communities that Gaines portrays in his fiction resembles Tzvetan Todorov's concept of cultural dialogue. In *The Discovery of America*, his study of the first meetings of Native Americans and Europeans, Todorov suggests ways to conceptualize the process of cultural interconnection. Unlike more programmatic studies of the Spanish discovery and conquest of the New World, Todorov's work investigates the multiplicity of ways in which Native Americans and Europeans interacted, and he describes a "cultural dialogue" in which neither group finds it necessary to "identify" with the other in the sense of giving up one's own identity. Nor does true dialogue imply a separatist conception of identity: "one does not let the other live merely by leaving him intact" (250). Todorov sees dangers in a contemporary attempt to "caricature" the experience of difference rather than engage in the give-and-take of dialogue itself: such caricature leaves the "other" not encountered but merely mythologized in terms that are unrealistic or patronizing. By contrast, "Gaines's narratives do not recount the doings of a single community; rather they record the spiritual, social, economic, political strivings of a people in the act of becoming" (Rowell 750). Gaines's "community"—for which we must read "communities" in constant process—changes inevitably and yet it coheres, through memory, through family, through local neighborhood. True community is the interaction of individuals who share a common history. As a state of mind more than an actual place, "community" assumes the "gathering" of persons, often of widely diverse identities but who share some commonality of experience. In the end toward which Gaines's narrative is always moving, community draws into itself individuals of diverse backgrounds, provided only that they are willing to "stand" as individuals first, which is Gaines's condition for all who would live inside a genuine community with others.

5

A Meditation on History and Ethics: Ernest J. Gaines's A Lesson Before Dying

Ernest J. Gaines's entire career has been marked by a search for a useful African American cultural tradition. Implicit in his narrative is the recognition that, while cultures change and evolve, the basis for any civilization is an inherited culture with roots in folk and popular tradition. In novels such as *The Autobiography of Miss Jane Pittman, In My Father's House, A Gathering of Old Men,* and *A Lesson Before Dying,* we see Gaines's efforts to lay bare a cultural tradition and to write narratives in which the past constitutes the basis for a progressive vision of the future. As an African American writer who focuses on the problem of representing a coherent cultural tradition, Gaines has faced the central problem of the African American Diaspora, in which a coherent African folk culture was fractured by removal to America and in which the possibility of an alternate New World culture has been undermined further by more recent migration out of the South.

In his own case, having as a teenager moved to California to live with his mother and stepfather, Gaines found that it was necessary to suppress his own rural heritage. In California he learned that "you were never supposed to tell people you came from the country," yet for Gaines this silence was a denial of his historical identity based on his childhood experience in "the Quarters" (the community that centered around the former slave quarters near Oscar, Louisiana) and his intimate contact with the storytelling and local knowledge of his elders: "Not only was he lying to himself, but he was denying knowing the others, the ones he had left, and wasn't that the same as denying who he was?" (Gaines, "Order" 250). Gaines never forsook his southern heritage entirely, but in his early writing he viewed that heritage with greater distance and irony than in his later novels. Unlike many of his contemporaries, Gaines never sought a direct African source as the basis for cultural order. The real source of coherence at the center of all of Gaines's writing is precisely that culture that he was told to conceal in California: the southern rural folk tradition.

In *A Lesson Before Dying*, Gaines adopts a more affirming attitude toward the entire range of southern traditional culture, and he finds in this culture, which includes African American religion, respect for elders, loyalty to family and neighbors, and commonsense morality, a useful and enduring cultural tradition that can be set against the fragmentation inherent in the long Diaspora. The importance of *A Lesson Before Dying* rests in the novel's acceptance of a southern folk culture about which Gaines has demonstrated considerable ambivalence through most of his career. In this novel, Gaines has achieved a greater clarity and perspective in his presentation of the workings of an entire cultural system. As a result of his discovery of the traditional culture as a basis for authority, he appears more hopeful. There is a real sense that the components are there to restore order to a fragmented culture.

In his effort to reverse the cultural alienation resulting from the Diaspora, Gaines adopts the model of nineteenth-century realist fiction. This tradition of classic realism, analyzed by Georg Lukács in *The Historical Novel* and other works, serves Gaines well as a model for illuminating the historical causes of cultural symptoms, and while the relation of Gaines's work to a Lukácsian conception of history is problematic at several points—for example, in Gaines's manifest effort at moral fable and in the static, assured chronicle of history suggested in some of his writing—the terms of Lukács's theory are nonetheless useful in understanding the work of this major contemporary author.[1] Gaines's place in this literary history comes late, well after the period of classic nineteenth-century realism, but I would suggest that his work, interpellated as it is with the evidence of cultural fragmentation, duplicates the progressive aesthetic of earlier realist texts. Gaines's novels link individuals to their social context with the explicit purpose of combating the alienation of capitalist and racist society. Gaines has never been content to replay the naturalistic mode of representation of other late capitalist texts, for beneath the sensuous detail of his novels rests the author's vision of social change. In interviews Gaines has frequently stressed that he is writing with the self-conscious intention of examining the course of American social history, not merely to represent this history in naturalistic terms but to change it.[2] Thus, his fiction aspires to and achieves a distinctive mode, fusing careful observation of social history with a forceful social vision.

A Lesson Before Dying may well be, as *Publishers Weekly* suggested, Gaines's "crowning achievement" (Maryles 21), for this novel is clearly the culmination of a sustained meditation on the larger issues of history and ethics. By focusing his narrative on the execution of an innocent man, and on the relationship of that man to his own marginalized community and to the dominant community that unjustly convicted him, Gaines is able to explore the structure of communal association and to imply the possibility for social change. Significantly, in a novel set in the 1940s in rural Louisiana, the issue of capital punishment has been displaced by an interest in relating and underscoring the positive resources of the traditional black community. Clearly, Gaines intends to locate his novel within a literary tradition in which the powerful subject of the execution of an innocent man is a familiar trope used to represent the broader repression of African Americans, but Gaines employs this trope in a way that carries the narrative beyond naturalistic representation focused on the past. Jefferson, his protagonist, is a dynamic character who, along with Grant Wiggins, Tante Lou, Miss Emma, and others, becomes a center of agency in the novel by virtue of his decision to reject a victimized status. Gaines treats the issue of capital punishment as a manifestation of an underlying cultural problem with roots in American history, which he carefully positions in historical terms.

Although he spent his early years in rural Louisiana, in several respects Gaines stands outside the tradition of southern African American narrative running from Frederick Douglass to Richard Wright. For one thing, it is important to understand that Gaines's perspective has never been specifically "southern." Like so many of his protagonists, Gaines was educated and lived much of his adult life in California, and as a result he brings a broader perspective to the southern African American historical narrative. Even as a teenager Gaines habitually saw racial issues in ameliorating terms. As he stated in an interview with Bernard Magnier, "I went to California when I was very young, to a decent, small town where I was completely integrated into the school" (Gaines, "Ernest J. Gaines" 7). In California, Gaines soon learned of more diverse communities than those of his childhood in rural Louisiana: "blacks, whites, Asians, Latinos—all the groups, races who were Californians at that time" (Gaines, "Order" 247), and though a good deal of conflict still existed, a progressive vision of racial cooperation was undoubtedly more available than in the South of that era. The "California perspective" is a significant element of Gaines's historical fiction, for it underlies his ability to read the southern past as a "pre-text" to the present, to use Lukács's phrase.

Gaines begins his novel with a conventional narrative of victimization, structuring his plot around an innocent black man who, without adequate legal representation, is convicted by an all-white jury of murdering Gropé, a Cajun store owner, yet Gaines's interest centers less on this injustice than on the restoration of Jefferson's human dignity. The hegemonic system that prosecutes him is nearly erased from the novel as Gaines shifts the sense of agency to Jefferson, Grant, and Paul, Jefferson's poor-white jailer. In restoring Jefferson's status as a worthy member of society, Gaines focuses in particular upon the importance of male role models in the family and community. In an interview with Charles H. Rowell, Gaines traced the fragmentation of African American family life back to the effects of slavery, in which families were routinely separated: "I feel that because of that separation they [father and son] still have not, philosophically speaking, reached each other again" (Gaines, "Louisiana Thing" 40). Grant Wiggins's relationship to Jefferson repeats a familiar cultural pattern in which an older male abnegates his responsibility for a younger one. Only at the insistence of his elders, particularly the female elders of his community, does Grant accept his responsibility to "teach" younger males. Grant has taken on the crucial role of "teacher" in his small community but has reneged on the responsibility to engage the community's indigenous system of belief. The task that Gaines sets for Grant and Jefferson is to free themselves from an enslaving myth based on past events—in Lukács's terms, to quit an antiquarian narrative of history, and to enter history as actors.

The essentially social nature of Gaines's fiction is everywhere apparent in *A Lesson Before Dying*. Significantly, all of Gaines's protagonists—indeed all of his significant characters—possess the sort of social relationship and "personal history" (the development from one stage of life to another and out of a contextualized setting and past) that Lukács identifies with realist characterization. The historicity of Gaines's fiction has compelling consequences. In Lukács's terms, the "concrete potentiality" evident in his fiction restricts rather than expands possibilities of abstract thought, and it is the limiting of potentiality that shapes great historical fiction and leads to positive development toward social ends. As Lukács recognizes, in life, situations arise in which people are faced with choices, and only through particular ethical choices does human character come into being. Similarly, in a realist work of literature, a character's decisions alter the future in concrete ways, and the acknowledgment of concrete potentiality implicit in realist aesthetics forms the basis for compelling narrative of social responsibility and moral account-ability.

Inseparable from Gaines's realist ideology is the severe transparency of his style. Nearly all critics of Gaines's work have recognized the "clarity" and "simplicity" of his writing, but it has not been generally understood that his style functions in opposition to a body of modernist and postmodernist writing in which aesthetic distortion reflects a static and ahistorical condition of existence and in which an incoherent surface displaces a coherent weltanschauung and ethical vision. Gaines is using narrative style in a very deliberate, self-conscious way, as evidenced by his comment: "I think of writing as well as I can—writing cleanly, clearly, truthfully, and making it simple enough so that anyone might be able to pick it up and read it" (Gaines, "Louisiana Thing" 49). By assert-ing "cleanly, clearly, truthfully" as his artistic standards, Gaines reveals a great deal about his position vis-à-vis modernism.

The "clarity" and "truthfulness" that Gaines insists on are possible only in the representation of a definite historical setting. Gaines's lan-guage is complex in its connotative richness, but his use of language is grounded in a historical community in which the layers of implied meaning are clearly understood. An example of this transparency of meaning within communal discourse is the children's rendering of the Nativity, a familiar pageant in which the words and imagery of the bibli-cal story are translated into the terms of local experience. With a hammer hanging from the loop of his overalls, Joseph looks down on Mary and the Christ child; the Three Wise Men kneel down, each placing "a penny on the bench beside Mary" (Gaines, *Lesson* 150). The shared dialect and sociolect are based on mutual assumptions and shared history as a point of reference, and these assumptions are understood by both black and white residents. As an educated black who is therefore automatically judged by both races to be a partial "outsider," Grant, at several points, violates the repressive code that prohibits blacks from using standard English. For example, he almost makes the "mistake" of properly pro-nouncing "batteries" with three syllables instead of the regional "battries" expected by Sheriff Guidry and other whites. The communal norms can be restrictive, but Grant's impulse is to dismiss entirely the importance of communal history, and in doing so he sets aside the belief in historical consequences that underpins all forms of social responsibility.

In opposition to Grant's modern skepticism, Gaines asserts the im-portance of belief in a coherent system of human responsibility. *A Lesson*

Before Dying is structured around the dominant metaphor of the "lesson," with its attendant figures of "teacher" and "pupil." Developing his metaphor of education, Gaines employs the idea of the "teacher who must learn." Grant Wiggins, the central consciousness in *A Lesson Before Dying*, is an elementary school teacher in the fictional Bayonne, Louisiana. Viewing his role as teacher in a purely mechanical way as he teaches reading, writing, and arithmetic and "drills" the class in preparation for the annual visit of Dr. Joseph, the school inspector, Grant's intention of making his class "responsible young men and young ladies" (39) must be taken as quite ironic. From the community's perspective, the teacher's knowledge must be reliable and comprehensive, and the teacher himself must be a "model" for his students; consequently, the teacher's lifestyle and demeanor are examined for imperfections. Through his outright dismissal of communal norms, Grant fails this high standard set by the community, and he must look to Jefferson as a model of learning that is based on more than "book knowledge." Ultimately Grant is willing to embody the community's values of moral education in his daily life, including a willingness to humble himself before his elders. Grant's accommodation with Reverend Ambrose, and his acquiescence toward Tante Lou and her friend Miss Emma, are crucial narrative actions, for they enact his changing attitudes toward the mores of a traditional community. By embracing his role within his own history, Grant finally becomes a teacher in the fullest sense: one seeking "to relieve pain, to relieve hurt," as Reverend Ambrose puts it (218).

From Grant's initial point of view, one of the "flawed" aspects of his history is the dependence of African American society on Christianity. Grant's conflict between religion and secular humanism, reaching back to his adolescent rejection of the church, repeats a familiar situation in Gaines's work, but in this novel there is more understanding of the function of Christianity within social community and a warning concerning the social, if not spiritual, consequences of its rejection. The religious calendar against which the novel's events take place, beginning one month before Christmas and ending the second Friday after Easter, introduces a meaningful annual cycle around which the local community organizes its life. The enactment of the Nativity, the passage of Lent, and the festivity of Easter Sunday are shared rituals that are passed down from one generation to the next; they form one basis of shared communication between individuals. Grant's condescending attitude toward the bible verses that his pupils recite is indicative of a more general complacency toward his people and their particular culture: "After listening to one or two of the verses, I tuned out the rest of them. I had heard them all many times" Grant says (33).[3] Yet in the crucible of events leading up to Jefferson's execution, Grant comes to understand the role of religion as a collective narrative of hope within a traditional community. Although Grant may never be convinced of the truth of Christian dogma, he does come to accept the value of belief as he sees it work through the agency of Reverend Ambrose, and he acknowledges its productive and unifying role within the community.

Grant's earlier denial of religious belief was connected to his denial of the potential for "heroism" in himself. To paraphrase the argument between Grant and Reverend Ambrose, any significant self-sacrifice in life, especially in the case of one faced with an imminent death sentence, appears to require faith in an existence that continues after death; in the context of the southern rural society, to deny the afterlife is to undercut the very basis of responsibility that holds the community together and that binds individuals to the community, educating them to norms of behavior based on an acceptance of social responsibility. What Grant sees as his own intellectual "honesty," his refusal to "lie" to Jefferson about his skepticism concerning the afterlife, amounts to an abnegation of participation in a particular community. It is a refusal to take seriously the belief system of the time and place in which he lives, and inevitably his skepticism becomes a corrupting model for others. In a sense, Grant is responsible for Jefferson's presence during the murder of a liquor store owner, and for the other youths who commit the murder. Once the binding of shared values is severed, discrete acts of irresponsibility and violence occur with increasing frequency. The individual is unable to invent a personal culture; human civilization is the shared creation of the human masses over time. Despite his air of narrow-minded dogmatism, Reverend Ambrose sums up this conception of cultural order with his remark to Grant that "long as I can stand on my feet, I owe her [Miss Ella] and all the others every ounce of my being. And you do too" (216).

Grant mechanically repeats this message of moral obligation to Jefferson: "No matter how bad off we are ... we still owe something" (139), yet Grant views this obligation in merely personal, not communal, terms (as evidenced by his consuming yet unfulfilling relationship with Vivian Baptiste, which ironically might lead to their "running away together"). He does not yet understand the more universal responsibility of human beings for others outside of an intimate relationship, and he has little if any sense of obligation to ancestors or descendants. Characteristically, as Grant gradually comes to understand the human need for shared belief, he does so by relating it to his literary education. After listening to the old men relating the exploits of Jackie Robinson, Grant thinks of James Joyce's "Ivy Day in the Committee Room," through which he discovers the universality of the need for heroes, whether in Ireland or in Louisiana. Only at the very end, however, does Grant connect his reading with the situation he now faces, of trying to convert Jefferson, and necessarily to convert himself, to the belief in responsibilities beyond his own immediate needs or feelings. Thinking of Jefferson just before the execution, Grant asks: "Have I done anything to make you not believe? If I have please forgive me for being a fool" (249). Reflecting on how Reverend Ambrose is able "to use their God to give him strength" (240), Grant thinks now of the "old man's" fortitude, yet he still refuses to kneel and pray with his students. Following the execution, a butterfly appears in the field of bull grass and flies away, signaling the passage of Jefferson's soul. Still uncertain of his own belief, Grant nonetheless tells his new friend Paul: "You have to believe to be a teacher" (254).

Behind the fabric of the novel one perceives Gaines's usage of his fable as a "lesson"—really a form of chastisement (a "lesson" in a remediating sense)—to instruct the reader in a fundamental truth about moral choice and historical contingency. Like Grant, and like Jefferson, all human beings are "condemned" by their involvement in history, facing the same "death sentence" by virtue of their mortality, and forced by their nature to become actors within a historical context that limits potentiality. Like Grant and Jefferson, all face a fundamental and inescapable decision: to choose to be actors within a flawed and unjust history or to withdraw from it as passive "victims" or onlookers. Grant's "lesson" leads him to adopt a more comprehensive and, paradoxically, more local perspective based on his own commitment to a particular place. His relationship with Vivian leads to a more earnest commitment to particular human beings, for after she becomes pregnant with his child, Grant's relationship to the entire community gradually changes. Since Vivian is required by the terms of her divorce decree to remain within visiting distance of her ex-husband, Grant is now also tied to the area. His dream of escaping the South, perhaps moving back to California (and, in fact, of fleeing all connection with particular human communities), is replaced by the necessity to remain and to change the social conditions of a specific place.

The conflict between Grant and Reverend Ambrose is subtly conveyed by their contrasting attitudes toward the radio that Grant brings Jefferson. Characterized as a "sin box" by Reverend Ambrose, the radio is viewed as merely "company" by Grant. At first Jefferson plays the "sin box" loudly enough to distract his mind from what Reverend Ambrose and Miss Emma are trying to do for him, but finally the radio, while still playing the night before his execution, is muted. As Grant increasingly reconciles with Reverend Ambrose, and as Grant's new influence is felt by Jefferson, the radio continues to play but ceases to be a distraction. Its muted play reflects the accommodation of Grant and Reverend Ambrose. More important than the radio, however, Grant supplies Jefferson with pencil and paper and suggests that Jefferson write down his thoughts, especially the thoughts that come to him at night. This gift leads to an important development in Jefferson's character: the beginning of his self-expression and communication with others.

The awakening of self-respect in Jefferson is paralleled by Grant's restoration as a responsible human being who believes in his own self-worth, especially in his role as a teacher. Watching the enjoyment of his fifth- and sixth-graders sawing and chopping wood (tasks familiar to their ancestors in slavery times), Grant had wondered if he had taught them anything. Repeating the lives of the older black men, the boys show little interest in the educational skills that, Grant believes, will lift them out of rural poverty. As one critic noted, "Grant's own struggle with self-contempt and hatred for his students" was in part the legacy of his teacher, Matthew Antoine, and this struggle "culminate[s] in his jailhouse mission to resurrect Jefferson" ("Review" 66). It may seem paradoxical, yet Jefferson's sacrificial death seems to be a necessary prelude to Grant's self-discovery, a transformation that emerges fully only at the moment of Jefferson's death. Jefferson's heroism not only restores Grant's faith and gives the dying Miss Emma someone "to be proud of"; it lifts the community as a whole beyond its habitual posture of "broken men." The very definition of a "hero," as Grant recites it to Jefferson, is of one "who does something for other people" (*Lesson* 191). Perhaps stated most directly and eloquently, "a hero does for others" (191). Implicitly this definition has been understood by Grant's students, if not immediately by their teacher, as they perform the Nativity pageant with its celebration of Christ as "a hero [who] does for others."

Implicit in Gaines's definition is the realization that heroic action implies social connection: heroism in the peculiar modernist sense of the isolated aesthete shaping a private mythology is unthinkable. Rather, heroism arises out of the hero's sense of relationship to a community (the most striking embodiment of such heroism within Gaines's fiction is the 110-year-old Jane Pittman's participation in a protest march at the conclusion of her life). The act of heroism, in fact, is collective, for it is impossible without the community's participation. In *A Lesson Before Dying*, women as well as men participate in and incite the heroism of Grant and Jefferson by a number of actions that reinforce their communal ties. In prison, Jefferson responds to Miss Emma by eating a bit of her gumbo, a ritual of communion that signals his acknowledgment of his social ties to her. Similarly, following his run-in with the two mulattos at the Rainbow Club, Grant is served food by Vivian as a mark of her concern. Again, Tante Lou sends Grant food when he feels most depressed. At the Rainbow Club the waitress Thelma, who loans Grant her hard-earned money to buy Jefferson a radio, insists on serving him food in a manner that reinforces their common beliefs and hopes. All of these examples of providing sustenance are ritual actions that suggest a faith in life. As David E. Vancil writes, Gaines associates a "sustaining resilience" with women: "Without the *hope* that these women provide through their belief in redemption in the future, life would be intolerable" (490). The serving and partaking of food is an elemental ritual activity, and the manner in which a meal is shared is closely connected with the idea of shared humanity, especially in the context of a person awaiting execution. Visiting Jefferson in the prison dayroom, Miss Emma and Tante Lou make a point of "setting the table" in a respectable fashion by bringing a tablecloth, silverware, and cloth napkins. The meal is not merely for sustenance but to embody in its performance a certain image of human existence—in this case, the choice to restrain animal impulses and to share a meal with dignity, an act that, to use the language of the novel, separates "man" from "hog." Thus, at the end, the "gallon" of ice cream that Jefferson at first requests is reduced to a "cup," to be consumed following a meal cooked by Miss Emma. Jefferson's final meal is dignified, not the gorging he had envisioned.

The lesson that Jefferson gradually discovers in himself and that others learn from him surely has to do with what it means to be a civilized human being. The "dayroom" is important as the setting for Jefferson's transformation, for in the dayroom visits can take place with a sense of dignity, as everyone can sit around a table instead of having to stand or crouch in Jefferson's cramped cell. Walking around the dayroom with

Grant, Jefferson begins crying because of his certainty that "lowly as I am, I am still part of the whole" (*Lesson* 194). This scene is the beginning of Jefferson's knowledge of a humanity learned only with the support of Miss Emma, Tante Lou, Grant, Reverend Ambrose, and countless others in the village. Appropriately, the novel ends with the establishment of several friendships, including that of Miss Emma and Jefferson, Jefferson and Grant, and Grant and the white deputy Paul, suggesting the fabric of community that is tied so closely to the ideal of education in the novel. Jefferson has never spoken of friendship to anyone, but on the eve of execution he not only declares it but begins to articulate its meaning in his crudely written but eloquent journal.

Of course, it is not only Jefferson who is in need of communal support, or who, in a larger sense, is "dying." Every human being is mortal and thus exists in need of the assuaging and supportive rituals that Gaines details in *A Lesson Before Dying*. As we have seen, Grant Wiggins's cynicism concerning human potential parallels Jefferson's despair following his trial. Those who are ill or dying are in equal need of support. After Miss Emma, distraught over the impending execution, takes to her sickbed, a crowd gathers at her house, now managed by Tante Lou. The universal practice of "visiting" to express support for the sick and/or dying is acted out in a way that demonstrates the communal mores. In another example, members of the community employ clothing to express their sense of deference for an important occasion. At the Nativity performance, all show up appropriately dressed in their "going-to-town clothes," different from "Sunday best" and from ordinary working clothes. Following the intricate regulations of a traditional community, human beings take responsibility for their own appearance on such important occasions. Through the use of such shared signals, a system of communal support and faith is maintained.

It is precisely this group involvement in the process of change that William L. Andrews stresses in his reading of Gaines: "the folk has assumed over the years an identity based on progressive struggle ... the struggle to recognize and conserve its spiritual and heroic folk traditions." As a social realist, Gaines pursues an aesthetic in which character is embedded in the process of a concrete social history and in which ethical choices are shown to have particular consequences. Given this artistic and social ideology, Gaines's fiction takes the form of a chastisement—a "lesson before dying" for the reader, who is equally involved in historical process. All images of chastisement (Grant's correction of his students,

Tante Lou's correction of Grant, Reverend Ambrose's lecture to Grant, Jefferson's restoration to dignity) are related and subsumed to the over-riding lesson of social responsibility, which itself is commensurate with a recognition of social change as dependent on human agency. The importance of the social community lies in its power to support and pass on traditional knowledge, particularly knowledge of ethical consequences. As a writer working within a classic tradition of social realism, Gaines has contributed to an understanding of the historical context of African American society, and he has envisioned progressive change through the agency of its members.

Notes

1. Throughout this essay I rely heavily on the narrative theory of Georg Lu-kács, particularly his essay "The Ideology of Modernism" and *The Historical Novel*. William L. Andrews, Jerry H. Bryant, Michel Fabre, and Charles H. Rowell, among others, have examined the aesthetic implications of Gaines's historical narrative.

2. See, for example, Rowell's interview with Gaines (Gaines, "Louisiana Thing" 39–51).

3. At the same time, Gaines remains realistic about the function of both white and black Christianity within the social and political order of the South. Filtering his commentary through Grant's consciousness, Gaines ironically notes the lack of true "sensitivity" among Christians toward the taking of life: "Always on Friday. Same time as He died, between twelve and three. But they can't take this one's life too soon after the recognition of His death, because it might upset the sensitive few." (*Lesson* 158). The date set for Jefferson's execution is delayed to April 8, two weeks after Easter.

6

Henry Roth's Narratives of Captivity

Henry Roth, who died in 1995 at age 89, was the author of *Call It Sleep* (1934), *Shifting Landscape* (1987), and a multivolume novel, *Mercy of a Rude Stream*, published between 1994 and 1998. Many of the significant questions concerning Roth's artistic career are suggested by what Roth himself called the "longest writer's block in history," and it is important to consider the reason for this blockage and the fact of Roth's recovery from it during the last two decades of his life. Roth's hiatus from writing—a remarkable period of silence for an enormously gifted writer who was widely praised for his first novel—should, I believe, be understood as symptomatic of a condition of subservience to an adopted national culture, a captivity from which Roth never significantly freed himself as the conflicting ideals of pride in his immigrant history and his drive toward assimilation left him no alternative but silence. The searing humiliation of Roth's childhood, beginning in the Lower East Side slums, resulted in an habitual identification with privilege and hegemony, an identification that Roth questioned only in retrospect. Even then, in the revisionary settling of accounts of *Mercy of a Rude Stream*, Roth anxiously adopted new sources of authority, even as he freed himself of earlier captivity.

Both Roth's writing itself, and the critical reception and promotion of his writing, must be positioned in relation to the control of hegemonic culture. The force of the national culture is everywhere evident in the critical reception of his work, from the ambivalence of contemporary reviewers of *Call It Sleep* (impressed by Roth's artistry but uncomfortable with his political tentativeness) through the novel's "rediscovery" after its reissue in 1964. Roth's work continued to attract critical attention, notably in Alfred Kazin's influential *New York Review of Books* essay on *Call It Sleep*. With the publication of the first volumes of *Mercy of a Rude Stream*, beginning in 1994, even greater interest in Roth's work emerged as evidenced by such influential essays as Irving Howe's review on the front page of the *New York Times Book Review*. The critical perception of Henry Roth's work, however, has remained consistent since the 1930s and has itself been, as Kazin points out, a product of the intellectual culture of the late-modernist period. As Kazin writes: "We can see now that [*Call It Sleep*] belongs to the side of the 1930s that still believed in the sacredness of literature, whether or not it presumed to change the world" (x). This interpretation, in which Roth is figured as a heroic sufferer in the cause of revolutionary art, continued to be echoed even in later poststructuralist criticism, such as an article on Roth's textuality by Wayne Lesser.[1] A third generation of critics, including Thomas J. Ferraro and Hana Wirth-Nesher, has positioned Roth in relation to new interests in immigrant and multiethnic literary studies. All of these readings, however, obscure the destructive force of hegemony as represented not by Roth in his narrative but in Roth's career itself. By enshrining Roth as a modernist, or poststructuralist, or postcolonial martyr, a Promethean figure by virtue of his ambitious first novel and subsequent silencing, the critical figuration of Roth's fiction has never confronted the destructive force of hegemonic culture, in his case embodied in his career, and thus has failed to comprehend its actual significance as a record of hegemonic power.

Perhaps the greatest injustice of the critical reception of Roth's works has been the inability of criticism to recognize the conflict of subaltern and hegemonic culture in Roth's writing as represented primarily by the conflict of Jewish immigrant and middle-class American culture. However ingenious, Wayne Lesser's response to this conflict—the central thematic and emotional tension of Roth's work—finally results in the undermining of its significance, since, as Lesser admits, in this reading David's search for meaning within "the religious, familial, and social systems most commonly assumed to possess such universal value ... leads nowhere" (164). All critical readings from within an ideology that represents the artist or intellectual in elitist terms as heroic, martyred, or powerful—which is to say, almost all readings of Roth's work following the initial reviews by Marxist critics—share Lesser's inability to find meaning in the conflict of immigrant and assimilated culture. Lesser is, of course, correct in pointing out that David is represented as "wish[ing] to establish meanings by discovering the semantic relations among the various signs of the world," but this is very far from proving the conclusion that David's "failed attempts" to discover a coherent system of signs "ultimately reveal[s] the mistake of assuming that the systems of the social world have an essential meaning and, thereby, possess any special moral authority" (165). Lesser is entirely correct in stating that David's "desire to create a personal-cultural identity and its end in failure" are "the text's organizing theme" (167), but in a move that is typical of liberal theory, he obscures the fact that there is an historical agency behind that failure, and that David's confusion, mirrored, as Lesser notes, by the "mass confusion of all in Chapter XIX" (164), results from the agency implicit in his rejection of the authority of his family's cultural tradition.

Foremost among his offenses is David's too eager dismissal of his inherited culture, a dismissal that has devastating aesthetic as well as human consequences. Chapter VII, Book III ("The Coal") begins ironically enough on "the morning of the first Passover night," a holiday when "one was lucky in being a Jew" (Roth, *Sleep* 242), yet by the end of the following chapter, David, having wandered aimlessly to the wharf on the East River and met a hostile trio of Irish youths, has denied that he is a Jew. At the end of this sequence David is forced to drop a "sheet-zinc sword" onto the electrified center rail of the streetcar line, thus setting off an explosion of power and "light, unleashed, terrific light" (253), an electrical discharge that the eight-year-old David connects with the description of Isaiah in a passage in which an angel touches Isaiah's lips "with a fiery coal that the prophet might speak in the presence of God" (Rideout 186). The fact that David should have been overwhelmed by a reading of Isaiah is understandable, as in Second Isaiah there appears the prophecy of redemption, the redemption of both the Jewish people from captivity and of each soul from the private captivity of sin. Roth implies, however, that David has not applied this prophecy to his people's captivity in poverty and cultural isolation nor to his own indiscretions, but only to his own ambitious image of selfhood—a "victory" *over*, and not of, his circumstances. David's attachment to the Polish-American boy, Leo Dugovka, is another instance of his readiness to escape his own background and to attach himself to the adopted culture. David finds that "he had never wanted to be anyone's friend until this moment" of meeting Leo, and even when Leo ridicules the Mezuzeh scrolls above Jewish thresholds, David feels only "a slight qualm of guilt because he was betraying all the Jews in his house who had Mezuzehs above their doors" (Roth, *Sleep* 306). It is with Leo that David feels, for the first time, the bliss of his own self-sufficient existence and will. Visiting Leo's house when Leo's parents are both working "gave him [David] a snug, adventurous feeling…. There were no parents to interfere, no orders to obey—nothing. Only they two, living in a separate world of their own" (319). Joking at the expense of his people and flattering Leo, however, prove too little to hold Leo's friendship; David is obliged to help Leo seduce his cousin, Estelle.

David's mounting betrayal of his culture is indicated, quite forcefully, by his loathsome act of pronouncing his own mother "dead" to Reb Yidel Pankower and Reb Schulim. After he also reveals her earlier affair with a Christian, David hesitates to return home, knowing that the rabbi has gone to chastise Aunt Bertha for having, as David suggested, informed the boy about his mother's past. Trapped in the dilemma of needing his parents' love and feeling shame and fear in their presence, David even imagines that he possesses the ability to disappear whenever necessary. "Ain't nobody. No place. Stand here then. BE nobody." (379).

David imagines the death of his mother, presumably because it is above all his attachment to his mother that stands between him and his ideal of assimilation. Even as an eight-year-old, David is ashamed of his mother's dependency and subservience, as her role is defined in traditional culture. In the scene after his father has been injured and has lost his job at the printing press, David attempts to conceal his mother's desperation from his friend Yussie. Love and shame tear at David, as momentarily he is thrust into total confusion by his conflicting emotions. At other moments this confusion hardens into "anger" (141). David becomes progressively more alienated from his parents' immigrant identity. As the narrative rendering of his consciousness shows, David feels an overwhelming sense of disgust with the crudeness and inferiority of his environment, and he seeks to transcend his physical and cultural situation through various means, including social assimilation, physical escape, religion, education, and, most importantly, art. Where else if not in bohemian literary culture would a thoughtful young man of Roth's time, brooding on the inferiority of his own cultural background, find a welcome reception for his talents and personality?

Even as he wishes to escape, David of course seeks security from his mother and from a nostalgic image of home. After his escape from the three menacing Irish boys, David finds temporary shelter in his home and community. Unfortunately, David cannot remain holed up within the few blocks of his Jewish neighborhood; nor is his mother strong enough to protect him from his domineering father. Not only this: David is "revolted" by the crudeness of his environment, especially by instances of unguarded sexuality as when Luter, his father's "best friend" and employer, attempts to seduce David's mother or when Yussie's sister, Annie, plays "bad" with David, kissing him and showing him "w'ea babies comm from" (53). There is also the narrow-minded prejudice of his own people, who seem to pass along the sting of their own suffering to other less assimilated groups. David's friends, Izzy and Maxie, who both live on his block, and to an extent David himself, make sport of Charlie Ling, the "Chinkee-chinaman" who operates the neighborhood laundry. "'Like a lady he looks,' said Izzy reflectively. 'Wod a big tail he's god on his head'" (175). David is not implicated in this prejudice to the extent of his friends, if only because he has begun to question his own ethnic and social identity. Or, to put it differently, he possesses no secure identity from which to arrive at judgments concerning others, however misguided. His immediate response to Charlie is neither amusement nor derision, but confusion: "Charley, American name. Just like Charley in school ... L-i-ng. Ling. Ling-a-ling. Is Jewish. Can't be" (174).

In retrospect, one can understand how the cultural and linguistic confusions of Roth's childhood could be adapted so well to the artistic purposes of modernist prose or how, moving in the other direction, a modernist sensibility could uncover and productively shape into narrative the confusions of immigrant experience. The style and technique of Joyce are stamped upon *Call It Sleep*, even to the extent of Roth's ending the work with a section ("The Rail") structured similarly to Molly Bloom's culminating monologue in *Ulysses* but suggesting as well Joyce's use of working-class speech in the Irish pub—in Roth's case, "Callahan's." As Malcolm Bradbury notes, David's immediate experience is continually transmuted into a "sign" and "a gift of tongues." The material facts of immigrant street-life are ultimately so ordered and subjugated to narrative form as to become choral voices, so much so that, paradoxically, the most patterned section of the novel is constructed out of the chaos of "the babel of politics and obscenity filling the street world" (Bradbury 131). As Bradbury states, "just as David's quest is for a linguistic revelation," so Roth's "task is to press through the barrage of discourse that surrounds him ... towards symbolic form" (131).

Above all, it is Roth's narrative distance from mass consciousness that links his novel to modernism. Unlike all his family and friends, in relation to his immigrant community David is an observer, not a participant. His personality, as Roth writes, reflects the incoherence of his historical existence: only David "knew how the whole world could break into a thousand little pieces" (Roth, *Sleep* 55). Unlike everyone else in the novel, David transmutes events into a production of language and symbolic form. Like Joyce, Roth abandons his indigenous culture, even as it serves as the basis for a revolutionary art. Like other modernist writers—one thinks of Faulkner's "creation" of his "postage stamp of native soil," a curiously imagined diminishment of home country to "postage stamp" dimensions—Roth intends to empower the artist as the agent of transcendent imagination, but it is a conferring of agency that results in an elitist relationship toward his own formative history.

As one might expect in a narrative of childhood, it is especially with his family that Roth's artist-hero must contend to control the materials of his art. Like many of her generation, David's mother is at the mercy of a modern American culture and speech that she does not fully understand. As a child, David commits the same cultural and linguistic errors, but unlike his parents, he determines not to be fooled. David's mother is constantly mistaken about the meaning of English words, as is David when he mistakes the English word "altar" for the Yiddish word for "old man." The very concept of a Christian altar must be described to David: "An altar is a broad stone—about so high" (120), his mother says. Later, after an episode in which he gets lost a few blocks from home and ends up at the police station, David is more careful about tracing his way through the maze of city streets. A similar resolve not to be deceived by authorized sources of knowledge underlies Roth's own turn toward hegemonic culture.

Even more so than his mother, however, David's father is identified as the enemy of assimilation and, by extension, the enemy of the national art to which he aspires. Albert Schearl is willfully unsuccessful in a series of jobs, and his defensive paranoia toward authority produces a suspicious and violent temperament, and one more often than not directed against his son. Walter B. Rideout refers to Mr. Schearl as "a truculently egotistical, almost paranoic father" (186), yet Albert is also a grand figure in his own way, and before David can defeat his father, he must destroy his father's image as a heroic victim. There is much in the novel to support this heroic image. Albert is economically enslaved, relegated to low-paying and monotonous jobs such as driving a milk wagon, and, as such, he takes on a quality of stoic heroism. David fully acknowledges the bitterness of his father's life, recording his suffering: his inability in winter to "see the stairs at four in the morning" and "the handle of the tray ... so frozen it burns through your gloves like fire" (Roth, *Sleep* 266). When Albert attacks the bum who has stolen milk from his wagon, he "towered above him, rage billowing from him, shimmering in sunlight almost like an aura" (281).

Albert's bitterness and paranoia, however, are less admirable when they are directed at David and his mother. At home David always dreads the arrival of his father for he feels the need to hide from his father's aggrieved expression and threatening demeanor. When Luter turns against Albert because Albert's wife has rejected his advances, Albert's anger is "terrifying." In the climax of the novel, David's mother admits her premarital affair with a Christian boy in Galitzia, and Albert discloses that he has suspected David's paternity and resented his presence all along. As Albert goes on to detail, the disruption of their marriage during immigration, in which he was forced to precede his wife by two years, led to his suspicions. The tremendous pressure of laboring at the bottom of society has scarred Albert's personality and corrupted his relationship to his family.

Because his father is so bitter and angry, the son must separate himself from the father and from the demeaning circumstances that produced him if he is to survive at all. When David is carried home by a policeman after his suicide attempt, it is his father who is singled out as responsible, accused of "quarreling" with his family and driving the son toward his death. Seeing his father's humiliation and defensiveness before his accusers, including the gentile policeman, "David felt a shrill wild surge of triumph" (434). After this triumph, David's relation to his father changes permanently. His father's footfall is now "dull, unresilient," and David even feels "vague, remote pity" (440). Contrary to Lesser's reading that this "triumph" leads to "a more mature comprehension of his family" and that "Davey seems to grow from his experience" and "attains a sense of equanimity" (Lesser 161), I find little to suggest that David ever understands the sources of his father's anger and rage or forgives his father for his abuse. At the end of the novel, David has escaped the father's dominance and entered "sleep" but not equanimity—a deliberately ambiguous ending for an unresolvable cycle of repression which the child, at this point, cannot begin to comprehend. Even as David aspires to being "fully American," he finds that the alternative to immigrant life is not really assimilation but cultural repression of a kind that Roth relates to his own later writer's block. Within the imagined structure of *Call It Sleep*, the alternative for David to his parents' culture is confusion, guilt, and self-destruction.

Roth has analyzed his own betrayal of immigrant culture in his autobiographical novel, *Mercy of a Rude Stream*, which identifies Ira Stigman's childhood separation from traditional Jewish culture as an im-

portant cause of his [Ira's] writer's block (although, significantly, he simultaneously identifies the source as sexual guilt). What is unusual in
Roth's case is not the betrayal itself but his extraordinary reaction against
his own betrayal and the period of stasis that his betrayal called into being. What other major writer's contempt for his own cultural assimilation
has led to a self-imposed exile from art of thirty-five years—and, even
more remarkably, to a courageous return to and analysis of the site of his
betrayal?

There are, however, a number of caveats to this positioning of Roth
as a courageous and transparent analyst of his own failures—an analyst
who reads his early work more perceptively than any of his critics. For
one thing, Roth's later rejection of modernism only leads him to embrace
other sources of authority. It is also convenient that Roth's enlightenment
concerning the failings of his early idols, Joyce and Eliot, should coincide with a period in Western literary culture when modernism has come
under significant critical scrutiny. As modernism and Anglo-American
literary culture cease to occupy a place of prestige, Roth has transferred
his loyalties to more fashionable hegemonies. One can't help but wonder
about a similar characteristic of David Schearl and later of Ira Stigman in
Mercy of a Rude Stream: both are keen observers who gain acceptance
by parroting the behavior of the more "refined," assimilated boys to
whom they are instinctively attracted. Both suppress the less prestigious
culture and language (that is, Jewish culture and Yiddish language) of
eastern Europe as they attempt to assimilate to American middle-class
life.

In the respect that they reflect the central movement of Anglo-
American literary culture, Roth's texts are not so clearly "polylingual,"
as Hana Wirth-Nesher insists, as they are monocultural, with literary
English in its modernist variant assimilating as many other languages and
dialects as possible within its own structural frame. If "polylingual" is
meant to suggest an interplay between, and equal status of, different languages or dialects, Roth's books are hardly polylingual in the sense of
more recent postcolonial texts, for his code-switching does not imply the
equal status of all languages and dialects. Rather, such languages and
dialects are arranged within Roth's prose, much as Irish working-class
speech functions in *Ulysses*, as markers of the alienation of the literary
consciousness from the vitiated speech of the masses. Even if *Call It
Sleep* is, in some sense, a polylingual novel as far as the author is concerned (and I am not so sure that this is the case, with regard to Polish,

Yiddish, Hebrew, Italian, and the other languages interspersed in the text—languages in which Roth was hardly fluent), it is largely monolingual for Roth's protagonist, who hardly understands anything of these languages. (As Wirth-Nesher correctly notes, "the hidden and entirely inaccessible language to David is Polish, which appears in the text only as gaps to be filled by the child's misguided speculations" [461 n].) Indeed, the novel is not so much about David's immersion in a polylingual or multicultural immigrant community as it is his resistance to, disgust with, and ultimate freedom from the cultural "babel" of the slums.

A few passages from Roth's writing may be cited to confirm this impression. In a crucial scene, both in a linguistic sense and in terms of David's personal and cultural history, David's mother discloses to Aunt Bertha the secret of her youthful affair and her subsequent loveless marriage to Albert Schearl. Since his aunt lapses into Polish ("Again meaning disappeared" [Roth, *Sleep* 192]) and his mother into the "alien thicket" of Yiddish (196), David comprehends only scattered phrases and sections of the account. It is through such scenes that the reader is faced with the harsh reality that David does not really share a language in which he can communicate with his parents or understand the experiences of the immigrant generation. As a result, Jewish immigrant experience is far more remote than the experience of assimilated Jews and of gentiles. Contrary to those who see Roth's "polylingualism" as an effort to "preserve" a traditional cultural legacy, or even to record realistically the immigrant experience in the early twentieth century, the textual evidence shows Roth using the Yiddish and dialectical English of his family in much the same way as other commodifiers of immigrant or regional culture, for the consumption of a readership not always sympathetic to that culture. With the publication of *Call It Sleep* in 1934, Roth's writing became part of the aggregation of cultures by the metropolitan culture, and the publication of *Mercy of a Rude Stream* has largely confirmed this impression.

If Roth believed that in *Mercy of a Rude Stream* he had "solved" his writer's block (if this meant understanding and acting upon the cultural politics implicit in his domestic drama), he was mistaken. In *Mercy of a Rude Stream* he has only become further entangled in a denial of his parents' world and has attached himself more firmly to an assimilated national culture. The suggestion that Roth himself repeatedly makes—that Ira's writer's block originated in his repression of the memory of incest—might appear to trivialize the issue by linking it to a psychological origin and deflecting attention from sources of much broader and greater consequence. Perhaps, however, such private markers signal paths to understanding his dilemma, as Roth suggests linkages between David's private motives and his historical context. Although Roth is scrupulously ambivalent on this issue, I would assert that Ira's memory of incest symbolically expresses the cultural bondage toward which Roth felt a paralyzing ambivalence. (It is not to be construed as "autobiographical," as Roth strongly asserts in a prefatory note to *From Bondage* and as Bonnie Lyons confirms in *Henry Roth: The Man and His Work*.) In *Call It Sleep*, for example, David's role as the procurer of his cousin for his Christian friend may be viewed as a rehearsal of David's relationship to the cosmopolitan culture and of Roth's relationship to readers from the "target" assimilated culture. His father's fierce punishment of David's act may be interpreted as a measure of the father's own resistance to assimilation and of his anger at his son and his wife's cultural and sexual betrayals, betrayals not only of him but of his people's history. David's electrocution is then an effort to escape from the presence of his father's wrath and the cultural conflict that underlies it, and from his own developing physical desires. However, it is not simply a psychological escape. Most importantly, it is an escape from full consciousness of his position, from the knowledge that comes too readily and too clearly to the child, into the dull "sleep" of adolescence and adulthood.

In Roth's highly romantic figuration, David's sleep is the tragic suicide of artistic sensibility under the pressure of society's demeaning reality, but his text suggests a multiplicity of readings. As at least one critic has recognized, *Call It Sleep*, a novel in which the author "is mostly content with an implied criticism of capitalist society" (Rideout 188), is "artistically" at the same time a more forceful record of the power of that same hegemony. In this sense, Lesser accurately characterizes David's discovery of the "textuality of his world," in which "'coherence' (personally or culturally considered) is a phenomenon of expressive language coming to terms with the world" (169–70). In Lesser's reading, however, such coherence is not a reflection of the historical condition but a linguistic manipulation resulting in an essentially ahistorical and privatized "equanimity." This reading seems accurate to the extent that Roth's first novel was a self-conscious flight from history into aesthetics: a novel in which Roth adopted the artistic methods of the central culture—"prose poetry modeled after Eliot" and Hart Crane; "arguably the most Joycean of any novel written by an American" (Ferraro 394–95)—to record realistically the voices and descriptions of an immigrant colony. One must admit that Roth's relationship to hegemony was, to say the least, very ambiguous.

While the four volumes of *Mercy of a Rude Stream* do not as forcefully present the dilemmas of Roth's personal history as does his first novel, they explicitly comment on the autobiographical revelations begun in *Call It Sleep*. Notwithstanding Roth's insistence that the work is "not autobiography," there are numerous parallels to Roth's first novel. As in the case of David Schearl, the problematic nature of Ira Stigman's identity inevitably leads to a crisis in which he feels great uncertainty over his future. As we learn in the second volume, *A Diving Rock on the Hudson*, even as a freshman at Stuyvesant High School, "Ira could no more define what troubled him than he could define a cloud." Roth's autobiographical novel is, however, no simple recollection of the author's youth but a shrewd reinventing and repositioning of his literary career. Roth never gives up his dream of achieving full self-consciousness, but in his later work he also deals with issues of culture and communication. The task of finding a "new creative form" and "a language of the self that will give him psychic and emotional wholeness in a fragmented world," is, according to Malcolm Bradbury, Roth's central motive in his first novel (130–31). In *Mercy of a Rude Stream*, however, he inevitably also begins to focus on the lost possibilities of his past life, including the failures attributable to his own moral weakness and aesthetic incapacity. Roth now understands that his task is not so much to construct a supreme fiction of ordered fragments, as to articulate a more timely heroic narrative disordered by the very social history it encompasses. If Roth had once comprehended everything in the terms of modernist art—David Schearl struggling toward the artist's first awakening to the significance of his future role within high literary culture—he now frames Ira Stigman as the subaltern, victimized by his position on the margin of cultural hegemony. In this way, Roth also positions himself as a new kind of "author," temporally, culturally, even technologically shaped by the "rude stream" of history.

For Roth's protagonist, Ira Stigman, adolescence necessarily involves the crucial moral failure of his existence: the long-term incestuous relationship with his younger sister that he identifies as a cause of his "blockage" as an author. Given the extent of his guilt, the narrator becomes absorbed with his own ruin. Ira's ruin, however, results not merely from personal weakness: it is related to and perhaps "necessary" to his (and to Roth's) self-conception as a modernist artist in exile from the repressive morality of inherited culture. Incest, in other words, is an effective figure to represent the closed culture, controlled by loyalties to tradition and to family, which Roth imagines in opposition to a "national" or international culture of modernism. At the same time, however, Ira's assimilation to modern American culture is also figured in his aggressively libertarian views, since it is freedom from customary restraints, more so than any other value, that demarcates Roth's assimilated "Americanness" from his traditional "Jewishness." Like David Schearl, however, Ira finds himself caught between Old World and New, overwhelmed by his own naiveté, not knowing "how to behave," seeking "refinement" among gentile and assimilated Jewish friends, awed by expensive possessions and cultured tastes. Yet from his position on the margin, Ira questions the American Dream with its emphasis on material success. Forced to choose between Cornell University and City College of New York, Ira faces the conflict over his future identity in America.

In the four-volume sequence of *Mercy of a Rude Stream*, *From Bondage* is the third published volume but the last composed, completed only in the final months of Roth's life. In this volume, Roth revises his earlier portrayal of the bohemian culture of the 1920s and 1930s that played an important part in the action of *Call It Sleep*. Yet even as Roth dismisses modernism as an authorized culture, he finds ways to confer new authority on his new authorial self. It is characteristic of Roth to cite classic, canonized texts as a structural parallel, and it seems particularly apropos for him to cite a classic text in which personal and national histories overlap. The plot and theme of *From Bondage* parallel in many respects those of *The Aeneid*, the epic narrative in which Aeneas flees a ruined life—in Roth's case, the culture of his immigrant ancestry—for a new existence within an ascendant culture even as he recognizes that he may not live to enjoy his existence within that culture. In Vergilian fashion, Roth intends to position his narrative in relationship to an historical epic of flight and resettlement with the implicit suggestion of a coherent, and in some sense imperial, future. Now, however, Roth, who as a modernist author seemed to have founded his art in opposition to the very confusion, fragmentation, and emotional disorder of his historical condition, asserts that his earlier novel had been drawn *from* the integral experience of a cohesive Jewish community and that his long writer's block resulted from the lack of any basis of secure identity that might replace his *cohesive* childhood community—the very community that had inspired such disgust and humiliation in *Call It Sleep*. As Roth now rationalizes it, the family's assimilating step from the Lower East Side slum to the more affluent Jewish and Irish section of Harlem was not an escape but rather the prelude to his psychological decline into depression and self-doubt.

Despite the questioning of modernist culture, redemption through art is still one of Roth's fundamental assumptions, and the frequent contrast of Ira's life and art with those of Joyce, Coleridge, and Beckett is meant to clarify his new understanding of his aesthetic—not to suggest any diminishment in his belief in the saving potential of writing. That redemption, however, is not achieved through Joyce's transmutation of life into words, or even through Coleridge's moralizing transcendence (as Ira at first interprets "He prayeth best, who loveth best"): Roth's conception of artistic redemption returns to primary experience—the "rude stream" of the novel's title—but finds "mercy" in the artist's resources, finally in the patient ability to reflect and order experience through language. If Roth's captivity to modernism involved the obligation to transmute experience into the purified idiom of art, his new aesthetic constrains him to the task of cataloguing and reviewing experience. Through memory, the losses of the past are retraced and retouched, the absurdity of one's history (both personal and collective) is revisited and rewritten.

Putting his own house in some kind of order is the figurative trope that structures *Mercy of a Rude Stream*. Looking back on a lifetime in its entirety, one is presumably able to order, to connect one event with another, to recognize one's own figure in the pattern. *From Bondage* relates Ira's college years as a student at City College of New York and dwells particularly on his extracurricular affairs: his continued intimacies with his cousin Stella, friendships with Larry Gordon and Gordon's New York University instructor, Edith Welles, and (his greatest "bondage") his now discontinued but still tormenting incestuous relationship with his younger sister, Minnie.[2] The self-absorption with his own "nastiness" is a permanent feature of Ira's nature, as his wife M stresses, speaking with Ira late in life. M says, "You're so involved with yourself that you're surprised when people ... get into your world" (Roth, *Bondage* 386). That obsession with self may explain why so many of Ira's involvements are incestuous. One of the more dramatic points of *Bondage* describes Ira's narrow escape from detection in his affair with Stella, his seventeen-year-old cousin. Even Ira's social relationships have an incestuous quality. A long stretch of *From Bondage* is concerned with Ira's budding relationship with Edith Welles and with Edith's ménage à trois (or quatre) consisting of Marcia Meede ("the foremost anthropologist in America," recently returned from the South Seas and presently teaching at Columbia), Marcia's ex-husband, Lewlyn Craddock, and Lewlyn's British girlfriend, Cecelia. Roth's account traces Edith and Marcia's rivalry for Lewlyn's attention and the lengthy revelation of the experimental mores of bohemian New York literary culture.

The degree of emphasis on self manifested in Roth's autobiographical fiction risks losing the reader's sympathy. Ira Stigman is himself ignoble, egotistical, and unreliable, and his intellectual tastes, which include his reading of Eliot's "Prufrock" and of Edith's smuggled copy of Joyce's *Ulysses*, a soon-to-be-canonical book that he immediately embraces but later rejects for its "evasion of history" (67), mirror his arrogance and immaturity. There is also the danger, as Roth notes, of suggesting that his life was representative of Jewish immigrant experience as a whole—a point that echoes early criticism of *Call It Sleep* as "introspective and febrile" (*New Masses* review, quoted in Rideout 189) in contrast to more socially purposive narratives such as Mike Gold's *Jews without Money*. This consideration points to one way out of Ira's self-absorption, through the new imperative of ethnic identity, and both Jewish immigrant history and Zionism become passionate interests in Roth's final years. If as a youth Ira aspired toward deracinated assimilation as part of the national culture, Roth's old age was absorbed with the fate of Israel.

Ira's (and Roth's) submissiveness to canonical ideas and texts should lead us to suspect something beyond a benumbed conformism of literary taste—the inglorious but exculpating figuration of immaturity and inexperience that Roth provides for his protagonist in *Mercy of a Rude Stream*—or the excusable ignorance that is suggested by the child-figure of David in *Call It Sleep*. What Edwin Seaver noted of David Schearl—that as a child, he is "pre-political" (quoted in Rideout 189)—seems almost as true of the much older Ira. Their creator, however, is the author of both novels, and it is his submission, first to canonical modernism and later to the new canonical altereity, that is troubling. It seems to reveal a lifelong insecurity or absence of an original and coherent artistic identity and the sort of identification with a hegemonic culture that Ngugi wa Thiong'o describes as the worst effect of imperial culture on the alienated colonial. At least in the first three volumes of *Mercy of a Rude Stream*,

Ira is still enslaved by his own immaturity, which is to say by the immaturity that his author imagines for him.

From Bondage necessarily breaks off inconclusively, something like Aeneas malingering with Dido in Carthage, and at this point in Ira's life, nothing is resolved. In the final volume of the novel sequence, *Requiem for Harlem* (1998), Ira Stigman moves away from his immigrant family and joins his mentor and mistress, Edith Welles, in Greenwich Village. This act ties his immediate future to the hegemonic modernist culture that Welles teaches at New York University and to the assimilationist program of national education and literary craft to which Ira aspires. Just as Roth eagerly set up Joyce, the most forceful of modernist writers, as the idol of his youth, he would construct a new idol to authorize the literary project of his old age. What we may learn from both of Roth's novels is how difficult it may be for any writer to break with the cultural idols of the time. In his search for agency, Roth was not a bohemian or revolutionary but a more representative figure reflecting the cultural aspirations of all too many subaltern people to align themselves with the power of the national culture: what Roth has done well is to write of his "captivity" with honesty and insight.

Notes

1. It is ironic, although predictable in a way, that criticism should cast Roth in a Promethean role, as Lesser does in captioning Roth as an example of "literature's revolutionary potential" (156). Lesser's article is particularly interesting as a transition piece, in terms of the critical response to Roth. As such, it assumes the same premises as earlier criticism, but recycles liberal ideology in a new critical language. Lesser's conclusion is that the novel ends with David's "liberating act of retaliation against the tyranny of [arbitrary social forms]" and with his reintegration following the recognition of his insight into the arbitrary and linguistically based nature of social "facts" (175). However, if David's acts are liberating and reintegrating, it is difficult to explain the fact that similar acts of "retaliation" on Roth's part result in such utter paralysis: how, in other words, does one explain the devastation of Roth's "writer's block," and indeed the much greater devastation of his psychological life, given the assumption that the autobiographical figure of David Shearl has achieved a revolutionary liberation nearly identical to that of his creator from "the repressiveness of arbitrary social forms" (Lesser 175)? It is precisely Roth's paralysis (and not his revolutionary

power), resulting from his exile from the meaningfulness of "arbitrary" social forms, that appears to be at stake in all of his writing.

2. One of the autobiographical parallels between Ira and Henry Roth that is elaborated at length is the developing intimacy of Ira and Edith, a relationship that is based on the relationship of Roth and Eda Lou Walton, the young New York University instructor with whom Roth lived while he was writing *Call It Sleep*. Like the fictional "Edith," Eda Lou Walton served as Roth's literary mentor, his lover and companion, and, equally important, introduced him to the work of modernists such as Joyce and Eliot. Reflecting on Ira's life with Edith, Roth compares that early period, so crucial to his emotional and intellectual development but ultimately so unproductive, with his later marriage to M: "with Edith, there was understandably not the same kind of treasured intimacy as with M, but real intimacy—over a long period of time, an entire decade" (*Bondage* 368).

7

Physical Disability and the Sacramental Community in Flannery O'Connor's Everything That Rises Must Converge

"Does one's integrity ever lie in what he is not able to do?" Flannery O'Connor wrote in *Mystery and Manners*. "I think that usually it does, for free will does not mean one will, but many wills conflicting in one man" (115).

Flannery O'Connor is a notable example of a physically disabled writer who found that the challenges resulting from her chronic illness (systemic lupus erythematosus) gradually came to enter the discourse of her writing and came to be "usefully" (a word she loved) translated into her fiction. Downplaying the considerable personal suffering and difficulty she endured in her private life, O'Connor nevertheless returned increasingly to the subject of physical disability; through her final collection of stories, *Everything That Rises Must Converge*, O'Connor's fictional world is permeated with the metaphorical figuration of illness and accident. What O'Connor may never have admitted was that her imaginative work afforded a channel for the exploration of emotional and psychological responses to disability, feelings that she strictly regulated in her public expression. A number of commentators would agree with Lee Sturma, who suggested that "the act of writing itself performed an expressive function for O'Connor which helped her to transcend the anger and pain she felt at her situation" (115). While it may well be, as O'Connor would certainly have wished us to think, that her disease played only a secondary role in shaping her fiction, it is also true that the discourse of chronic illness and physical disability enters many of her stories after *Wise Blood* and becomes an important metaphoric vehicle in her stories.

Flannery O'Connor's extraordinary letters, first published as *The Habit of Being*, are filled with repeated references to her illness and its physical repercussions. As she received more frequent and prestigious speaking engagements, for example, O'Connor found herself scheduling her appearances around the limited air service available in the 1950s. After checking on flights to St. Louis, where she lectured in 1958, O'Connor wrote to a friend: "There's a train but I can't ride them on account of the crutches" (*Works* 1068). Even air travel was extremely tiring, as she found especially after her only trip to Europe. O'Connor did not enjoy driving and considered herself a "horrible" driver (flunking the Georgia driver's examination on her first try), although she did acquire a refitted automobile and learned to drive so that she could transport her elderly mother to town in the event of an emergency.

Still, O'Connor frequently vented her irritation at suggestions that her illness in any way limited or "determined" her work, and it is certain that her religious beliefs would have found powerful expression in her writing, even if she had not contracted lupus. Her friend in Milledgeville, Mary Tate, described O'Connor's appearance as "unassuming" and "her disability inconspicuous" (33), and O'Connor herself, downplaying the influence of physical limitation, once commented on Henry James's famously obscure ailment: "as for James' physical infirmity, that is negligible in the Christian order of things and it is not good to carry it over and make a criticism of his work" (*Works* 1096). As Richard Gilman (under the pen-name "Robert Donnor") wrote, "When she was describing her illness to me, her tone was remarkably matter-of-fact, without a trace of self-pity" (O'Connor, *Conversations* 47).

While her illness may not have determined the thematic directions of her fiction, O'Connor did make notable use of the language and imagery of disability. The title of one of her finest stories, "The Lame Shall Enter First," was perhaps a sardonic jest at her own treatment by the airlines (prior boarding for disabled passengers) as well as a biblical reference; her last great story, "Revelation," refers obliquely in the matter of Mrs. Turpin's swine farming to her medication, derived, as she wrote Maryat Lee, from "the pituitary glands of thousands of pigs butchered daily in Chicago, Illinois, at the Armour packing plant" (*Works* 1063). O'Connor's compassion toward all adversity, and her openness toward all human difference, result from the conjunction of her religious beliefs and her physical ordeal—a tension between selflessness and feeling that appears to underlie much of her finest work. As Edward Kessler indicates, O'Connor understood that all human life, as well as all natural being, was in the "process of becoming more than itself" (101) and as such was participating in an evolutionary spiritual process, a development set forth in Catholic doctrine but also confirmed through scientific observation. Not merely the "acceptance" but the positive *beauty* of all human individuality is implied in such stories as "Redemption," in which, as Kessler notes, "beauty is not a stable surface to be appreciated but a hidden power that demands the destruction of social and linguistic preconceptions before it can be seen" (107). That O'Connor has in mind a transforming and in a sense radical vision is implied in the climax of this late story, in which the "ugly acting" Mary Grace causes Ruby Turpin to ask "How am I a hog?" Ruby's conventional and static definition of beauty is undermined and finally replaced by a true visionary sight that prompts her compassion toward socially defined "others."

The artistic climate of her time biased O'Connor's aesthetic theory toward the same tension between physical particularity and unifying transcendent mythologies. Echoing New Critical discourse, O'Connor was certain that good fiction must be "concrete," by which she meant that it must be dramatized through particular incidents and images, yet her aesthetic practice paid particular attention to the role of the universal and immaterial. The tension between the particular and the universal enters her fiction in the emphasis on transformation—the evolutionary moment marking the gap between, but also the identity of, the immanent and the transcendent. In "The Nature and Aim of Fiction," O'Connor noted Joseph Conrad's statement that "his aim as a fiction writer was to render the highest possible justice to the visible universe…. It means that he subjected himself at all times to the limitations that reality imposed, but that reality for him was not simply coextensive with the visible" (*Mystery* 80).

In her case, O'Connor's illness provided a convincing vehicle through which to dramatize the tension inherent in a process of radical transformation. The relevance of her illness, which limited her energy and curtailed her mobility, to her fictional discourse can be glimpsed if we consider her description of the importance of self-denial as a preparation for the sort of change that she termed "grace." It was self-denial or suffering, one side of the tension between the physical and the ideal, that O'Connor observed as missing in the writing of some of her contemporaries, particularly in the works of the Beat writers: the issue was at once an aesthetic, ethical, and religious one, for in seeking to avoid suffering or to minimize its significance, readers and believers alike have removed themselves from the posture of acceptance. Without an acknowledgment of the necessary existence of suffering in a world circumscribed by sin and death, there can be little understanding of the need for grace.

One of O'Connor's fundamental metaphors is that of Christ's body existing in history in the life of his church: "the Church is the body of Christ, Christ continuing in time" (*Works* 1099). This fact requires O'Connor to represent human beings, those "inside" the church and those drawn to it, whether consciously or not, as replicating Christ's wounds, the broken body and spilled blood of communion. At the very center of the sacramental life of the Catholic Church is the Eucharist, and the body and blood embodied in bread and wine were the focus of O'Connor's daily meditation for the twenty years of her adult life. As Dan Curley notes, O'Connor's stories replicate the Pauline conception of "justification by faith" in which grace, in a dramatic moment of recognition, is recognized and accepted by a sinful human being. Curley writes: "This idea of grace through imperfection is an outgrowth of Miss O'Connor's belief that the true communion of saints is not a communion of love but a communion of suffering" (quoted in Paulson 160). In the terms that O'Connor repeatedly employed, the disabilities of her characters replicate the action of Redemption through the Crucifixion and may put them "in the way of being receptive," although their physical ordeals do not in themselves bring about conversion: only a willing spiritual change within an individual can accomplish this.

A second crucial element of O'Connor's metaphoric system is associated with the importance of patience and humility, an emphasis that surely had much to do with her own chronic illness. If O'Connor's aesthetic necessitated an extreme bifurcation of physical and spiritual being, the act of grace is the resolution to this opposition, and the expectation of grace, as represented in her stories, involves mounting anxiety and impatience, and the need for patience, on the part of its human recipients. As one might expect, the most common trope for this necessary forbearance and for the expectation of growth over time is illness itself. As in the case of Asbury Fox in "The Enduring Chill," the victim of illness experiences gradual intimations that something is amiss, and while these symptoms are often dismissed by the conscious mind, the disorder becomes the focus of the victim's subconscious dreaming and motivation. As it gathers hawk-like to assault its object, the resolution to a lengthy period of illness resembles the pattern of the revelation of Christ in time, a divine unfolding of possibilities that is both transcendent and immanent. As a metaphor also for Christ's patience toward man, illness and disability work slowly to transform man's "ignorance," just as Asbury, that "very ignorant boy," has been since childhood witlessly observing the water-stain in the shape of an enormous bird descending toward his bed.

O'Connor writes in a letter to Ted Spivey in 1959 that "if God intends for the world to be spared … all this is accomplished by the patience of Christ in history and not with select people but with very ordinary ones" (*Works* 1099). In some ultimate sense, despite her just evaluation of her extraordinary gifts and her pointed critiques of those contemporaries whom she must have considered at best obtuse, O'Connor needed to feel herself "very ordinary." In O'Connor's personal life, her impulse was to remind herself of the need for moderation and patience, this in the face of her own moments of impatience and pride in dealing with those close to her. She was ever conscious of her limitations as a person and as a writer, of the narrowness of her gifts and of having to work within artistic as well as personal limitations, yet paradoxically this discipline and sense of confinement might be useful if it necessitated change. "I am usually out of my depth," she wrote to John Hawkes concerning the characterization of Rayber in *The Violent Bear It Away*, adding that the five years spent writing *Wise Blood* and seven on *The Violent Bear It Away* resulted from having to "try it every possible way…. What you are really twisting about in is your own limitations, of course" (*Works* 1109). In the final years of her life, O'Connor found less and less energy available for her work, usually devoting only two hours per day to her fiction. Though limited in time and energy, her patience seemed unbounded. Early on, O'Connor realized that living with lupus would necessitate restrictions in her working habits, but she also found very quickly that the brief time she spent writing was more intense. In the final months of her life she was working even less but with a sense of great pleasure.

O'Connor's attraction to the writing of Teilhard de Chardin, whom she first read in December 1959, was connected with the ways in which her illness informed her writing. As Karl-Heinz Westarp writes, "Teilhard's discussion of 'passive diminishments' in the second part of *The Divine Milieu* exerted a particularly strong attraction on Flannery" (97). As an ardent and orthodox believer, O'Connor felt that her writing was strengthened by the "living Christ" within her, a sustaining power that was inexhaustible. The importance of Christ's example in O'Connor's life is nicely expressed in her letter of July 20, 1955, to "A": "if you believe in the divinity of Christ, you have to cherish the world at the same time you struggle to endure it" (*Habit of Being* 90).

O'Connor's own pain also provided insight into the suffering ever present in her characters in their process of moving toward or resisting change. She emphasized to readers that though she wrote *about* the grotesque, her beliefs were the *opposite* of grotesque. Quoting St. Thomas, O'Connor declared that "the artist is concerned with the good of that which is made" (*Mystery* 65). The grotesque, "masochistic" penance of Haze Motes in *Wise Blood*, of young Tarwater in *The Violent Bear It Away*, the internalized anguish of Rufus Johnson in "The Lame Shall Enter First" or of Asbury Fox in "The Enduring Chill" are victories because they prefigure fundamental change. O'Connor called resignation to suffering "one of the fruits of the Holy Ghost" (*Works* 925), meaning that adversity brought with it an enrichment of experience and an occasion for selflessness and contemplation. In his self-blinding, Haze Motes turns to this "inner vision," just as for O'Connor "everybody, through suffering, takes part in the Redemption" (*Works* 921).[1]

In the course of his superb analysis of O'Connor's fiction, Richard Giannone offers considerable insight into the relationship between O'Connor's illness and her creative process. Giannone's reading of "The Enduring Chill" stresses the "caring" of others necessitated by the fact of illness: "as a chronically sick person who will need help, [Asbury Fox] will have to accept the kindness and love of others" (Giannone 192). The force of sickness is to undermine the individual's self-sufficiency and self-confidence, and to urge communion with others. Illness is also humbling in a productive way and may lead to a greater tolerance for others. Forced to reassess one's own powers, the sufferer may be led to reassess his or her own merits in relation to others. In the case of Asbury, "sickness has value and can offer a way to others and to God" (Giannone 192). The biographical facts of O'Connor's return at age twenty-five to her mother's care in Milledgeville, Georgia, resemble in many ways the details of "The Enduring Chill." Asbury Fox's homecoming from the North, where he had been a failed writer, retraces O'Connor's involuntary return from the artistic centers of New York and Connecticut, and the ironic humor with which Asbury's illusions are undercut may have been self-directed as well. Returned to the household of his loving but self-satisfied and unreflective mother, and of his perceptive but harsh older sister, Mary George, Asbury is entrusted to the "personal care" of the wise and exceedingly tenacious Dr. Block. A countryman with a "drill-like gaze" ("two cold clinical nickel-colored eyes"), Block resembles O'Connor's self-description as an artist: self-effacing, intellectually unpretentious, but "staring" with obsessive curiosity at her subject. As a fictionalized persona of the artist herself, Dr. Block takes samples of Asbury's blood and examines his body with a probing gaze, his eyes seeming "to glitter at Asbury as if from a great distance" (*Works* 557). To Asbury, however, the "idiot" Block staring him down from a distance suggests his deceased father, about whose "stupidity" (as the type of the local businessman) Asbury complains.

O'Connor subtly connects the details of Asbury's convalescence with the physical vulnerability of human beings in the broadest terms, including references to the worst contemporary acts of evil. When Asbury arrives home, "dying" as he believes with an undiagnosed fever, Mary George exclaims: "The artist arrives at the gas chamber," a reference to the Holocaust that is intended to deflate Asbury's preoccupation with self at the same time that it directs attention to the much greater suffering in the world outside. Mary George understands her brother all too well, for he is indeed a self-absorbed prima donna who has never shown much sympathy for others. As Giannone points out, Asbury's "self-worship" has destructive consequences for his writing as well as for his greater spiritual health. His "failure" as an artist results from his disregard for the created world, for without an interest in what is outside and greater than himself, Asbury's writing "excludes God and creation, the source and evolving affirmation of life" (Giannone 186).

Although Asbury's suffering is inconsiderable in relation to that existing in the world at large, as the culmination of a young life of failure and alienation, it is enough to open his eyes to the source of his misery—his egotism and narcissism. Since it concludes with such recognition, the story conveys a tone of joyous transformation. Interestingly, Mary Tate has described the local literary evening at which O'Connor read her just completed manuscript of "The Enduring Chill": "As she read, she savored every humorous line and watched to be sure that we laughed in the appropriate places" (32). Like Asbury's mother, who, at the news that Asbury's disease is not life-threatening, experiences "the only smile of unqualified joy in all of O'Connor's fiction" (Kessler 48), O'Connor is able to "laugh," in her case because she sees more than her characters do; she understands their pain in the context of what O'Connor took to be Teilhard's sense of evolutionary history, and she understands that all suffering was shadowed by joy and that "in us the good is something under construction" (*Mystery* 226).

Among the many forms of suffering that are present in O'Connor's fiction, perhaps the worst is the condition of spiritual torment resulting from the denial of God's love. To deny the worth of oneself and others, and to ignore the work of the created world is to reject the basis for loving communion. The result of this condition of "sin" is an inability to recognize or accept the possibility of love and happiness. Without knowledge of the foundation of such happiness, the agonized sufferer is open to the worst sorts of misunderstanding, often taking the form of a travesty of religious ritual and dogma.

In a harrowing story of spiritual denial, "The Lame Shall Enter First," O'Connor portrays two characters who, each in their own way, reject the world of love that is offered to them. Although he understands the possibility of goodness and love, which has been taught him by his loving and pious grandfather, Rufus Johnson "chooses" to live a destructive, antisocial existence. Clearly, Johnson intends to devote his life to a vicious, alienated pursuit of evil. Despite this choice, however, he lives within the framework of a religious sensibility that Sheppard denies. "As Johnson tells Sheppard, good intentions and actions are irrelevant in the face of rightness and truth, and clearly being right means being one with Christ" (Brinkmeyer 98). Like Rufus Johnson, Sheppard lives in alienation and denial of love, but his suffering is the result of an even greater separation from God. As a result of this separation, Sheppard lacks the means to comprehend his own grief after the death of his wife, and he has no way to explain the death to his grieving son Norton. With no method of explaining his condition of loss to himself or others, Sheppard falls back on the fragmentary and unconvincing teachings of modern psychology that instruct him to "control" his sense of loss and to direct his "unhealthy" grief toward more positive ends. In following this course, however, Sheppard is led to deny the very basis of loving communion that exists in the needful condition of human mortality itself, and without a basis for love, he denies the agonizing need for love in himself and his son.

Sheppard is a representative of the philosophy of secular rationalism that rejected an objective basis for ethics. In making Sheppard into one of the least attractive characters in her fiction, O'Connor intended to critique the social scientist's relativist ethics. "In the relationship that Sheppard tries to develop with Rufus, we see O'Connor's most explicit rebuttal of the notion that upbringing and environment ought to excuse bad behavior," writes Paulson (23). Although he has suffered from a difficult childhood, Rufus Johnson is not the product of his environment; as Rufus insists, he has "chosen" to be delinquent. His worst act, promoting the death of the helpless Norton, is a vicious example of evil for its own sake; Rufus gains pleasure in his control of Norton, and with Norton's suicide, he gains revenge against Sheppard. As Dan Curley writes: "Whatever else may be obscure in Flannery O'Connor's work, her opposition to moral relativism is clear and unchanging from first to last" (quoted in Paulson 159).

O'Connor's religious beliefs involved certain definite ethical conclusions, among them not only the rejection of relativism but also rejection of the modern faith in social and scientific progress. The naive belief in human perfectibility, suggested in the character of Sheppard, has ethical consequences that are brought to light in the course of "The Lame Shall Enter First." Significantly, Sheppard's embrace of the cult of perfectibility is motivated by his unwillingness to admit the enormity of his own and his son's suffering after the death of his wife. In the process of attempting to avoid the consequences of the human condition of mortality, Sheppard is led to commit heinous acts of family neglect and denial of love. Sheppard's condescending effort to "save" Rufus changes to hatred of the delinquent adolescent when it becomes clear that Rufus will never relinquish his fundamental conception of human evil. In Sheppard's recognition of his neglect of his son Norton (in a crisis of "agonizing love" described as "like a transfusion of love"), he is brought at least to the beginnings of self-understanding, for Sheppard, suddenly "paralyzed" by his thought, must at last see that he, not the lame and delinquent Rufus Johnson, is more limited and in greater need of rescue.

In her humorous way O'Connor explained how, as in the case of Tarwater at the climax of *The Violent Bear It Away*, the force of evil may press one toward understanding. In a letter to Mrs. Terry on Aug. 27, 1962, she explained: "Those who see and feel what the devil is turn to God. Tarwater learned the hard way but he has a hard head" (quoted in Giannone 256). In the case of many, but not all, of her characters, a similar climactic confrontation with evil leads to a recognition of the necessity of a philosophical or religious means of comprehending and transforming the human condition. For O'Connor, Christian doctrine could never be understood "outside" or "above" the world of human existence since its explanatory and transformational powers always functioned simultaneously inside and outside the created world. In this sense, Brinkmeyer is particularly astute in pointing to the "dialogic" nature of O'Connor's writing: "In not closing herself off from the variety of voices of her self and the world ... O'Connor deepened her faith and her art" (194).[2]

O'Connor's view is at once intensely "moral" and at the same time skeptical of the human ability to form ethical judgments. As Richard Gilman prefaced an early interview, "what stands out in Miss O'Connor's writing is its moral quality, wedded to a high order of imagination" (O'Connor, *Conversations* 44). As Gilman recognized, however, in conventional terms O'Connor "was the furthest thing from a moralist," for her "moral judgments" were always, at the same time, "philosophic" or "aesthetic" in nature (54). An example of this kind of moral thinking is O'Connor's belief that virtue necessitates "struggle." As O'Connor stated in an interview with C. Ross Mullins, Jr., in 1963: "What makes the sensibility good is wrestling with what is higher than itself and outside it. It ought to be a good bone-crunching battle" (*Conversations* 105). What becomes evident is that O'Connor is, at the same time, skeptical of transient or idiosyncratic ethical theories *and* completely assured of the existence of a firm basis for objective moral judgments within the classical Christian tradition.

In her "Introduction" to *A Memoir of Mary Ann*, the biography of a child cancer patient who spent nine years at Our Lady of Perpetual Help Free Cancer Home in Atlanta, O'Connor clarified her view that suffering could be an enrichment to the sufferer and an inspiration to those around her: "Mary Ann's diminishment was extreme, but she was equipped by natural intelligence and by a suitable education, not simply to endure it, but to build upon it. She was an extraordinarily rich little girl" (*Mystery* 223). Encapsulated in Mary Ann's story, O'Connor discovered all the elements of her own most vital experience, all that she was attempting to dramatize in her fiction. Through her native intelligence and supported by doctrinal instruction, Mary Ann chose to make of her life something positive and indeed triumphant. She lived in a community with others whom she affected decisively by her very existence. As O'Connor pointed out, the caring relationship to others in which Mary Ann lived "is a communion created upon human imperfection" (*Mystery* 228). The loving community that Mary Ann helped to create around herself pointed toward "the vision of heaven as a communal feast" (Gentry 147) of the sort which Old Tarwater passed on to his great-nephew in *The Violent*

Bear It Away. It is the pleasure of "coming home" to which Asbury grudgingly yields in "The Enduring Chill" and that Asbury's mother celebrates in her smile of unqualified joy.

The acceptance of grace of the sort metaphorically associated with disability is, of course, available to all. In a thoughtful article comparing the lives of O'Connor and Simone Weil, who from adolescence suffered physically disabling headaches, Lee Sturma points to O'Connor's membership in a "community of believers" as one crucial difference between the two writers. O'Connor was not predisposed, as was Weil, to seek additional pain or martyrdom (as a Jewish woman, Weil's request to be sent "under cover" to the Continent during World War II was, consciously or not, suicidal). With a greater sense of humility, O'Connor sought to escape her pain through a series of new treatments, as her doctors tried various therapies and dosage combinations. As Sturma puts it, she "knew what to do with her suffering," struggling to alter what could be changed and accepting what could not.

Flannery O'Connor's illness contributed much to the hard-won resolutions of her late fiction. The stories in *Everything That Rises Must Converge* and the final works such as "Revelation" result from more than a decade of reflection focused on her disability and its mysteriously enabling agency. A careful reading of Flannery O'Connor's stories alongside her essays and letters reveals just how substantial was her use, in terms of fictional incident and image, of the everyday detail of disability. Moreover, it shows how profound was her understanding of the need to turn her existence away from her illness and toward creative and charitable purposes.

Notes

1. O'Connor's considerable interest in the civil rights movement was connected in some sense with her own chronic pain that paralleled the suffering of African American people in the South. She wrote in a letter dated May 4, 1955, that her stories point to "the redemptive quality of the Negro's suffering for us all" (*Habit* 78).

2. If O'Connor's writing is dialogic in relation to social reality, this is *not* to say that her work suggests an opposition between religious and historical realities of the kind proposed in *Flannery O'Connor and Cold War Culture* by Jon Lance Bacon. After reviewing the "general tendency in O'Connor

criticism: assigning priority to the 'universal' religious themes," Bacon asserts that his "interest lies elsewhere—in the process by which a particular historical moment could shape the expression of perennial human concerns" (5). Bacon's work provides much valuable context information for reading O'Connor's fiction, from an analysis of American foreign policy to the treatment of the "necessity" for defending the domestic sphere from corrupting intrusion. Nonetheless, its fundamental conception of "religious versus historical" is at odds with O'Connor's own view of the unfolding of Christ's church *within* history. Driven by the thesis that O'Connor's radical vision connected her with antibourgeois and antinationalist activists, Bacon's analysis offers little insight into the *truly* radical aspect of O'Connor's writing, which is to be found not in her opposition to American colonialism or capitalism, or in her ambivalent racial sympathies, but in her vision of the transforming power of Christian belief when set against the transient concerns of history. If O'Connor took a "dark view" of contemporary America, it is likely that she also was dismissive of the radical politics with which Bacon's criticism wishes to connect her. Bacon's statement that O'Connor's "literary subversion of the domestic ideal reflects her critical perspective on the American way of life" (49) seems to be at odds with O'Connor's actual motive in satirizing domestic life—her wish to disrupt the spiritual complacency implicit in the valorizing of any form of earthly contentment. Certainly, as Bacon writes, "the fanaticism of characters like Hazel Motes [in *Wise Blood*] points to a moral standard at odds with consensus ideology" (86), but this fanaticism, which was clearly shared by the author, also rejects the liberal ideology that critics such as Vance Packard, Paul Goodman, or David Riesman would employ as the basis of their critique of middle-class America. Nor does the notion of the Catholic church as "the locus of cultural resistance" really square with O'Connor's idea of the church as the communion of Christ. The view that the church's primary role is to resist domesticity, consumerism, and nationalism is a truncated conception of O'Connor's art, for surely she intended more for her "transcendent concerns" than to "[bring] them to bear on contemporary American culture" (Bacon 144). Although it is true that O'Connor engages in a critique of the materialism and complacency of modern America, in none of her works of fiction is the baseness of that contemporary culture the primary object of artistic concern. Indeed, in a sense that baseness is itself necessary, for (as in "Revelation") the intolerable condition of practical existence serves as impetus toward an acceptance of grace.

8

Race, Class, and Redemption in *Walker Percy's* The Last Gentleman

Edward J. Dupuy's study of autobiographical elements in Walker Percy's *The Last Gentleman* helps us to understand the role of social or "intersubjective" communication in his narrative. As he focuses on the autobiographical genre that, in Percy's case, comprised practically a conversation with the self, Dupuy clarifies the limited extent to which Percy's existential search involved, indeed required, an extension into intersubjective relationships and envisioned a reconstituted, authentic social community. Before this could take place, however, the complex dialectic of Percy's social thought necessitated a skeptical interrogation of all social relationships; this "destructive" phase would be followed by a rebirth of modest but at least authentic discourse. In this theory of social communication, Percy relied on a synthesis of modern existential philosophy, especially that of Nietzsche and Heidegger, and orthodox Catholic doctrine influenced by the thinking of Gabriel Marcel and other Christian existentialists.

In particular Percy appears to develop Marcel's investigation of the uniqueness of the human person apart from function and to repeat Marcel's insistence on the special ontological status of "mystery" versus "problem:" Many of Percy's philosophical explorations appear to recast Marcel's concern for "the loss of the creature," that is, the loss of an individualized self in an increasingly bureaucratic and technological society. As Percy warned, "the sector of the world about which science cannot utter a single word is nothing less than this: what it is like to be an individual living in ... the twentieth century" (*Signposts* 213). Stated in different terms, the loss of the creature is the loss of selfhood within an increasingly communal and bureaucratic society, yet it is important that Percy conceives of "authentic" social community in highly idealized terms, as a community of believers in a corrupt modern society.

Daniel Schenker focuses on the radical nature of Percy's thought as he asserts that America as a "dynamic society ... has changed the definition of what it means to be human" (96) and that the antidemocratic, Agrarian, and "spiritual" aspects of Percy's work are necessitated by the "inhumanity" of the scientific-technological order which his work opposes. Only an apocalyptic phase of destruction, coming like the "fortunate" hurricanes that Percy depicts in several novels, will sweep away the corruption and make possible what Percy in "The Culture Critics" termed "quality in politics, science or art" (quoted in Schenker 84). Central to Percy's thought is a "diagnosis" of cultural malaise specific to modern Western culture—Binx Bolling's perception "that people are dead, dead, dead" or Thomas More's consciousness in *The Thanatos Syndrome* of "spiritual death ... the way people are closed off to one another" (Percy, quoted in McCombs 818), but, if the crisis is one of bourgeois culture, Percy understood subaltern groups, within Western culture, and presumably outside Western culture as well, to be moving toward the same crisis. As Percy stated in an interview with Ben Forkner and J. Gerald Kennedy, "something has gone wrong, and it has to do with the paradox between the good life, the affluent life, a wealth of perception on the one hand, and yet a sense of poverty at the very base of this wealth" (Percy, "Walker Percy" 6).[1]

From first to last caricature is a staple of Percy's technique, and it is illuminating simply to list the topics that are subjected to typing. How are we to respond to the astounding, and apparently straightforward remark in his essay "A Novel About the End of the World" that "[t]he Okies were too hungry to have 'identity crises'" (*Message* 103)? What, after all, does one make of the derisive satire of Levittown, the New Jersey suburb populated by Mr. Gallagher and Mr. Shean "cranking up their Toros and afterward wisecracking over the fence" (*Gentleman* 115)—the very image of the low-brow Irish descending to pub-talk after their bit of exercise? How should we read the caricature of the Jewish writer Mort Prince, "a pleasant slightish fellow with twirling black hair which flew away in a banner of not absolutely serious rebellion. He wore a black leather wristlet and, as he talked, performed a few covert isometrics on the beer can" (*Gentleman* 115).[2]

In a certain sense, Percy's destructive caricatures did, I believe, express an intensely committed ethical concern, but it was a concern that Percy found difficult to express directly and that his admirers have not always explained very well, for this concern assumed a highly skeptical view of human potential and, as such, it often involved derisive and even nihilistic attacks on less radical positions. Percy clarifies his intention in an interview with Jo Gulledge, in which he states that, given the culture of alienation out of which he writes, "one of the best things that ever happens in my novels is when the loneliness is bridged." Percy refers to the epitaph from *The Last Gentleman* in which Romano Guardini describes the end of the modern world and the beginning of a new era, when, in Percy's words, "the world will be stripped bare of all the old togetherness, even of love." This deconstruction of existing modes of social discourse opens a space for authentic social communication: "bad as it is and lonely as it is, it's going to be honest, clean, no bullshit, and there will actually be a possibility of one lonely person encountering another one, really encountering another one and perhaps even God in a way that hasn't been possible before, even in a culture which sets every value on togetherness, groups, and relationships" (Percy, "Reentry" 115). The difficulty of this conception is suggested, however, in his statement to Gulledge that the destruction of present social existence will open the way for "encountering another one and perhaps even God": in a characteristic manner, Percy defines social community in terms of what remains a private encounter between two individuals or, in an even more idiosyncratic sense of "community," an encounter with God. Although he reaches a different conclusion than I will concerning the import of this solitariness, Jay Tolson substantiates the claim that Percy lived a very private existence—"what seems to have been a life of subdued provincial domesticity" (13). Indeed, according to Tolson, Percy "felt tremendously content within his domestic world. Its snugness and security were something he had never experienced in his childhood" (327).[3]

Percy relies on caricature and derisive satire in his portrayal of social groups since individuals who comprise social groups, in Marcel's and Percy's terms, have an "incarnated" existence that is always mysterious and unclassifiable, and thus cannot be "summed up" by social categories.[4] It is this "summing up" that Percy invariably treats with derision since, from his perspective, group allegiance is a manifestation of the modern abdication of the self to abstraction and is also seen as destructive of the intersubjectivity or authentic human social interaction that Percy desires to restore. Taken to an extreme, group identity undermines what Marcel defined as the fundamental human "urge to make ourselves recognized by some other person" (Marcel in *Homo Viator* 14; quoted in Howland 13).

Percy himself claims to have treated all social groups with equal derision (claiming at the same time to "like" individuals of all groups).

Even so, among the many social groups caricatured in his writing, there is one group never subjected to satire. That social group is precisely Percy's own—the white southern elite, known in the latter nineteenth-century South as the "Redeemers" (otherwise, the "Bourbons"), a class that included Percy's maternal and paternal ancestors. As Percy characterizes them in both fiction and essays, the southern elite are deemed a noble, civic-minded, responsible, and relatively selfless group whose intelligent leadership heralded a period of stability and progress in the South after the Civil War. One of the most important contributions of the Redeemers, in Percy's view, was to moderate the climate of race relations in a period of potential violence ("the fact is that Negroes enjoyed considerably more freedom in the 1880s [in Mississippi] than they do now" [*Signposts* 45]). The Redeemers, however, became politically irrelevant in the wake of a period of democratic social change that led to the rise of poor whites to positions of political and economic prominence. Percy laments the collapse of the political alliance between white moderates and blacks, for in the rise of the white working class he sees a cultural devastation similar to what Faulkner described in his Snopes trilogy. Against this powerful tide of social change, the Redeemers were paralyzed by their faith in an ideology of stoic pride and individualism— a philosophy that, as Percy points out, "was never really social or political but purely and simply moral in the Stoic sense" (*Signposts* 46). Against the simplistic message of Huey Long—a potent message of class self-interest—the Redeemers were impotent.[5]

The position of African Americans and of other marginalized groups within Percy's reading of southern social history replicates their role within the political alliance of the Redeemers, and Percy's attitudes toward race recycle in many respects the historical sympathies of his ancestors. Percy seeks the same moderate climate of race relations that characterized the 1880s, but he recognizes that such a climate cannot be brought about by the leadership of a southern cultural elite that is now weakened by the democratization of the South. Paradoxically, the potential for racial progress lies in two apparently quite opposed bases: the expanding influence of the business class in the South ("Racial injustice is bad business. There is no segregation in the stores" [*Signposts* 97]), and the still vital force of southern religion (not so much in the institutionalized churches but in the benevolent ideology of Christianity itself).

Percy's most impassioned and direct addressing of racial issues occurs in an essay, "Mississippi: The Fallen Paradise," published in

Harper's in 1965 at the climax of the civil rights movement in the Deep South. Percy had been appalled by the University of Mississippi riots of 1962 and by subsequent violence by southern whites opposed to integration. In the essay, he decries the attacks on James Meredith and Medgar Evers carried out by white students. Percy leaves no doubt as to where his sympathies lie in this instance, yet his reading of the *causes* of southern bigotry has the result of deflecting attention from the southern upper class, for, as Redeemers' rhetoric had always done, it shifts the responsibility to the poor white class (the class that Percy's cousin and guardian William Alexander Percy in *Lanterns on the Levee: Recollections of a Planter's Son* sometimes referred to as "peckerwoods") and to the new bourgeois descended from that class. In no uncertain terms, Percy expresses his contempt for the "mob" attitudes that have fueled the opposition to civil rights. The ugliest incidents of racial violence have taken place in the Deep South—in Mississippi and Alabama—rather than in the seaboard South of Georgia and the Carolinas. In Percy's view, the reason for this difference lies in the "frontier culture" of the Deep South in which politics devolved into a "corrupt Populism"—"the demagogic racism of Vardaman and Bilbo" (*Signposts* 44–45). In Mississippi, the "responsible leadership" of the "old moderate tradition of the planter-lawyer-statesman class had long since lost its influence" (*Signposts* 44).[6]

Among Percy's novels, *The Last Gentleman* is a central text for discussing his social ethics, for it is the novel in which we find the clearest articulation of an individual's relationship to social communities and the most expansive casting of social types. Narrated from the perspective of Williston Bibb Barrett, the novel takes on an allegorical quality as it follows Barrett on his journey from New York City to his home in Ithaca, Mississippi, and finally to the New Mexican desert. Will Barrett's bewildering confusion and lack of engagement reflect the confusion of the modern period of history (or perhaps, as Sutter Vaught notes in his diagnosis, the confusion of human identity itself: "your trouble is due not to a disorder of your organism but to the human condition" [*Last Gentleman* 276]). Sutter, for his part, reflects Percy's belief that contemporary society is so corrupt and unhinged that one cannot apply "partial solutions"—the only solution, in Sutter's phrase, is "lewdness" or salvation. Barrett's tolerant and bemused attitude underlines the absurdity of human attempts at "authentic" communication unaided by a recognition of the human relation to a transcendent level of being—his conviction that *he*, not the world, is afflicted. Since there is no cure for his imagined affliction, short of redemption of the world as a whole, Barrett is left to drift between "fugue states" of detachment and inconsequential fantasies of "settling down" and "living a life." In a meaningless world, almost all human relationships are rendered pointless and accidental.

A curious exception to this condition of social malaise appears to be Val Vaugh's teaching in a rural Alabama school for African American mute children. Turning her back on a middle-class environment that she recognizes as inauthentic, within her limited social enclave Val has actually achieved a sort of meaningful social community, though one based on a potentially patronizing relationship toward severely disadvantaged children. In Percy's theoretical terms, however, Val is nonetheless "on to" the crucial fact of the triadic nature of symbolic language (for a discussion of this theory in Percy's essays, see among others "The Delta Factor" and "The Fateful Rift: The San Andreas Fault in the Modern Mind"). Briefly, Percy's triadic theory of language follows the philosophy of Charles Peirce in stressing the existence of a "third element" in symbolic communication, unique to human beings, that distinguishes symbolic language from signs or dyadic communication. In "Symbol, Consciousness, and Intersubjectivity," Percy defined the crucial role of intersubjective communication within his philosophical system: it would serve as the logical crux on which behaviorist and empiricist models of existence must break down, for neither of these models could account for the scientist's own participation in the symbolic production of language—the "narrative," so to speak, of the symbolic act itself. "I am not only conscious of something; I am conscious of it as being what it is for you and me," Percy wrote. "If there is a wisdom in etymologies, the word *consciousness* is surely a case in point; for consciousness, one suddenly realizes, means a knowing-with! In truth it could not be otherwise. The act of consciousness is the intending of the object as being what it is for both of us under the auspices of the symbol" (*Message* 274).

In Percy's view, the possibility of authentic communication is dependent on the rejection of a discredited rationalist ontology and the recognition of the triadic basis of human language. Such recognition would entail radical consequences, since it would force the acceptance of the category of "mystery" as the basis of human consciousness. Short of such a revolution, however, Percy's treatment of social issues is disturbingly indifferent. There is little impulse to work within the

unredeemed society, as it now exists, as such effort seems only to fore-
stall what is seen as the inevitable collapse of that society. Percy's reader
is thus left with a disturbing ethical chasm: on the one hand, the reader
notes Percy's ardent commitment toward redeeming society and restoring the basis for authentic community; on the other hand, Percy is
indifferent at best toward conventional avenues of social reform.

By no means is the disadvantaged condition of African Americans
singled out for what may seem indifference (indeed, Percy's greatest
distaste is reserved for southern poor whites, who are mercilessly caricatured in numerous passages, including the depiction of Beans Ross and
Ellis Gover in *The Last Gentleman*, small-town sheriffs who are, respec-
tively, sadistically racist and slow-witted). In Percy's fiction, the social
conditions of women, immigrants, Jews, and the poor are all depicted as
inevitably worsening in the context of the general decline of twentieth-
century Western civilization. The crucial scene in *The Last Gentleman* in
which Barrett returns to his childhood home in the Delta—the site of his
father's suicide—provides a clue to the origin of the narrative's disen-
gagement with social change. The suicide of Will Barrett's father
resulted from his reaching the "dead end" of the stoic faith in a purely
individual code—the elite code of honor and goodness by which his father had lived.[7] While in this novel Barrett never resolves the issue of the
legacy of stoicism, he appears to sense the need for a less individualistic
basis for living ("I think he was wrong and that he was looking in the
wrong place. No, not he but the times" [*Last Gentleman* 260]). Barrett
realizes that his father had been the victim of "the times," a historical
culture in which the upper class performed the solitary duties of noblesse
oblige but held itself aloof from other groups.

Unfortunately, Barrett's analysis never proceeds beyond this point,
as Percy indicates by what happens next. Immediately following the
moment of recognition—his intuition that his father's culture was
doomed by its dependence on an alienating code of private honor—a
young man of Barrett's own age passes by him, but Barrett has no more
to say to his African American contemporary than did his father: indeed,
he has less (even if his father's words were largely part of a patronizing
ritual). Then a curious explanation for their silence occurs to Barrett:
"The engineer looked at the other as the half second wore on. You may
be in a fix and I know that but what you don't know and won't believe
and must find out for yourself is that I'm in a fix too and you got to get
where I am before you even know what I'm talking about and I know

that and that's why there is nothing to say now. Meanwhile I wish you well" (260).

This passage suggests a remarkable diagnosis of race relations in the mid-1960s and an extraordinary rationale of the speaker's inability to participate in changing the racial climate. Barrett recognizes the inequality of African Americans but warns that when they "get where I am" (in terms of both socioeconomic progress and spiritual decline), they will not find happiness; they will be in an even greater "fix." In wishing his black contemporary well, Barrett implies his recognition of the unfairness of the southern racial system, but he also silently asserts that his own problem of spiritual alienation is "greater" than the socioeconomic problems of other groups. There is nothing to say, in Barrett's view, because black and white Americans find themselves at distinct stages of existential crisis. In his view, African Americans have not yet arrived at the point of alienation that whites reached some time ago.

A major difficulty with Percy's apocalyptical scenario is that, short of revolutionary change and the formation of a new basis for human justice, it offers no solution to existing social problems—problems that Percy himself asserts are at a point of crisis. Percy's hesitancy to address social issues has been noted by many of his critics. In his negative assessment of *Love in the Ruins*, L. E. Sissman went so far as to write in *The New Yorker* that Percy "has given up on man as a fit subject for rehabilitation" (quoted in Tolson 359). In a more balanced analysis of the same novel, J. Gerald Kennedy stressed the inevitable dualism of Percy's orthodox religious doctrine, which views human society as irremediably fallen. In "Walker Percy and the Myth of the Innocent Eye," Panthea Reid Broughton reviewed Percy's place within a romantic tradition in which the "innocent eye" of the child displaced the rational vision of "corrupt" adults. Broughton concluded that, while all of Percy's protagonists attempt a "quest for a vision-clearing experience," any attempt to redeem the physical world is futile: by definition, the humanistic level of experience is "alienated" and all efforts at enlightenment "*only* open one to participation in this world" (Broughton 105; emphasis added). The separation of spirit and world is nowhere better illustrated, as Broughton recognizes, than in the character of Lancelot, who tells Percival that "it will be your way, or it will be mine" (Percy, *Lancelot* 257). Broughton's gloss is that "either *seeing* reveals the meaningless venality of this world and converts one to it or it convinces one of the limits of all that is finite" (108). The implication for Percy's social thought is that for the time being—a period that might last for years, decades, or centuries—a failed and unjust society is left to follow its own course.

The southern racial system during the period depicted in *The Last Gentleman* was one greatly in need of reform, for it was an apartheid system supported by a mixture of repression, paternalism, and resistance to change. Percy's representation of this system is quite realistic, as black characters are repeatedly shown to be intimidated, patronized, and ignored. In acute vignettes in *The Last Gentleman*, such as the beating of Sweet Breeze by two local sheriffs or the hunting episode involving Uncle Fannin and Merriam, his black retainer, Percy offers a portrait of southern race relations of a sort unchanged since the days of Jim Crow, yet the novel's implied commentary on race relations in the South is quite ambivalent, at times recalling what Percy wrote in "Mississippi: The Fallen Paradise" about the fact that "despite the humbuggery about the perfect love and understanding between us white folks and darkies down in Dixie, whites and blacks in the South do in fact know something about getting along with each other which the rest of the country does not know" (*Signposts* 51). There is little doubt that Walker Percy as an individual bemoaned the continuing failure of his region to reform its racial system, but for this reason it seems all the more puzzling to find that in his fiction and essays he generally ridiculed organized efforts to promote change.

In fact, Percy's divided sensibility was not unlike that of other southern moderates of his time who recognized the tragedy of southern racism but who believed that a solution could not be imposed on the South from the outside. In a 1957 essay of the same title, Percy defined "the Southern moderate" as "a man of good will who is aware of the seriousness of the problem, is searching for a solution, but disagrees that the solution is simple and can be effected overnight" (*Signposts* 95). Noting ambiguously that "the cure" for racial injustice could be "worse than the disease," Percy asserts that "the real role of the moderate is, not to press for a quick solution, but to humanize, to moderate, the solution which is surely coming" (97). Unlike the liberal from the North or the South, the southern moderate is realistic enough to appreciate that "any enforced cultural change" cannot come overnight. It is "the social and sexual consequences of integration" that most concern the white southerner: even moderates in the South are disturbed, Percy believes, by the prospect of school integration, for this involves the potential for cultural damage and even sexual intimacy. Percy insists that the southerner is justifiably worried that "the crisis of school integration should coincide with the crisis of juvenile morality and with the upturn of crime statistics among urban Negro populations" (98). In response to this apparently intractable conflict, Percy offers a familiar solution, essentially a variation on the "separate but equal" doctrine of southern opposition to integration. Given that integration of the schools is inevitable—mandated by the Supreme Court and enforced by federal troops—Percy's proposal, as a southern moderate, is integration without social mixing.

Percy's own relationships with and attitudes toward African Americans were equally tied to the culture and values of his region and family. Percy gradually came to support a moderate program of racial reform, although even his most outspoken essay on civil rights ("Stoicism in the South," which appeared in *Commonweal* in 1956) speaks of blacks as "the mob" and seemingly "insolent" in their demand for equal rights, even as it supports the ultimate goal of desegregation and equality. The relationship of Will Barrett to John Houghton—the Vaught's gardener in *The Last Gentleman*—provides some insight into Percy's complex attitudes, for Houghton's character is modeled on that of the person of Elijah Collier or "Lije," a house servant who befriended the Percy boys during their unhappy childhood in Birmingham and who later reappeared to work for William Alexander Percy in Greenville. As the fond description of Houghton suggests, Percy's memory of Lije was affectionate but also "paternalistic" (Tolson 89). Tolson, in fact, believes that "at the center of [Percy's] attitudes is a certain historical fatalism: Blacks, having suffered at the hands of whites, have acquired a certain dignity and wisdom, but any effort to lift themselves out of their less-than-desirable station in life involves a compromise of their best 'black' qualities" (131).

According to the moderate view, only an authentic "change of heart" by southern whites (a change that would eventually come about on its own) could bring about meaningful racial integration. Barrett, in fact, is a good example of the well-intentioned southern moderate who nonetheless is not yet prepared for social integration. From childhood he has felt uncomfortable around black servants, including his own family's "mammy" and cook, D'lo, and when he returns briefly to his home, he still feels the "distance between them" (Percy, *Last Gentleman* 262). The blacks with whom Barrett is accustomed to dealing are almost all servants. As such, they are not likely to initiate change in their relationship to whites. Indeed, the absence of communication between the Vaught and Barrett servants and their employers is striking. D'lo is a mammy figure who avoids conflict by "a good-humored letting [Barrett] be" (262). John Houghton, the Vaught's gardener, is perceived by Lamar Thigpen as an Uncle Tom ("The Vaught retainers seemed to remind Lamar of an earlier, more gracious time..." [215]). Certainly Percy recognizes the unreality and inadequacy of this social system, as is evident in his shrewd analysis of servant "manners" in his depiction of both households.

The exception to this unruffled discourse of social equivocation is the figure of David Ross. Whether through rebellion or ignorance, seventeen-year-old David does not adopt the subservient manners of previous generations of blacks in the South. Unlike his mother, Lugurtha, who sticks carefully to the role of contented mammy ("All she wanted in the world was to find fervent areas of agreement" [159]), David precipitates conflict as he projects his own vulnerability. As Barrett explains it, David "invites" the violation of whites who are inherently "not that bad" (159). David "irritated the engineer" (157) because he brings to the surface those racial conflicts that have been veiled by an elaborate code of manners. Believing that a new basis of trust can operate between the races, David ignores the conventional manners and thus exposes himself to repeated humiliation and abuse. Significantly, the trust in which David believes—a simple faith that human nature is benevolent and that other human beings will treat him fairly—is shown to be naive. In Percy's theological terms, David's trust in human nature is misguided because it ignores the sinfulness of human beings and because it relies on a rationalistic faith in human justice rather than on a justice grounded in religious redemption.

In any event, Percy argues that in the contemporary South, racial problems per se are no longer of paramount importance to the novelist. In an autobiographical essay, "Coming Back to Georgia," Percy notes the changed racial climate—the absence in cities such as Atlanta and in the South as a whole of "what was uniquely oppressive for both white and black and which has now vanished" (*Signposts* 29). In any case, the racial problems that remain in the South are no longer specifically sectional in nature since with the large-scale migration of blacks from the South to the North, "southern" racial conflicts have become *national* problems. The contemporary southern novelist in this view simply does not find racial issues, in and of themselves, to be of paramount significance. The focus of interest now rests on "the successful middle class," and for the middle class in America "something has gone badly wrong here, something which has nothing to do with poverty or blackness or whiteness" (*Signposts* 36).

A significant aspect of Walker Percy's narrative is devoted to the signifying of this shift, as Percy sees it, from an ethical model in which race, class, and other social conflicts mattered to a model of society and art in which they are irrelevant. On the final page of *The Last Gentleman*, one reads the description of Sutter's car, an old Edsel "spavined and sprung, sunk at one corner and flatulent in its muffler, spuriously elegant and unsound, *like a Negro's car*, a fake Ford" (319; emphasis added). Among the seven pejoratives describing Sutter's Edsel, the inexplicable characterization "like a Negro's car" is inserted. One might argue that in the mid-1960s, many African Americans did indeed drive older cars and thus Percy's phrase is merely descriptive. To understand Percy's technique of satiric caricature, however, it is necessary to grasp his philosophical point: it is not *some* women who are characterized as "attractive" or not; it is not *some* Jews who are "special"; it is not *some* blacks only who drive old and unsound automobiles. Within Percy's model of narrative practice, all human beings within groups devolve into caricature, and they do so for the reason that they must if the "truth" of the significance of middle-class spiritual malaise is to be foregrounded. All apparently "successful" forms of social interaction, whether within gender, ethnic, or social class groups, *must* be undermined if Percy's dialectic of destruction and redemption is to be validated. Everyday social existence *must* be understood as radically unsuitable in order for the dialectic of redemption, in Percy's radical sense, to be necessitated.

The treatment of race and class in *The Last Gentleman* must be positioned within the larger context of Walker Percy's cultural critique. To appreciate the severity of Percy's representation does not, of course, diminish the sense of his artistic accomplishment, but it should lead us to admit the radical nature of his ethical vision. Ultimately, Walker Percy stands as a major figure who, as Jay Tolson notes, led an intense and conflictive life of spiritual quest and who transformed his own inner disputes into narrative at every turn.

Notes

1. In another interview, Percy diagnosed the spiritual dilemmas among residents of the "new affluent society" at Hilton Head Island, South Carolina, in

whom Percy detects "a good deal of malaise, a despair that does not know itself" (Percy, "Talk" 17).

2. Percy counted Jews among his closest friends and literary associates, and he particularly admired the work of contemporary Jewish writers such as Saul Bellow and Bernard Malamud, yet what Tolson describes as Percy's special attraction to Jews (30) suggests at the same time a certain one-dimensionality in his thinking. As Percy wrote in "The Delta Factor," "[w]hen one meets a Jew in New York or New Orleans or Paris or Melbourne, it is remarkable that no one considers the event remarkable. What are they doing here?" (*Message* 6). Although this passage has been taken out of context, in which it serves as an illustration of a larger argument, it is nonetheless significant that Percy fixed on the Jew (as representative of the anomaly of an ancient sect's survival in the modern age) as exemplary, and that he would argue that meeting a Jewish person in a modern city would give rise to such a peculiar thought. Even the character of Max Gottlieb in *Love in the Ruins* and *The Thanatos Syndrome*, modeled on Sinclair Lewis's character of the same name in *Arrowsmith* (itself based on the actual Jacques Loeb of the Rockefeller Institute), comes across as a stereotypical figure: "a good scientist and ethical man" in Tolson's phrase (108). Is there not something patronizing in the figure, just as there is hostility in the treatment of Mailer? In assigning a special significance to the existence of Jews in America, and in discerning a special role for the productions of Jewish writers and critics, Percy was expressing a complex psychological bond and bondage. Like Percy—the Catholic convert in the Protestant South—the Jewish writer was (in Percy's conception) an outcast in American society, and like that of his ancestors, Percy's "defense" of Jews was part of a patrician's struggle against the unprogressive forces of society: the Ku Klux Klan, the Citizen's Councils, and the rest.

3. Percy recognized that the condition of solitude was a significant issue in his writing and that his insistence on portraying the solitary nature of modern existence posed problems for even his most discerning readers. Caroline Gordon, an early and sympathetic critic, read *The Last Gentleman* in proof and criticized the opening paragraphs for dealing at such length with the solitary figure of Will Barrett. Percy replied that "with the times being what they are, one almost has to begin a book with a solitary young man. All my writings, for better or worse, take off from ... solipsism" (Tolson 329).

4. Mary Howland demonstrates the extent to which Percy relied on the philosophy of Gabriel Marcel in his theory of social relations, but she does not specifically analyze the treatment of race relations in *The Last Gentleman*.

5. For a more objective reading of the role of Redeemers in southern politics, see Chapter One in Ayers.

6. Paradoxically, in an earlier essay "A Southern View" (published in July 1957 in *America*), Percy defended a similar "Southern heritage" originating in "the frontier and the farm" and "possess[ing] a prevalent democratic temper that to an amazing degree destroyed class feeling" (*Signposts* 91). As Percy in 1957 described this "agrarian" heritage, it was "a tradition which at its best enshrined the humane aspects of living for rich and poor, black and white" (*Signposts* 91).

7. It is not accidental that Walker Percy should have understood so well the dangers of individualism. Percy's family history, and the southern upper-class culture in which his family played a role, taught lessons of stoic individualism and aristocratic reserve. Percy's cousin and guardian, William Alexander Percy, began his memoir *Lanterns on the Levee* with a memorable description of existential solitude: "Below on the road stream the tribes of men, tired, bent, hurt, and stumbling, and each man alone." Among Percy's guardian's tenets of life, Jay Tolson writes, "the first is Will's belief in the solitary character of human existence" (65). As Lewis Baker notes in his study of the Percy lineage, patrician reserve and a sense of noblesse oblige were family traits passed down to Walker, who in his private life as philosopher and novelist "has withdrawn behind the innermost wall of individuality" (176).

9

The Risks of Membership:
Richard Ford's The Sportswriter

In the first two sentences of *The Sportswriter*, Richard Ford sets forth those issues with which his novel will be most concerned: a man, his work, his home and sense of place, his relationship with family, and his expectation of "the good life." Since Ford's writing has begun to be compared with that of Walker Percy, it would be well to consider the first sentences of *The Last Gentleman*, perhaps Percy's most canonical work and a book that announces its very different concerns: "a young man thinking," the emptiness of physical existence, and the issues of ontology and perspective represented by the young man's telescope. It is not until the eleventh paragraph of Percy's novel that another *human being* enters the narrative, a fact that suggests the most important contrast between Percy's and Ford's sensibility: despite Percy's interest in theories of language and "intersubjective" communication, his fiction envisages quests in which reflection, whether solitary or dialogic, comprises the protagonist's supremely important activity. Richard Ford's central characters, however, are engaged in quests of a far less private, less individualistic, and less metaphysical nature. Indeed, Ford's writing expresses an urgency concerning the collective future of American society, and, through his continual process of humorous satiric deflation, he suggests the absurdity of private reflection as a solution to the malaise of contemporary middle-class existence.

Richard Ford's essay review of *Lancelot*, "Walker Percy: Not Just Whistling Dixie," is an important statement of Ford's artistic relationship to Percy. The essay might be viewed as evidence of a substantial indebtedness to Walker Percy, but it is in fact a "tribute" that one must read with particular care, alert to what is said and not said and to the way in which Ford turns Percy's kind of sardonic irony on Percy himself. Ford begins with large praise for Percy's ability as a stylist: "From a writerly point of view, I'd rather read a sentence written by Walker Percy than a sentence written by anybody else I can think of. Percy, to my mind, is the best sentence-writer around" (Ford, "Walker Percy" 558). The initial emphasis on (and limitation to) the "writerly point of view" should raise an alarm (as should the sardonic praise of Percy as "the best sentence-writer around"), and indeed Ford proceeds in terms that clearly restrict his praise to the level of style and technique, as in his concluding assessment of Percy's "lovely facility for writing prose, the very thing he does best" (564). Furthermore, Ford qualifies his approbation by raising certain questions about Percy's ideas and attitudes. What Ford says, in sum, is that he has learned from Percy's example as a stylist, especially from his use of "voice" and descriptive language, but that he is skeptical concerning the direction of Percy's moral philosophy, especially in the novels appearing after the publication of his first novel, *The Moviegoer*.

In fact, what Ford says about Percy's ethics and social vision is highly ambivalent. Of the character Jamie Vaught (a character that Percy appears to treat with the utmost seriousness in *The Last Gentleman* and, significantly, one whom Percy connects most explicitly with the religious theme of that novel), Ford could quip that he is one "who passes out good advice and good vibes throughout the book and, before he dies, makes everybody feel better" (560). If, as he stated, Ford admires Percy's "faith" in the traditional basis for a unified and healing vision, he suggests that he may not share with Percy the same sources of belief. Discussing Percival as a character who is extraordinary as one who seems to retain qualities of piety and virtue, Ford adds that it is "chiefly *Lancelot*'s 1970's update of the dolorous knight's tale," with his "worldly" and "fleshly" calling, "that provokes our interest"—not Percival's role as virtuous healer (562). Of "Lance's windy disquisitions" (the apocalyptic rage that Ford explicitly identifies with Percy as well as Lancelot), Ford writes that "we've simply heard it before, most of it long before the Sixties' glibness made it a cliché" (563). Indeed, Ford writes that *Lancelot* is "a novel which Percy seems to have handled without a great deal of certainty or much real interest in the ideas he passes on as truth" (563). Ford concludes his negative assessment of the novel by stating unequivocally: "I think it all just got too grim for Percy; the specter of his own mean and incomplete vision flew back at him, and he tried to make it a joke, but it was too late" (564).

Again, there is plenty of evidence for Percy's technical influence on Ford, and Fred Hobson in "Richard Ford and Josephine Humphreys: Walker Percy in New Jersey and Charleston" (published as Chapter 3 in

The Southern Writer in the Postmodern World) has furnished a convincing review of it. A careful reading of Hobson's essay, however, shows that he focuses on Percy's "writerly" influence largely to the exclusion of thematic issues. As Hobson demonstrates, Ford's narrator in *The Sportswriter*, Frank Bascombe, resembles Percy's narrator in *The Moviegoer*, Binx Bolling: Frank "is another in that line of reflective and somewhat paralyzed well-bred, well-mannered, and well-educated young southern white males who tell their stories in the first person and are moved by the need to connect" (Hobson, *Southern Writer* 55). Both narrators are given to inventing or appropriating terms to explain themselves and their views of the world, such as Binx's "everydayness" or "certification" and Frank's "forgetting," "literalism," and "factualism." There are other similarities of character and plot: both Binx and Frank are "watchers: one watches movies, the other watches sports" (56), and "beyond that, it is the tone, the language, the cadences, the detailed social observation, the attention to southern types that links Ford with Percy" (57). I would maintain, however, it is *not* the ideas—the ideological or philosophical grounding which, more so than literary style or narrative technique, define the author's identity and relationship to the world. As Hobson admits, "there is much more one could say about *The Sportswriter*, particularly how this novel, which is so much like *The Moviegoer* in certain ways, is so very different in others" (57).

In contrast with Walker Percy's central figure of the "wayfarer" embarked on a quest of existential identity, Ford's protagonists are less decisive but more tolerant, focused not on the problem of one's very existence but on getting by, helping others in the small ways that one can, and going on to the next day. Unlike the more expansive quests undertaken by Percy's heroes, Frank Bascombe never really leaves Haddam, New Jersey. What he may be said to be seeking is "solace," and solace, in contrast with "mystery" or "being," implies a context quite different from that of quest. The context in which one seeks solace is pain that is not amenable to redemption. A reading of *The Sportswriter* uncovers the sources of Frank Bascombe's pain, not in an existential and religious context but in those complicated relationships of family, intimacy, and labor that are suggested in the novel's first lines.

The distinction between Percy's and Ford's sensibilities is suggested by Ford's theorizing of the writer's task. In several interviews and essays, as in his fictionalized comments, Ford consistently stresses the untranscendent nature of literature, its limited and minor quality in relation to experience.[1] For Ford, writing is always a matter of attention to the "small" and less ponderous matters of existence; in his view existence is open-ended and inconclusive, the pleasing "frame of mind" of "not knowing the outcome of things" (*Sportswriter* 369). The only truth, Ford writes, is "life itself—the thing that happens" (374). As in his merciless satire of the literature faculty at Berkshire College, Ford's narrator is angered by the travesty of literature involved in its misuse for conveying "ideas" and the illusion of permanence ("time-freed, existential youth forever" [222]). Speaking with uncharacteristic directness through his narrative persona in *The Sportswriter*, Ford writes: "Some things can't be explained. They just are. And after a while they disappear, usually forever, or become interesting in another way. Literature's consolations are always temporary, while life is quick to begin again" (223).

One misreads Ford by sacralizing or allegorizing the secular language that his narrative employs. There are, for example, such clues as in the novel's derisive satire of Easter service at Haddam's First Presbyterian Church, where Frank slips in for a few minutes only to find that "nothing here could matter less than my own identity" (237). Leaving the service of "confident, repentant suburbanites," Frank reflects that he is "'saved' in the only way I can be (*pro tempore*)" (238). In an angrier mood, Frank imputes that Jesus is the cause of "misery" for many in contemporary life whose problems are more complex than Christian teaching would prepare one for. These fictional passages are echoed by Ford's comment to Kay Bonetti that *The Sportswriter* is "not a Christian book. The kind of redeeming that goes on in that book is entirely unreligious; it's really Frank figuring out ways to redeem his life based on nothing but the stuff of his life" (Ford, "Interview" 85).

Frank Bascombe is shown striving, often unsuccessfully, toward an understanding of social reality. In the course of representing this striving, Ford has his protagonist indulge in the use of abstract terminology and descriptive generalization that resembles that of Percy's heroes, but in Frank's case his grandiose philosophizing seems trivial and inconsequential, and his caricatures of everyone around him, from "cheerleader" Vicki Arcenault to Haddam banker, Carter "Knot-head" Knott, seem a means of avoiding rather than connecting with others. It is as if, in a subtle maneuver of style and content, Ford has turned Percy's sardonic style upon itself. In contrast with his essential goodness and good sense, Frank's philosophical discourse is flawed and escapist, as in his facile distinction between a "literalist," "a man who will enjoy an afternoon watching people while stranded in an airport" and a "factualist," one who "can't stop wondering why his plane was late" (*Sportswriter* 132–33). In contrast with this sort of flippancy, Frank is capable of the most sincere feeling, as in the understated description of his relationship to his beloved and now deceased parents, who during his youth permitted him to enjoy a childhood pleasantly oblivious of the adult world: "They simply loved me, and I them. The rest, they didn't feel the need to blab about" (205).

One of the superficial similarities between Percy's and Ford's writing rests in their mutual appreciation of the absurdity of American political rhetoric. Percy's writing is marked by attacks on liberal ideas, as well as by disdain for southern conservatives. Ford also writes some very entertaining satire at the expense of liberals, but equally his ridicule is directed at conservatives such as Frank's ex father-in-law, Henry Dykstra, "somewhere to the right of Attila the Hun" (122). The thrust of Percy's politics, however, is more radical in its effort to reinstate the authority of a religious community. According to Percy's analysis in "The Loss of the Creature" and other essays, the rise of a scientific and rationalistic culture in the nineteenth century led to an increasingly alienated culture in which human beings lost a meaningful relationship to their own being. The sense of "creatureliness" can only be restored following an apocalyptic crisis leading to the restoration of a relationship to the "everydayness" of existence. As Percy portrays this "return" at the conclusion of such novels as *The Second Coming* and *Love in the Ruins*, it coincides with the establishment of an "interpersonal" relationship with another human being. Percy implies that the recovery of everydayness—the recovery from a condition akin to "suicide"—points to psychological and spiritual reintegration, including the apprehension of the "mystery" of human existence.

In a meticulous and insightful essay, Edward Dupuy points to a similar dialectic of loss and return operating in *The Sportswriter*. For example, Dupuy cites the poem that Frank Bascombe carries to Ralph's grave, which he describes as "a poem about letting the everyday make you happy—insects, shadows, the color of a woman's hair" (*Sportswriter* 19). Dupuy characterizes Frank's attitude at this point as "the freedom and dispensation of the ex-suicide," and his emotion is said to reflect Frank's "relenting nature" ("Confessions" 96–97). Although Dupuy does not explicitly identify Percy as the source, the terms in which he discusses Ford connect Ford's references to "relinquishment" with Percy's dialectic of loss, crisis, and acceptance of "mystery." It can be demonstrated, however, that these are not always the terms in which Ford writes: to cite one of many examples from *The Sportswriter*, Frank is shown to be mocking the sort of existential anxiety that informs Percy's novels and such essays as "The Man on the Train" in *The Message in the Bottle* when he derides the sense of being "anxious in the old mossy existential sense" (*Sportswriter* 145) or describes crazed Herb Wallagher as "alienated as Camus" (208). Frank's anxiety is of a different order, the product of cultural and social disturbances rather than the disturbance of "being itself." One would have even more difficulty fitting Frank Bascombe's later history in *Independence Day* into Walker Percy's mold: surely by this point, a dozen years after the conclusion of *The Sportswriter*, Frank must have learned an acceptance of mystery, if he is ever to do so, yet it is clear that his pain has not been relieved by his relenting, perhaps because the historical world continues to impinge markedly on Frank's private existence. Even if he has learned a greater degree of "acceptance" in his own affairs, as he enters middle age Frank finds himself more and more engulfed in the difficulties of others (represented primarily by his son's emotional distress).

Indeed, the term "mystery" suffers a process of comic deflation in *The Sportswriter* since, for Ford's rather ingenuous hero, "mystery" is a condition not that much different from a romantic adventure. A conspicuous example of mystery in this sense is Frank's one-semester affair with Selma Jassim, Berkshire College's resident literary theorist. Frank is attracted to Selma in part because of their similar skepticism (like Frank she "preferred to stay as remote as possible" [227] from other people, particularly from other altruistic Christians on the Berkshire faculty). Frank comments that "mystery emanated from her like a fire alarm" (229), and in Frank's case mystery leaves him with only a nostalgic remembrance of happiness at a quite human level.

Frank's potential loss of contact with society, following the death of his son and the ensuing divorce, remains an issue, but after the novel's climax in the weeks following Walter Luckett's suicide, Frank is shown as reestablishing more meaningful human contacts. However he may ridicule Walter's hapless psychological condition, the fact of Walter's searing despair intrudes, as Frank thinks repeatedly of "poor Luckett" over Easter weekend. Later Frank realizes that he "might've warned" Walter that he was making "a terrible mistake" (304). Indeed, it is Walter's death that "has had the effect on me that death means to have; of reminding me of my responsibility to a somewhat larger world" (368). Visiting Walter's apartment with X, Frank feels for a moment that he shares "the grief poor Walter must've felt alone here but shouldn't have" (335). In the lonesome night after Walter's death, Frank drives to the Haddam train station where, watching reunions of passengers with family and friends, he realizes that "[t]o take pleasure in the consolations of others, even the small ones, is possible" (341). Walter's suicide note, which he later reads, causes him to consider how "we get bound up with people we don't even know" (350). By the end of the novel, this larger world includes even a new contact with his deceased father, through the intermediary of Frank's forgotten cousins in Florida. Uncharacteristically, Frank comments toward the end of the novel: "I have taken the time to get to know them" (370).

Frank's own heritage is clearly within the provincial and working-class culture that his cousins still inhabit: his parents, originally from rural Iowa, have moved about from one working-class job to another before settling on the Gulf Coast of Mississippi. When Frank's father dies in 1959, his mother remarries the plebeian if modestly successful Jake Ornstein of Skokie, Illinois. Frank's character is shaped by his family's misfortune, but also by its integrity, and by his own discomforting position on the margin of the American Dream. The major elements of his personal history—his working-class roots, the premature death of his father, his separation from his mother after her remarriage, the relatively early death of his mother, his lonely schooling at Gulf Pines ("Lonesome Pines") Military Academy, his chance ROTC assignment to the University of Michigan, his marriage and divorce with X, and the tragic death of his son—are all inseparable from the social and historical context in which he has lived; they are not merely idiosyncratic events in a personal history but reflect the shared history of his generation. By assigning his birth-year as "1945" (a highly significant one year later than Ford's own birth), the year marking the end of World War II and the beginning of a new collective history, Ford suggests the representativeness of Frank Bascombe's story. His unabashed sentimentality concerning love and family, his nostalgia for the carefree misdemeanors of frat life, his fatuous odes to pastoral suburban existence, his tendency toward boosterism, his inspirational talk, and even his pomposity—all are Ford's means of assembling the novel from the collective voices of postwar American culture.

Frank does suffer from a sense of alienation, of course, as well as a gentler condition of abstraction that Ford terms "dreaminess," but these conditions have a cultural or social, not an existential basis. The confusion and incoherence he feels result from the disjointedness of his cultural roots; due to his transient and disjunctive family history and the national history of dramatic social change during his lifetime, Frank is alienated from home, family, and local culture. He is an apologetic and indifferent southerner, and like many in his generation it is difficult even to speak with any assurance of his "home." His life lacks a historically grounded sense of identity based on local or regional connections, and as a result Frank reacts to all crises with benign fatalism, denying the pain he has lived through. Significantly, Frank's existence is missing the very sorts of human connection, especially that of intimate and sincere friendship that both Wayne C. Booth and Martha C. Nussbaum insist upon as a condition of ethical development. That Frank's life and to a large extent the suburban culture in which he grows up lack coherent significance is attested by the superficiality of his social relationships at the beginning of the novel, as the narrative ironically asserts the "meaningfulness" of Frank's least sincere attachments: for example, his weekly visit to Mrs. Miller, the palm-reader who for five dollars offers him a simulation of friendship and concern. If Frank finds particular solace in his palmist, *"the stranger who takes your life seriously"* (100), he is generally content with even more ritualized relationships or with solitude. In a particularly droll passage, Frank lauds his family's use of catalogue shopping as "the very way of life that suited us and our circumstances ... we were the kind of people for whom catalog-buying was better than going out into the world" (195). Surely it is not just Frank Bascombe and X who are the comic butt of this mocking narrative voice—it is likely the reader, who may live in a similar suburban neighborhood.

The relationship of social connection to moral self-improvement, and to what Nussbaum terms "perception," is reiterated in *The Sportswriter*, as for example in the account of Frank's brief friendship and correspondence with Peggy Connover (ironically, a friendship that proves the immediate cause of his divorce from X). In the supportive, asexual relationship of man and woman, Frank discovers a reward of happiness, and of the letters from Peggy that follow their brief meeting he says, "it pleased me that somewhere out in the remote world someone was thinking of me for no bad reason at all, and even wishing me well" (147). From a complicated series of signs, Frank begins to infer that "life ... is not as disconnected and random as it might feel" (143). Yet the problem of his almost total isolation from others continues to worry Frank to the point that he rationalizes its advantages. This posture is certainly undercut by derision, but it simultaneously acknowledges Frank's recognition of the origin of his predicament. As he admits not long afterward, however, it is cynicism of a particularly selfish kind: "lifelong self-love and the tunnel vision in which you yourself are all that's visible at the tunnel's end" (172).

It is hardly coincidental that the incoherence and isolation of Frank's life are mirrored in the lives of many others in the novel, as Frank discovers (though never fully admits) that his own despair is symptomatic rather than individual. In Wade Arcenault, Vicki's father, Frank encounters another who shares the grief of sudden loss: Wade's first wife, Esther, died suddenly when Wade was forty-nine, casting him into a lifelong despair that Wade buries in his "devil's dungeon"—the basement workroom where he locks up all pain. Another important example is Herb Wallagher, an ex-pro lineman from Walled Lake, Michigan. Herb's paralysis resulting from a ski-boat accident duplicates the freakishly accidental, arbitrary quality of Frank's own inexplicable loss of a child. The narrative of Frank's visit with Herb, his well-masked double, bears close scrutiny, for if it is one of the more significant of Frank's failed attempts to establish connection with others, it may also mark the beginning of his difficult journey back to social and ethical selfhood. From the moment the day begins with an unexpectedly heavy snow falling from an overcast sky, the meeting of Frank and Herb is singled out as portentous. Herb's residence turns out to be less imposing than one would expect of an ex-pro lineman, and Herb himself (perhaps doubling Frank's moral nature) is "much smaller" than Frank thought he would be. Frank senses that neither Herb nor his wife, Clarice, has found much happiness in life, and indeed that Herb has drifted into angry self-pity, having given up his job as "spirit coach" of other athletes. Herb, in fact, turns out to be dangerously unstable, living in a state that is "too close to regret" (164)—the sort of regret that Frank must avoid at all costs. For Frank, the significance of this encounter is surely something of a lesson in the despair to which he also is susceptible. It is a warning about the consequences of withdrawal from society—a bunkered isolation and a ruined life seeking refuge at "Walled Lake," and, thus, it seems appropriate that Frank should flee from Walled Lake in the comfortable fellowship of Mr. Smallwood's cab. For his part, Smallwood is on to

Herb Wallagher and, for that matter, on to the insanity of suburban existence altogether, with its barely repressed violence and ubiquitous anger.
Back with Vicki at the hotel, Frank senses a new wariness and "gloomy
remoteness" in their relationship, but Detroit itself, with its unpredictable weather, is perversely capable of inspiring hope as well as loss. As
Frank puts it, "You can never completely count on things out here. Life
is counterpoised against a mean wind that could suddenly cease" (171).

There has always been an element of solidarity in Frank's unusual
degree of sympathy with social outcasts—his willingness to cross social
boundaries, to empathize with the excluded, and to submit the class assumptions of his suburban community to critical examination. Indeed,
Ford represents Frank Bascombe as a "human weak link, working
against odds and fate" (254)—a man capable of ethical sympathy with
other weak links. A failure himself in the profession of creative writing,
Frank sympathizes with failure in the world around him. His social tolerance naturally involves him in conflict with his own class, although
Frank's "class" is more ambiguous than it might seem at first. From *The
Sportswriter* one learns that at age twenty-four, Frank moved into "a
large Tudor house" at 19 Hoving Rd., Haddam, New Jersey, from profits
from a movie contract for his first book. The section of Haddam where
Frank lives is upper middle class and culturally elite, yet Frank has
"nothing in common" with his neighbors, the Deffeyes. His preference is
for companions like Vicki Arcenault, a matter-of-fact, working-class
woman newly arrived in the northeast by way of Waco and Dallas.

Surprisingly, perhaps, in Vicki—whom he has originally typed in the
most dismissive fashion—the narrative suggests that Frank begins to respond to some reality of feeling outside himself. During the argument
that ensues after he is caught jealously looking through her bag, Frank
records his imagining of her suffering, and he broadens his imagination
of human pain beyond Vicki and himself to include everyone who has
felt emptiness and loneliness. At this point Frank cannot, however,
imagine Vicki other than in condescending terms, as his trivializing of an
imagined future marriage shows. Even so, if Frank, at this point, lacks
the moral imagination to perceive his own role in relation to others, the
narrative reveals that his imperfect imagining is interrupted twice by
emergency sirens in the city, as if to connect Frank's wounds with those
of others. It is indeed "outside" that Frank needs to relocate his imagination, for Frank is at least enough of a loner for X to accuse him of being
one. Certainly it is significant that the best he can do in the way of

friendship is a relationship like that with Bert Brisker, an acquaintance with whom he has nothing in common.

Despite his irresolute and flippant manner, Frank is represented as a figure with serious ethical concerns. One of the most striking moments in *The Sportswriter* is his memory of a dream in which "someone I knew ... mentions to me—so obliquely that now I can't even remember what he said—something shameful about me, clearly shameful, and it scares me that he might know more and that I've forgotten it, but shouldn't have" (144). The representation of "shame," so striking in its appearance in Ford's novel, is hardly fashionable in postmodern art, for the reason that it implies a stable social culture out of which an act can be judged "shameful." Of all ethical intuitions, shame is the most historical. It is asserted out of a coherence of social responsibilities—a continuity that, as Charles Newman notes, is necessarily discounted in postmodern art in which language constitutes its own reality, but in which, paradoxically, "[a] truly autonomous language could convey no human relations whatsoever" (81).

It would be interesting to speculate as to the location of the ethically stable culture out of which Frank is enabled to judge a "shameful" act for what it is. Regardless of its origins, an ethically coherent vision certainly underlies Ford's emplotment as we hear Frank interrogate "the good life" of postwar America. The peculiar seductiveness of this culture, with its promise of limitless opportunity and freedom, is suggested in Ford's description of "the bricky warp of these American cities.... Choices aplenty" (7). Frank's relationship with X marks his entry into bourgeois American culture—a culture that from the start he finds distasteful. Clearly, Ford is interested in analyzing the moral bankruptcy of bourgeois culture in its relationship to "the rest of the world." Dupuy accurately notes that when Frank returns to Haddam at the end of *The Sportswriter*, he sees suburbia in a new light—no longer "neutral" and comfortable but "a lie ... it tries to provide closure while at the same time excluding the ultimate closure—death" ("Confessions" 102–3). Frank particularly notes the deceptive optimism of the suburbs—not just the deception of a way of life that excludes the existential consciousness of mortality, but the everyday lie of middle-class culture itself, the promise of a bounteous and happy life that rests upon the assumption of an ever-expanding base of wealth and power. Ford's interrogation of the superficiality and oppressiveness of the suburbs is conveyed, for example, in moments of vacuous praise, including Frank's unctuous ode to "the suburbs I love" (14). Early in his married life, Frank objected to the disingenuousness of bourgeois communities like New Lime, Connecticut, but his complaint now extends much further. Haddam itself is full of affluent men such as the five members of the Divorced Men's Club, among whom Frank sometimes feels a profound sense of despair. Frank says flatly that "the suburbs are not a place where friendships flourish" (79), and his unfortunate relationship with Walter Luckett, who weirdly imagines Frank to be his "best friend," is evidence of this.

It is of course an index of Frank's pain that he seeks a "neutral" place in which to live. Haddam, however, is not merely neutral—it is dangerously unreal, as even Frank admits. The unreality of suburban existence can be gauged by its effect on Frank's children, particularly on his son. Who is more the product of suburban society than Paul, Frank's delinquent, antisocial teenage son? Even in *The Sportswriter* Paul Bascombe was shown to "display a moody enthrallment" (107); by the time period of *Independence Day* his moodiness has shifted dangerously toward fierce detachment and instability. Who better than Paul to illuminate for his middle-aged father the insincerity of middle-class life? Their trip from New River, Connecticut, to the Basketball Hall of Fame in Springfield, Massachusetts, and the National Baseball Hall of Fame in Cooperstown, New York, is an ironic pilgrimage to the shrines of American national pastimes (shrines as well to the increasing commercialization of those pastimes)—but it is a pilgrimage of a postmodern and not a medieval sort, conducted by a pair of tight-lipped, streetwise, cynical detectives bent on unmasking the contradictions of American culture at century's end. Within this culture, purportedly the land of opportunity and universal happiness, father and son encounter their own troubled images in the mirror of American society: a homeless, transient father and daughter living out of an automobile; a succession of middle-class, professional types befogged by their own "success"; an African American truck driver searching without a clue for the "right place" to settle his life. Most importantly, they encounter their own grief and despair (metonymically focused on the threatened loss of Paul's eyesight, but encompassing as well the loss of Ralph and the divorce of Frank and X, and expanding to embrace American suburban society as a whole). They are faced with the need to divest themselves of their security and complacency within a deadening suburban environment, and to take on risk, involvement, and pain—the attributes of true responsibility and membership.

In *The Sportswriter* Ford is not content to represent Frank's experience in existential terms, as that of a quest for personal identity, although he does present his character as that of a man frequently nostalgic, reflective, and lost in "dreaminess"; in the sequel, *Independence Day*, the narration is even less focused on the inner self, as Frank, now well into middle age, is entangled to a greater extent in a web of social responsibilities. A rich cast of memorable secondary characters peoples the novel, suggesting that Frank's life is inseparable, as indeed it is, from all those in his family and community. Prodded by such meetings, and by Frank's openness toward others, the narrative moves eventually from grief to healing, from reflection and solitude back to society. In *Independence Day*, Frank attempts, with heroic courage and will, to step back into the roles of father and husband, and he reenters the community of Haddam and the world as he engages a host of friends, associates, and strangers in purposeful communication. Not surprisingly, Frank's interest in "mystery" is largely absent in this sequel; he is too busy attending to the intricacies of selling real estate, developing a stable relationship with Sally Caldwell, and, most importantly, nurturing his troubled children. If there is mystery during the "Existence Period" of middle age that Frank has entered, it is in the possibilities of human kindness and love.

I began this chapter by reading the opening lines of *The Sportswriter* and contrasting them with those of *The Last Gentlemen* as a way of suggesting the considerable difference in sensibility in the writing of Walker Percy and Richard Ford. It seems appropriate to conclude by examining the final paragraph of *Independence Day*, which would take us as far along with Frank Bascombe as we can yet go. Watching the Fourth of July parade in Haddam, Frank reflects on his own independence: the prospect that his son will come to live with him in the future, that he may "soon be married," that he will inevitably enter the "Permanent Period," the "long, stretching-out time" that leads past middle age and ends with death. Significantly, however, watching the parade that involves so many of his townsfolk, Frank now sees that "[i]t is not a bad day to be on earth" (450). Frank joins the crowd along the curb just in time to catch the end of the parade—just in time to "see the sun above the street, breathe in the day's rich, warm smell" and, in the final words of the novel, to "feel the push, pull, the heave and sway of others" (451). Immanence, in this conception, is quite opposed to Percy's treatment in *Lancelot* or *The Last Gentleman*. If Sutter Vaught in the latter of these novels seeks "descent" into immanence as an alternative to salvation,

Frank Bascombe finds that "pleasure" is "eighty percent" of life's good (he doesn't specify the source of the other twenty percent). If immanence is the dead end of despairing figures such as Sutter Vaught or Lancelot Lamar in Percy's novels, it is the positive good in Ford's, one reason why Frank Bascombe has landed in "gloomy New Jersey" to begin with and stayed put at 19 Hoving Rd. in Haddam for nearly a quarter of a century, by the time of *Independence Day*. The present and here-and-now are never perfect, but they may possibly prove to be enough.

Note

1.   See, for example, Ford's comments in an interview with Kay Bonetti and his discussion of art's relation to "lived life" in his essay, "The Three Kings."

10

Representing the Subaltern Figure in *William Styron's* The Confessions of Nat Turner *and Thomas Keneally's* The Chant of Jimmie Blacksmith

There are intriguing similarities between the careers of the two best-selling historical novelists William Styron and Thomas Keneally. One of Keneally's early novels, *Confederates*, deals explicitly with southern history and is set in Styron's home state of Virginia. Another novel, Keneally's *Schindler's Ark* (1982) (the basis for the film *Schindler's List*) resembles Styron's *Sophie's Choice* (1978) in that it deals with the Holocaust and specifically in its focus on the possibility of survival. Most importantly, Keneally's *The Chant of Jimmie Blacksmith* (1972) was published five years after the controversial success of William Styron's *The Confessions of Nat Turner*, a novel similarly based on the life of the leader of a famous subaltern rebellion. Despite these similarities of subject matter, there are significant ideological differences that distinguish their writing, and these are particularly apparent in *The Confessions of Nat Turner* and *The Chant of Jimmie Blacksmith*.

The problems involved in any literary representation of the subaltern have been suggested by postcolonial critics including Gayatri Spivak and Doris Sommer. As Spivak notes, implying the near impossibility of a nonsubaltern writer ever achieving accurate representation: "No amount of raised field-work can ever approach the painstaking labor to establish ethical singularity with the subaltern" (xxiv). At the same time, Spivak insists that such effort to establish singularity is an obligation of literature. In the terms of Spivak's theory, both Styron and Keneally, to the extent that they are Western authors attempting "to establish singularity with the subaltern," are in the position of writing subjects that they can never know well enough, and from this theoretical perspective their efforts at representation must be viewed as "failures," though as necessary failures. Considering their works in the terms of Spivak's theory, however, leads not only to a recognition of the difficulties of their authorial positions but also to the complexities inherent in the formation of subaltern theory itself. The categorization of Styron and Keneally as "Western" authors, of their subjects—an American slave leader educated in Western texts and an Australian of mixed indigenous and Western heritage—as subaltern, and, perhaps most of all, the unpacking of what is intended by ethical "singularity" are unavoidable problems of subaltern criticism. Reading such highly ambiguous texts problematizes theory itself, even as theory complicates the ways in which we read those texts. A reading of Styron's and Keneally's cross-cultural texts should also problematize the essentialized conception of ethical singularity: does any social or "unity" group, to employ Jacques Derrida's term, ever achieve singularity with another, and can it be expected to do so? Does any individual ever achieve singularity with another, or even with oneself, given the multiplicity of motives and interests that comprise each human being? In light of this, we should modify Spivak's insight and speak instead of achieving sympathy, or respect, or simply knowledge of others. By these standards we may more fairly evaluate Styron's and Keneally's achievements.

Employing a version of Doris Sommer's conception of the narrative resistance of subaltern texts to mainstream readers, we might further conceptualize the resistance of the text—in this case, the text of subaltern history (the "actual" Nat Turner and Jimmie Blacksmith)—to efforts at representation by all authors, but particularly by those Western writers whose novels are intended for a mainstream popular audience. Just as subaltern fictions, in Sommer's terms, inscribe their own terms of resistance in relation to Western readers, the subaltern historical subject refuses to give itself up to the Western author—a fact that seems painfully obvious in the responses of subaltern critics to Styron and Keneally. Soon, however, difficulties similar to those encountered with Spivak's theory emerge in the effort, necessary in this critique of subaltern resistance, to identify the "authentic" text of subaltern history. For example, the contemporary 1831 "confession" of Nat Turner, reputedly dictated to one Mr. Gray while Turner was awaiting execution, can hardly be accepted as an accurate or complete account as dictated, or even as an account that has been faithfully transcribed or reproduced; nor are the contemporary newspaper accounts of Jimmie Blacksmith's rebellion in any sense unbiased reportage. In both cases the reader is left with only the theorist's assurance that one "knows" the resistance of the subaltern subject when one sees it, but it is more difficult to demonstrate conclusively where this resistance lies.

From the beginning, I would note the paradoxical outcome of Styron's attempt to "speak for" the subaltern subject: based upon a substantial amount of research and artistic commitment, Styron's representation of the legacy of American slavery nonetheless reflects to a large degree the conventional view of postwar American liberal historians, not so far as we can determine the point of view of the subaltern himself. By attempting to narrate the consciousness of an indigenous Australian, Keneally also attempts to "speak for" the subaltern, even if he does so apparently with a greater sense of ironic self-consciousness. Like Styron (whose southern regional identity comprised a subaltern subject in its own right), Keneally approaches the subaltern from his own colonial heritage. As a reading of his recent historical work *The Great Shame, and the Triumph of the Irish in the English-Speaking World* makes clear, Keneally brings sympathies based on his extensive knowledge of Irish colonialism to his understanding of indigenous Australia. Noting that Irish transportees carried carbines for use against Aborigines, Keneally points out the irony that, "given that [Hugh Larkin, an Irish transportee] and many of his fellows had been transported for 'Being in Arms,' this must have struck Hugh as a divine satiric turn. It was from the weapons of these hair-trigger dispossessed of Europe that the natives received the thunderous news of their own coming dispossession" (*Great Shame* 86). Keneally depicts Australian settlers at the same time as victims and victimizers: horribly abused by the terror of English imperialism and blindly abusing indigenous people, whose condition in some ways approximates what theirs had been in Europe. The implication is that the recognition of this analogy, to be gained through a scrupulously honest examination of history, is crucial to changing political attitudes and ending damaging legacies of past colonialism.

In both *The Chant of Jimmie Blacksmith* and *The Great Shame*, as well as in other works that bear upon colonialism (including *The Fear* and *A River Town*), Keneally suggests many similarities of Irish and Aboriginal history—a comparison of Irish repression and transportation with subaltern experience that he broadens in *The Great Shame* to encompass the history of American slavery. Quoting Wakefield's *England and America* (1834), Keneally refers to transportation as "slavery in disguise" (*Great Shame* 43). Beginning in chains, the months-long voyage of convict ships from Ireland to Australia resembled the Middle Passage of African slaves from Africa to America, and the role of convict labor paralleled that of slave labor: "What slave cotton was to the American South, convict wool would be to Australia. The mills of Britain had an illimitable hunger for both" (55). Once transported convicts had settled in Australia, however, there was no awareness of "communal cause" between themselves and indigenous people, and violence was instigated on both sides (56).[1]

Although they reflect significantly different conceptions of relationship to the subaltern, *The Confessions of Nat Turner* and *The Chant of Jimmie Blacksmith* are similar novels in some specific respects. In terms of plot, both novels deal with the career of a subaltern figure who leads an armed rebellion against hegemonic society. Jimmie Blacksmith's position as an indigenous Australian educated by a Christian missionary mirrors that of Styron's Nat Turner, a slave prodigy who is educated by his master as an experiment in "progressive" social reform. Unlike Keneally, however, Styron repeatedly injects hints of the potential for racial understanding and amelioration, as in Nat's comments on his "devotion" to his first master, Samuel Turner (a master who, through financial imprudence, nonetheless ends by selling Nat into the hands of less scrupulous owners). In the worn-out small farms of Virginia (unlike the more brutal plantations of the Deep South), Styron's narrator finds that "there was still an ebb and flow of human sympathy—no matter how strained and imperfect—between slave and master, even an understanding (if sometimes prickly) intimacy" (*Confessions* 258). Through his experience of various masters, from the kindly Samuel Turner and the "fair" if stern Thomas Moore to the coarse and "barely tolerable" Rev. Eppes, Nat comes to realize that the attitudes of slave owners are not monolithic: although some like Rev. Eppes were capable of subjecting slaves to extreme deprivation and violence, others, perhaps the majority, at least intended to treat their slaves with humanity, even if they often failed to do so.

Strikingly absent in Styron's novel, however, is any suggestion of the white master's sexual attraction to blacks. Unlike Keneally, who wishes to undermine the idea of the superiority of Western "civilization" by stressing Rev. Neville's hypocrisy, Styron depicts masters like Samuel Turner as genuinely well intentioned, if inept, egoistic, and unfortunate. This difference is one of the first indications of an opposed intention in the two novels. If the institution of slavery is completely dehumanizing, enough to render African Americans a prostrate class during and after

slavery, individual slave owners were, in the view of Styron's novel, often sympathetic and even admirable. Indeed, the majority of slave
holders in Nat's experience are, like Joseph Travis, "decent and sympathetic" (326). This recognition is a significant basis for the program of
racial cooperation that the *Confessions* wishes to promote: as individuals,
whites are capable of moral action, even within the context of dehumanizing institutions.

Early in the novel, Styron inserts the proposition that as a house servant—and thus removed from contact with the masses of slaves—Nat
has been particularly fortunate. In contrast with his friend Wash (himself
the son of one of the Negro drivers and thus a level above that of the field
hand), Nat is said to possess a language with which to reflect on his condition while "Wash has almost no words to speak at all"; he possesses
only a "poor crippled tongue" (144). The novel, in other words, concep-
tualizes Nat's cultural development as resulting largely from his
fortunate association with whites. As a house servant, Nat becomes an
"eavesdropper" to the conversation of whites, so much so that he begins
to imitate not only their speech but their manners. As Nat tells us,
"[a]lready my mother teases me for the way I parrot white folks' talk—
teases me with pride" (144). As a house servant, Nat has advantages that
approximate those of whites, and in his portrayal as a house servant, Nat
is attached inextricably and unquestioningly to the cultural ideals of
Western society.[2]

As we see, Styron's *Confessions* is a revisionary narrative of southern slavery, presumably with the intention of supporting a liberal
program of civil rights politics. This subtext of racial amelioration is absent in Keneally's novel, in which one finds a caustic satire of Australia's
Aboriginal policies. While Styron implies a "progressive" view of American history, implying that liberal policies will integrate blacks into
"mainstream" culture, Keneally's assumptions are not assimilationist:
Keneally's novel stresses the tragic costs of all colonial history: the
forced migration of whites *to* Australia and the mistreatment of indigenous peoples *within* Australia. Ironically, Keneally's settler-people
occupy a historical position as colonized immigrants that corresponds to
what would become the subaltern position of indigenous Australians under immigrant rule, a correspondence suggested by the surprisingly
ambivalent newspaper accounts of Jimmy's outlaw career. "Diabolical"
yet almost heroic, "abominable" yet cunningly intelligent, Jimmie is figured as both savage and mythic hero. Keneally's narrative develops these

similarities and affinities with the effect that the figure of Jimmie Black-smith comes to embody the historical oppression of both indigenous and settler peoples; his fumbling rebellion, confused flight, and inevitable death signal what Keneally understands as the self-consuming and self-destructive nature of all narratives of human subjection. Of course, in practical terms it is important that Keneally's whites are generally un-aware of the similarity of their condition to that of Aborigines, for their failure to understand the commonality of their situation as colonized out-casts leads to many grotesque consequences, such as the perverse fas-cination of the public with the death penalty, the communal means of disciplining the rebellion of unassimilated peoples.

For its part, Styron's narrative also perceives an identity between European and African Americans, but one that implies African Ameri-cans developing *toward* the position of their European counterparts (that, in effect, views African Americans as "white men in black skins," to em-ploy an infamous phrase from Kenneth M. Stampp's *The Peculiar Institution: Slavery in the Ante-Bellum South*). Styron's view, in other words, projects the liberal ideology that both African and European Americans share a common humanity, but that slavery and its legacies have degraded the humanity of African Americans so that only a process of education and enculturation will allow them to "rejoin" whites within enlightened society.[3] The overriding plot of *The Confessions of Nat Turner* involves the "education" of Nat, from the inhuman condition of the slave to the intermediate stage of rebellion, and to the final stage of Christian (and cultural) redemption. One might note that Nat's story, as fashioned by Styron, is not unlike that of Frederick Douglass: after his sale by his hypocritical master, Douglass is reduced to a "thing" by a se-ries of slave breakers, regains dignity following his violent rebellion against Mr. Covey, and finally, after a period of labor and education, gains admission to liberal society following his flight to the North.

An important stage in Nat's development involves his growing awareness of the inhumanity of slavery in its reduction of black people, as the novel portrays it, to an animalistic and brutal condition. The *Con-fessions* pictures Nat's disgust at the cruelty and coarseness of his own people and shows him moving "beyond" their subaltern condition and toward the condition of whites. As Nat grows up—"a pet, the darling, the little black jewel of Turner's mill" (169)—he is equally the household's "spoiled child" (169) and one who "began more and more to regard the Negroes of the mill and field as creatures beneath contempt" (169). In contrast to Jimmie Blacksmith, who remains in at least partial relationship to his indigenous family, Nat becomes progressively more distant from all of his race. One consequence of this depiction is that, from the perspective of Styron's novel, it is impossible to ironize Western society toward the level of enslaved blacks, for the reason that, like Stanley Elkins, Styron's narrative views the condition of slavery as utterly reductive in relation to a supposed normative condition of Western civilization. The inhumanity of slavery derives, in this view, from the complete powerlessness of the slave, a condition that Nat first observes when his mother is assaulted by the overseer McBride. Later (especially after he has witnessed his mother's capitulation and assent), Nat is overcome by a realization of the white's "terrible authority, filling me with dread" (151). Shortly afterward, he is caught with the stolen copy of a book (ironically, in the case of a slaveholding family of very ambiguous ethical qualities, a copy of John Bunyan's puritan moral allegory *The Life and Death of Mr. Badman*), and brought before a group of curious whites whom he figures in terms of the "oppressive and fearful presence of white people" (154–55). After he is "loaned" to Rev. Eppes for one year, Nat finds himself even more powerless as the solitary black in Shiloh, Virginia, a hill country town of thirty-five whites among whom he is passed around as virtual common property.

Unlike more recent scholars, including Eugene Genovese, who demonstrate the existence of a resilient slave culture transferred in part from Africa, the *Confessions* accepts Stanley Elkins's view that the condition of slavery implied the virtual destruction of human culture: in spite of the master's "efforts to teach a fundamental cleanliness," slave cabins are filled with odor and filth. The novel goes to great lengths to depict African American life as permanently dehabilitated by the effects of slavery, so completely that, in the terms of the novel, black Americans appear incapable of achieving economic and cultural renewal on their own. This view of the legacy of slavery points toward the liberal doctrine that, given the destructive effects of slavery, descendents of slaves are unable to rectify their own condition and must be rescued by whites. These assumptions may seem extreme, but a similar historical conception was shared by James Baldwin and by scores of liberal writers in the 1950s and 1960s. At the conclusion of "Notes of a Native Son," the morning after his father's funeral, Baldwin faces the same "legacy" as he ponders his father's desperate life of alienation: "That bleakly memorable morning I hated the unbelievable streets and the Negroes and whites who had, equally, made them that way" (94). Like Styron at the end of *The Confessions of Nat Turner*, Baldwin suggests the necessity of finding a meaning for his existence beyond the destructive legacy of hatred that he has inherited.

If the condition of slavery is utterly dehumanizing, it stands to reason that rebellion against this condition must involve Nat in grotesque distortions of humanity and develop only through confused gestures of rage and fear. As Nat comments in reference to the character of his friend Hark: "Though it is a painful fact that most Negroes are hopelessly docile, many of them are filled with fury..." (Styron, *Confessions* 67). It is not possible to develop from an enraged slave to cultured Virginian without passing through a nightmare stage that, from the point of view of enlightenment, one later regrets. Nat becomes heroic, in Styron's terms, because he transforms at the end into a "redeemed" rebel who embraces Western civilization. In fact, a major point of the novel is that African Americans such as Nat may be "redeemed" only after they have worked through the antisocial rage that they have accumulated during slavery. Styron's novel, however, may imply *more* than the liberal reading of the dehumanizing condition of slavery since, in an unanalyzed narrative move, the narrative conflates the identity of slave and subaltern: it is never suggested that the debasement of American slaves was preceded by a condition of African civilization. Before they disembarked in America, as the *Confessions* would have it, African slaves possessed no history. Furthermore, in the emplotment of Styron's novel, the subaltern's rescue or redemption implies a reciprocal obligation: the acceptance of patronage and a performative acknowledgment of it.

In contrast, Keneally's depiction of Jimmie Blacksmith's rebellion shifts the narrative focus so as to question the basis of settler civilization as well as the adequacy of Jimmie's model of assimilation. Jimmie Blacksmith's depiction as one tragically alienated from both black and white society would appear to be a version of the "tragic mulatto" figure that can be traced back to nineteenth-century literary tradition, since Jimmy's experience of tribal life, including his relation to his mother Dulcie Blacksmith and his maternal uncle Jackie Smolders, is troubled by the knowledge that he is the "pale" one, the son of an unknown white who visited his mother in the Brentwood blacks' camp in 1878. However, Keneally problematizes the assumptions of the "tragic mulatto" by stressing that it is not Jimmie's biological race but his society's assumptions concerning race and its construction of racial identity that are significant. Although he grows up within a native community, under Rev. Neville's influence Jimmie comes to "question its value" (Keneally, *Chant* 5). Unlike his cousins and his half brother Mort, Jimmie is skeptical about tribal beliefs and rituals such as the origin of life in Emu-Wren (the tribal totem), the knocking out of the initiation tooth, or the stone-knife circumcision. He begins to see his own people through the distorted perspective of many whites—as immoral, alcoholic, lazy, and primitive. Ironically, Jimmie's naive plan of assimilation is conceived by the Rev. H. J. Neville as a propitiation for Neville's own failure in having abandoned his missionary post in favor of a white parish in which he will be safe from a secret "weakness"—that of sexual attraction toward Aboriginal women.

In fact, one of the closest similarities between the depiction of Nat Turner and Jimmie Blacksmith rests in the common narrative emphasis on their adolescent sexual experiences, but these experiences lead ultimately to entirely opposed results. As an adolescent, Nat has little contact with female slaves outside the Turner household: his sexual needs are satisfied by masturbation accompanied by fantasies of an affair with an anonymous blond-haired white woman. Some time later, Nat's fantasies are centered on the figure of Miss Emmeline, the youngest daughter of Samuel Turner—a young woman of twenty-five whom Nat idolizes as the plantation ideal of purity and perfection, until he stumbles across her in the wanton embrace of her lover and overhears that she has prostituted herself in Baltimore before returning to her father's plantation in Virginia. Nat's sexual outlets also include his homoerotic experimentation with a slave boy, Willis—one of the aspects of Styron's depiction of Nat Turner that scandalized many critics.

Although Nat is attracted to white women and to black youths, he dies a virgin, and, more to the point, he is never really attracted to black women (his only such fantasy involves "a light-skinned kitchen maid" [330]). Such an attraction to black women would, after all, entail a connection to slave society that Nat detests. Overwhelmingly it is Margaret Whitehead who is the object of Nat's sexual fantasy and exclusively so after his capture since she is the principal one "that showed me Him whose presence I had not fathomed or maybe never even known" (403). Margaret's innocent love, and Nat's idealized fantasy of marriage with her, are suggested by the narrative's final image of the morning star as "bright and fair" (404). Styron's having cast Margaret as Beatrice to Nat's Dante is in a sense evidence of the sincerity of his defense of the novel: clearly, Styron viewed Nat Turner as "heroic," but heroic within a distinctly narrow cultural paradigm.

Unlike Nat's idealized fantasies, Jimmie's first sexual experience is entirely corporeal. At the end of a hellish night of drinking and copulation with an indigenous woman named Lucy, Jimmie is bailed out of jail by Rev. Neville. In reaction to his "corruption," Jimmie purifies his body by washing outdoors in the freezing cold, and, in emulation of the presumed morality of whites, he resolves never to repeat the event. In narrating Jimmie's early sexual experiences, Keneally underlines the confusion and hypocrisy inherent in his position as one hailed by Western culture into its ambiguous ethics, a posture that continues even after Jimmie's rebellion against settler society. Since Jimmie finds himself in the anomalous position outside both indigenous and European society, one of the ways in which he begins to understand his identity is as "outlaw," a mythic figure who survives beyond all society, and he begins to compare himself with those legendary outlaws of the past, including the Australian folk hero Ned Kelly. After discovering his caricature in the *Bulletin*, Jimmie realizes that he is becoming a well-known personage—a devilish fugitive with 5,000 men hunting him, yet in this figuration, Jimmie is further controlled by white society, becoming in fact the figure that the press reports him to be.

Jimmie Blacksmith's master, the ironically titled Rev. H. J. Neville, B. A., encourages his protégé with dreams of "escaping" his "primitive" condition and becoming one whose children, or at least grandchildren, will pass for white. In order to accomplish this dream Neville encourages Jimmie to gain a Western education, convert to Christianity, adopt settler work habits, acquire property, and, of course, marry a white wife. To this end he takes a job setting fence posts "up river" with an Irish farmer, Mr. Healy, a harsh man who finally swindles Jimmie out of part of his wages, and whom Jimmie eventually repays with death. Despite this determination to succeed in the terms of Western society, Jimmie repeatedly "falls into sin" and between the extremes of sensuality at Verona camp and the morbid deprivation of Healy's farm, Jimmie grows more and more angry and disappointed in his hopes to assimilate.

Acquiring a proper wife, as Jimmie realizes in the case of the seductive Mrs. Healy (one of the first objects of Jimmie's fantasies), is conditioned by one's status within a capitalist culture of production and consumption. As Keneally's narrator ironically puts it: "Jimmie wished impossibly that Mrs. Healy might stray with him when he became a recognizable man, an owner of things" (21). Jimmie's "act of fantasy" (21) is not primarily sexual in nature: it is the choice of the white woman as the signifier of his acceptance in Western culture. Casting Mrs. Healy in the role of the "ideal landowner's wife" (21), Jimmie does not in any way perceive Mrs. Healy herself as an individual human being. In this respect at least, Jimmie's racial fantasies are identical to those of Nat Turner, in Styron's depiction. Conscious of his sexual attraction, Jimmie is paradoxically unconscious of his more important motive—that of ownership and social standing. It is of course significant that Jimmie's contract with Healy involves the construction of fence lines: the securing of property is as urgent a business for the ambitious young Jimmie Blacksmith as for the mature Mr. Healy.

In the case of Nat Turner, the attraction to Margaret Whitehead, as Mary Kemp Davis shows in "William Styron's Nat Turner as an Archetypal Hero," may be considered in one sense to be the crucial "test" of his heroic struggle, so much so that Styron injects a fantasized marriage at the end of the novel to indicate the completion of Nat's process toward "redemption,"[4] although it may also be read, as Styron's critics recognized, as a debasing suggestion of the cultural or even racial superiority of Western/white femininity. Jimmie's attraction to white women is also a crucial element in Keneally's novel, but its result hardly proves redemptive: in Jimmie's case, his determination to marry a white woman without regard to her character helps to seal his destruction. His marriage to Gilda leaves Jimmie with a wife toward whom he feels contemptuous superiority and a frustrated sense of humiliation. "Very frail," "thin-hipped," and "sickly" (*Chant* 67), Gilda is the emblem of the failure of his policy of racial assimilation. Jimmie's marriage not only confirms the fact that he cannot gain acceptance into settler society, it makes apparent how false are the racial assumptions that Jimmie uncritically adopts.

Despite the interrogation of assimilationism, Keneally's portrayal of Jimmie's role as tragic mulatto at some points underscores the truth of Spivak's thesis: Keneally's characterization of indigenous culture is constructed in descriptive terms that mirror popular images—in light of his reading audience, perhaps necessarily so. If Jimmie is ambitious and self-controlled, qualities admired in bourgeois society, he finds these qualities strangely undermined by the inexplicable persistence of an Aboriginal memory that is figured in popular discourse. For fortnights at a time, he is overcome "by a bad spirit, lassitude and submission he could not account for" (24). Unlike his half brother Mort, however, Jimmie cannot enter the sense of love as something "written into the order of his day" (27). Instead, for a time at least, he leans toward the sort of love common among settlers: a "mere visitor," as Keneally terms it, that occupies a brief period of life before it is displaced by an interest in family status and property. After killing Mr. and Mrs. Healy, to take another example, Jimmie expected a "slump of spirits," but instead he feels pride and contentment in the "effective" manner in which he has acted, having "manufactured death" for his overbearing and haughty enemies (96). Jimmie's exaltation in being *effective* in *manufacturing* death is a feeling learned from settler society, not from tribal society. In contrast, his half brother Mort's tribal morality is appalled by the horror of himself having wounded the Healy's serving girl and Jimmie's having killed Mrs. Healy and several women at the Newbys' (Mrs. Newby, her daughters, and the teacher Petra Graf).

Nonetheless, whatever its limitations of depiction, Keneally's treatment points toward the need for a sobering collective meditation on the errors of Australian history, the errors of transportation as well as those of mistreatment of indigenous people, and it suggests the need for a more conscientious reading of the past. Unlike Styron's novel, which promotes a liberal program of assimilation within an authoritative Western culture, Keneally's work mocks pretensions to authority of all sorts as he probes the legal, economic, and cultural means by which settlers establish boundaries—literally and figuratively setting up fences between themselves and indigenous people even as, in some cases, they urge the assimilation of these same people. As in the case of Nat Turner, in which a travesty of legal process is carried out preceding the inevitable execution, the sham of citizenship enjoyed by the Blacksmith brothers before their crimes is ended with the "Bill of Outlawry," stripping Jimmie and Mort of all their "legal rights." Keneally pursues the especial irony that the hunt for Jimmie Blacksmith coincides with the last phase of federation talks, high-sounding debates over Australian independence that are reported alongside newspaper accounts of Jimmie's enraged rebellion and society's feral response. Keneally ironizes the *Bulletin*'s account of Jimmie's capture, including its stress on the mercenary aspects of justice (the £2,500 reward), and he reproduces vindictive letters to the editor such as that from one Tom Dancer, who writes in opposition to the visits of compassionate jailhouse parsons, who may, by offering "the prospect of heaven to a repentant sinner" (175), ease Jimmie's guilt and thus his sense of punishment. A letter from Rev. Neville offers further layers of irony: admitting his part in Jimmie's failure, Neville questions whether Aboriginal missions should continue and, in a culminating stroke, asks all readers "to pray for the repentance of this murderer who once lived under my roof" (176).

One of the more revealing characters, in terms of the relationship of Australian colonial identity to its indigenous population, is that of the schoolteacher, Mr. McCreadie. Angered at hearing the teacher telling the children that "Australia is ... [the] dearest land of all" (133), Jimmie takes the teacher hostage, but by never accepting the role of victim, and by refusing to be silenced, McCreadie, weak as he is physically, retains some of the authority of the colonial teacher. As Jimmie comes to see, the teacher "understood—perhaps from the classroom—the ways control shifted from one to another" (135). Jimmie's paradoxical desire to enjoy a "genial self-reflection" in the teacher's presence is thwarted by McCreadie's refusal to submit to Jimmie's control. In a doubly ironic reversal of roles, the white hostage struggles to maintain his individuality and self-integrity while the black warden seeks dominance and control even as he desires the good opinion of the authoritative teacher. Dominance, however, is never in any situation stable or final: as Keneally writes, "people are never passive mirrors" (139). Turning Michel Foucault about, we may say that there is always resistance to the gaze of authority, even amid the oppression of colonialism. In a conception that resembles Doris Sommer's notion of textual resistance, Keneally's conclusion is that the mirror of the Other actively resists monocultural readings and subverts imperial culture.

Ironically, McCreadie, who is an amateur student of indigenous culture, in some ways appears more respectful of tribal customs than Jimmie. It is McCreadie who suggests that they test whether the murderous brothers have been cursed by visiting the initiation cave or "womb" of another tribe, and he is more appalled by the desecration of the site— used as a popular picnicking ground by whites—than is Jimmie. For McCreadie and Mort, if not for Jimmie, the desecration of a sacred site, with the breaking of *tjuringa* stones, replicates the broken history of indigenous peoples in Australia as a whole. As Keneally's narrator states, Australian history has included the "acquiescence" (150) of indigenous Australians to the power of white settlers, an appalling record of social repression involving alcoholism, imprisonment, death, and despair.

The novel teases the reader with the notion that Jimmie, like the "redeemed" Nat in his prison cell just before his execution, may at the end be "restored" to society, only to withdraw this speculation with the more mundane and practical suggestion that "he might as an alternative simply go to bed" (171). As he nears capture and inevitable death, Jimmie thinks back to his biological conception, suggesting his continuing confusion of racial genetics with the social construction of racial identity. Contemplating the terrible bullet wound to his mouth and the difficulty with eating and drinking that it causes, Jimmie thinks again of his birth, but he is incapable of thinking in other than racial terms. The shape of his mouth, he believes, has even now "turn[ed] against him in his final crisis" (172).

Just as Styron stresses Nat Turner's regret over Margaret's murder, Keneally emphasizes Jimmie's "regret" and bitterness, along with his desire to return to an idyllic tribal life that putatively existed before any contact with white settlers. Almost as a comment on the positing of Nat's redemption in the *Confessions*, however, Keneally's account of Jimmie's regret is broadly ironic, as Jimmie is finally discovered by his pursuers in a "dignitary's bed" in a convent bedchamber reserved for a bishop. In the end, Keneally employs Jimmie Blacksmith as a means of reflecting on the historical record of colonial Australia's treatment of its indigenous population and, by extension, as an ironic meditation on the factitious nature of all assertions of cultural or racial identity. Unlike Styron's hopeful vision of the "morning star" shining brightly into Nat Turner's prison cell on the morning of his execution, Keneally concludes his novel with the grotesque and thoroughly ironic personage of Mr. Hyberry, Jimmie's fatuous and self-important executioner, obliviously going about his work of human destruction.

Notes

1. Similarly, most Irish immigrants in America, many of whom had fled conditions of near-enslavement, displayed little sympathy for the cause of abolition. Within the Democratic Party in the 1850s, Irish immigrants aligned themselves with southern slaveholders in opposition to abolitionists and Know-Nothings alike. John Mitchel's writing in the *Irish Citizen*, published in New York in 1854, supported the cause of slavery and pointed to the dangers of abolition in freeing a large number of laborers who would compete for employment with Irish workers. See Keneally, *The Great Shame* 270 ff.

2. James Baldwin in "Stranger in the Village" analyzes the historical origins of the loss of identity that Styron posits for Nat Turner. Concerning his relations with Swiss villagers, Baldwin notes that "I, without a thought of conquest, find myself among a people whose culture controls me, has even, in a sense, created me, people who have cost me more in anguish and rage than they will ever know, who yet do not even know of my existence" (139). In the same essay, Baldwin asserts that "the American Negro slave ... is unique among the black men of the world in that this past was taken from him, almost literally, at one blow" (144). Like Styron, Baldwin views American slavery as a condition in which the slave was cut off from African origins and found it necessary to invent or adopt a new "American" identity.

3. Again, compare the analysis in "Everybody's Protest Novel" in which Baldwin imagines for the newly arrived slave the same loss of identity and the same necessity of discovering identity anew within the culture of the New World: "Thus, the African, exile, pagan, hurried off the auction block and into the fields, fell on his knees before the God in Whom he must now believe; who had made him, but not in His image. This tableau, this impossibility, is the heritage of the Negro in America: *Wash me*, cried the slave to his Maker, *and I shall be whiter, whiter than snow!*" (16).

4. In a useful reading, Mary Kemp Davis situates Styron's figure of Nat Turner in the archetypal symbolism of the uroboros (the circle, sphere, womb, or mandala). Drawing extensively on Erich Neumann's *The Origins and History of Consciousness* (1954), Kemp demonstrates how Styron's depiction of Nat Turner parallels the archetypal hero's conflict with the primal or "dragon" mother, and in his differentiation from the uroboros he wins and marries the "captive" (the feminine distinguished from the "dragon" mother; his own creativity, his soul), allowing for the reintegration of the hero within a society that includes women as well as men. Davis, who sees Nat as "an archetypal hero in Christian garb" (71), shows how Nat gradually identifies Margaret Whitehead—the ambiguous, seductive, mysterious female—with the "Infernal Feminine" side of the Great Mother. Despite the fact that she is "indeterminate," Margaret is perceived as a threat. According to Davis, Richard Whitehead [Margaret's brother] "projects the threat of castration via his Mission Sunday sermon. In preaching submission to slavery, he would condemn the slaves to the timeless world of the uroboros, or the unconscious" (77). Davis sees Nat Turner's act of murdering Margaret as returning him to the unconscious. As Davis notes, "A central irony of Turner's situation is that the murder that was supposed to liberate him from the egolessness of slavery brings about the death of the ego" (80). Thus, in Davis's reading, Nat Turner's journey is a "circular" quest (80). As Davis

suggests, earlier Turner has figured Margaret as the infernal feminine; now in his cell, he realizes she is the captive—an identity close to his own soul: by marrying her in fantasy Nat successfully ends his quest and is psychologically "redeemed."

11

Obligations of the Dispossessed: The Ethical Vision of Kaye Gibbons's Ellen Foster *and* A Virtuous Woman

The critical temper of Western writing since the 1960s can be comprehended by briefly considering the major theoretical propositions of
poststructuralist criticism, which would include, among others, Roland
Barthes's classic conception of the "death of the author," Jacques Derrida's "trace" (the signifier of absence and *difference*), Paul de Man's
critique of referentiality, and Hayden White's insistence on the random-
ness and irrationality of human experience, an experience so bereft of
presence that it can only find meaning in the metanarrative that images
its absence. In opposition to this philosophical emphasis on absence,
Kaye Gibbons imagines an unfamiliar fullness of life and a potential for
human fidelity based on the simple efficacy of moral conduct. In this regard, Gibbons's fiction is part of a highly significant cultural initiative
that reasserts growth, coherence, meaning, and even faith as ethical and
aesthetic terms. Her writing is indeed fresh and original, for it stands in
opposition to a generation of American culture for which cynicism and
despair had become nearly reflexive responses. By some magic of imaginative transformation, Gibbons's writing conjures a new era in which the
failures and divisions of the past have been exchanged for hopefulness
and contentment. It is as if Norman Mailer had awakened from a long
dream, driven South, and sat down to write of biscuits and gravy, picnics
on the lawn, and the lessons of love and fortitude.

To accomplish its revisionist task, Gibbons's writing employs the
genre of moral fable: brief allegorical narratives that both satirize immoral behavior and illustrate a moral thesis. In the context of a poststructuralist and postmodern literary culture, Gibbons's novels serve a
rhetorical function as they promote a certain ethical perspective that is
also connected with the perspective of a particular social milieu. Gibbons
is hardly alone in this shift away from postmodernist literary culture: her

writing has affinities with earlier fiction by Flannery O'Connor, Raymond Carver, and Joyce Carol Oates, to name a few, but Gibbons is original in the particular ethical vision she presents and in the clarity and simplicity with which her fiction embodies this vision. These qualities are particularly evident in Gibbons's first two novels, *Ellen Foster* and *A Virtuous Woman.*

All of Gibbons's novels have the fairy-tale quality of stories of a lost world in which innocent children—and adults with the vulnerability of children—have been set adrift. In this desperate condition, characters such as Ellen Foster or Ruby Pitt are truly abandoned, beyond the nurture of responsible and cohesive families or communities. Thrust into an environment in which ethical priorities are deeply confused or entirely obscured, individuals such as Ellen and Ruby must locate their own sources of order and integrity. As Veronica Makowsky stresses, Gibbons's heroines are resourceful enough to discover methods of self-nurture, a self-empowerment that is signaled by their skillful preparation of food. It should be emphasized, however, that self-nurture is not enough for the development or happiness of these characters. Rather, as adult members of society they can only be nurtured adequately by carefully observing the destructive effects of an existence conceived as random and senseless and by reclaiming the ethical order of a traditional society that is still available in their experiences. Their vision of a "straight" world in which people are careful with others and with themselves, not given to social experimentation, and content with simple and familiar truths is an antidote for a postmodern world in which the force of conventional moral precepts has been lost.

Ellen Foster is the story of the moral development of an eleven-year-old girl from a poor southern family. To understand the evolution of Ellen's moral sensibility, it is necessary to trace the extreme conditions under which she lives. Ellen's parents are codependent partners in a damaging marriage in which the father plays the role of the "baby" demanding a level of attention that can never be satisfied and despising himself at the same time for his immaturity, while the wife is the self-sacrificing maternal figure, excusing her husband and soothing his wounded ego. The weakness of Ellen's parents is obvious to her: her father is "a big mean baby" (3), and her mother is worn down by the father's demands for attention and by his abuse. Ellen recognizes the destructiveness of her parents' relationship, but unlike her mother she does not excuse her father. With the examples of her parents' deaths before her, their "wild ride" breaking apart before her eyes, Ellen learns early in life about the consequences of irresponsible behavior, and she finds that only self-respect and purposeful action can prevent her own destruction.

Significantly, Ellen develops an aesthetic sense that is closely tied to her social condition. Like Gibbons's own writing, Ellen's model of art is one that is forceful, moralistic, and essentially realistic, though not strictly representational. She prefers oil paint to watercolors: "to paint something the way it is supposed to be not all watered down but strong" (52). Her "experimental" painting of "brooding oceans" is hardly innovative in modernist or postmodernist terms, but it has the virtue of a coherent vision: "how the ocean looks strong and beautiful and sad at the same time" (106). Ellen's appreciation of life is grounded not only in a knowledge of its potential tragedy, but also by a hopeful sense of its beauty and, perhaps her central value, an admiration of moral strength. Not surprisingly, Ellen attempts to shape her life on the basis of a similar vision. Out of necessity, she develops a quality of strength and self-sufficiency. Her need to excel and to be respected are clearly related to her awareness of life's potential for neglect and weakness. "I am not just a face in the crowd," Ellen insists (116).

Ellen's very emphasis on security—her fixations on food and money, her attention to bathing, grooming, and orderliness—are understandable in light of her family upbringing. The list of what she likes about her foster home (the availability of food, stability, safety, and kindness) is a catalogue of what was lacking in her parents' household. What Ellen desires above all else is a secure "home." In reading Gibbons's novels, we come to understand much about the essential physical and emotional needs of human beings, especially the needs of those like Ellen Foster who are developing in the most difficult social conditions. In order to provide adequately for these needs, it is necessary for adults like Ellen's parents to act resolutely and faithfully on behalf of their families, and for this action to take place, parents must be held accountable to a code of moral conduct.

Gibbons's novels make the consequences of a lack of accountability abundantly clear. A character not unlike Ellen's father is John Woodrow, Ruby Pitt's first husband in *A Virtuous Woman*. John Woodrow is an example of a southern male whose character has been warped by attitudes of dependence and inferiority. In a post-Civil War society in which few opportunities existed for working men, and in which the legacies of prejudice against white southerners permeated the national culture's attitudes, southern men were particularly vulnerable to the enfeebling influence of a defensive and self-indulgent regional culture. As the South continued to suffer from the legacies of colonization for many decades, southern working-class men retreated from their communal and family responsibilities, and southern women took on a more important position not only within the domestic sphere but within the social, political, and economic arenas. In what, in many cases, amounted to a near subsistence economy, males became dependent on traditionally female-centered domestic production. A pattern of matriarchal culture was established, at least among the poorer classes in the South, that continues to pervade southern society.

Within such a matriarchal culture, males were deprived of their former sources of identity as breadwinners and meaningful participants in community life. In such a condition they came to seem childish and helpless, both to others and to themselves (a helplessness that all too often found approval from forceful matriarchal mothers or wives), and their psychological states were marked by a conflicted sense of self-disgust and aggressive defensiveness. John Woodrow, who grows up within a poor farming family, is an example of such a disenfranchised and embittered southern white male. Filled with self-hatred and attempting to compensate for his weakness by aggressive "meanness," John Woodrow depends on Ruby even as he abuses her: as Jack Stokes tells us, "half the time he wouldn't work. They'd have to depend on what she could go out and do and bring in" (*Virtuous Woman* 21). In his treatment of Ruby, John is clearly engaged in a retributive cycle of abuse that derives from all of the repressive elements in southern working-class society: economic and cultural inequities, patriarchal repression and abuse, and matriarchal protection and extenuation. John is "passing along" to Ruby the stings of humiliation that he has accumulated during a lifetime of failure within such a system.

In an acute analysis of the same sort of cultural prejudice against which poor southerners struggle, Gibbons describes how Jack Stokes in *A Virtuous Woman* is constantly having to correct, or attempting to correct, the prejudiced assumptions of middle-class people, as when Jack shows off his National Rifle Association membership card: "Seems like I'm always having to take something out and show somebody the truth about something they don't want to believe. I guess if you have on a new suit or drive a new car or live in town you might could get somebody to believe you" (22). While Jack Stokes is by nature gentle and responsible, even he cannot escape the distorting influence of society. Like John Woodrow, Jack's response is a defensive pride—in his case, involving the ownership of a gun that he acquired from Ruby. His pistol practice and NRA membership are assertions of selfhood (despite his awful marksmanship); the gun is a symbolic affirmation of his right to exist. Regardless of the rationality or efficacy of gun ownership, it is a form of resistance to the sort of social prejudice that has always been felt to be demeaning for people such as Jack.

Similar assumptions—in her case, of incapacity, deception, and meanness—control middle-class society's opinions of Ellen Foster. Against these assumptions, Ellen protests to her grandmother: "All the people who said things about me were wrong" (*Ellen Foster* 78). Part of Ellen's "identity problem," as her school counselor calls it, is her fear that she may become like her father. In this sequence of thought, surprisingly enough, Ellen views herself, like her father, as another victim of matriarchal violence. After living with her grandmother, she understands how her father's destruction was hastened by her grandmother (though, she insists, her father would have destroyed himself in any case). While her father is "weak as water" (76) to begin with, the grandmother is a controlling and aggressive force that harms both Ellen and her father: "she would come rolling in a wave over you and leave you there on your behind choking on the thing you had intended to say. And she could keep coming with her flood and stand laughing at you struggling in the waves of your forgetting" (76). Like the matriarchal voice that Tonita Branan analyzes in "Women and 'The Gift for Gab': Revisionary Strategies in *A Cure for Dreams*," Ellen's maternal grandmother employs words to control and ridicule others, though in this case the relation between "female characters and discourse" is hardly "productive" (Branan 72), as it is in the case of Lottie Davies in *A Cure for Dreams*.[1]

In her description of her mother's family, Ellen Foster gives an incisive account of the dynamics of the southern matriarchal system as it operates among the working class and poor whites. Ellen is terrified by the vengeful strength of matriarchs such as her grandmother, and she is appalled by the weakness that she sees in men like her father. As she says, "[m]en and daddies are not supposed to be like that" (*Ellen Foster* 76). As Tonita Branan and others have demonstrated, Gibbons acknowledges the power of southern matriarchy in her portrayal of women such as Lottie Davies. What is not so evident is that Gibbons also reveals the extent to which matriarchy, in its more extreme forms, can be destructive to women as well as to men. It is understandable and admirable that southern women should when necessary support their dependent families. As Ruby says in *A Virtuous Woman*: "See, I know now that this world is built up on strong women, built up and kept up by them too..." (13). Jack's mother was one such matriarchal figure: "a tough, hard woman" who was part-Indian but who dies when Jack is fourteen. His response to her death, however, is instructive, for as a male who is emotionally dependent as a child, his life afterward is emotionally empty and immature: he lives among his male peers, shy of women and yet in their absence lacking both happiness and ambition. It would seem that, as depicted in Gibbons's fiction, an abusive and controlling matriarchy is no better, for women or for men, than a repressive patriarchy. In her fiction, Gibbons appears to promote a more balanced vision of gender relationships: female characters such as Ruby admit their need for "somebody to take care of me" (*Virtuous Woman* 143), just as Jack speaks of his dependence on Ruby and his desolation after her death. The virtue of human love transcends the limitations imposed by the social order.

If the values of responsibility and love are essential in Gibbons's treatment of matriarchy, they are equally important to her presentation of interracial relationships. In her friendship with her African American neighbor, Starletta, Ellen Foster overcomes her racial prejudices and accepts Starletta as a valued friend. Further, Ellen discerns the similarity between her own cultural dispossession and that of Starletta's family (and later that of Mavis, a field-worker for Ellen's grandmother), to the point that she comes to identify with African Americans in general. As Ellen says, "I was cut out to be colored..." (*Ellen Foster* 85). Working in the fields with a black crew, Ellen is so tanned that she thinks she "could pass" for a black person (66). Like working-class African Americans, Ellen lacks economic security, is abused at school and in the community at large, and is the object of patronizing indulgence. Since Ellen's entire social environment conspires to destroy her self-respect, it is no wonder that she is drawn to African Americans and that she spies on Mavis and her family in the evening in an attempt to understand how a family can survive in conditions of abuse and neglect.

The account of Ellen's relationship with Starletta is not actually very significant for what it has to say about southern racial relations; rather, it *is* significant as an example of the value of friendship based upon a healthy and sustaining moral system. The importance of Ellen's friendship with Starletta is not that she finds a *black* friend but that she finds a friend whose values, nurtured in a secure and ethical family, are identical to the sort of ethical self-definition toward which Ellen progresses throughout the novel. Indeed, as a narrative of racial friendship, Gibbons's account of Ellen and Starletta's friendship is merely a pastiche of what Fred Hobson has analyzed as the "southern racial conversion narrative," the autobiographical genre in which southern writers from Lillian Smith to Pat Watters "confess racial wrongdoings and are 'converted,' in varying degrees, from racism to something approaching racial enlightenment" (*But Now I See* 2). As Hobson speculates, the contemporary southern writer may not "feel quite the same intensity in writing about race, the same anguish and tension in his or her telling, now that telling the racial truth about the South and about oneself" involves little risk (121). As a narration about race per se, Gibbons's novel accomplishes nothing new; one could say that it is in *not* speaking about the issues of race, class, and gender but instead in addressing what *is* a new concern in American cultural debate—the desperate need for a coherent system of ethical beliefs and priorities—that Gibbons's work is most original.

Gibbons acknowledges but downplays the importance of the deterministic social factors that have preoccupied literary theory since the 1970s. Underpinning almost all recent social criticism is the single issue of "oppression," a critical emphasis that John M. Ellis in *Literature Lost: Social Agendas and the Corruption of the Humanities* traces to the immense influence of Michel Foucault. It is a "narrow" focus that Ellis finds troubling, since a critical theory that allows only one avenue of interpretation, and that begins the reading of texts with a single admissible reading already in place, can hardly be regarded as open-minded scholarship. Ellis finds that "social agenda" criticism, while purporting to promote the interests of the disadvantaged, is in fact based upon an elitist premise, since it images the "marginalized" subject as radically "other"—outside the borders of conventional behavior, institutions, and even consciousness. Thus, in this conception, "the poor" are said to be disadvantaged by virtue of their class origins and, what is more significant, the economic, cultural, aesthetic, and ethical components of their lives are understood to be largely determined by their class.

Ultimately, Gibbons's moral fable is not class- or gender- or race-based, but rests on a traditional ethical teaching that has the capacity to transcend the social origins of her characters. Indeed, the harshness of social conditions as described in her fiction necessitates the existence of a transcendent code of ethical behavior: one's response to denial and abuse can be either to accept the controlling mythology by which the abused are imaged as helpless or to reject it. In *A Virtuous Woman*, Jack and Ruby dismiss the idea that "modern society has to take some of the blame for what happened to [Roland, Tiny Fran's son, who is convicted of rape]" (111). Such an argument is identified by Jack and Ruby as the ethical perspective of "folks in town" who, Ruby says, "in general try to think too goddamn much" (112). Jack's judgment of Roland—that he is "mean" and has been "twisted" by his mother (112)—seems to Ruby closer to the truth.

On the basis of their inherent goodness and strength, some of Gibbons's characters transcend their social limitations while those who are weak and irresponsible are destroyed or destroy others: Jack Stokes achieves happiness for himself and others, despite his origins in the tenant class, while Tina Fran Hoover spreads misery to her husband and children, especially to Roland. John Woodrow declines, even from the class of poor farmers into which he was born, while Ruby Pitt, having left her stable family to live among migrants, later "rises" after her marriage to Jack. Gibbons's perspective is not based on class or economic hierarchies but on the viability of ethical beliefs that she sees as the basis for human happiness. Such views are explicitly moralistic, as are those of the British novelist, Samuel Richardson, and perhaps for the same reason: both are shaped by similar Protestant, working-class origins and by a system of ethical belief within which character and fortune are nearly identical. In terms of Gibbons's moral fable, there is more than a little similarity between Ellen Foster and Pamela, and between Ruby Pitt and Clarissa Harlowe.

Indeed, Gibbons's ethics stems from the culture of the southern yeoman class, a culture transported to the American South by English and Scottish immigrants whose descendants have always comprised the bulk of southern white society. With its insistence on individual responsibility, this culture is suspicious of corporate or governmental assistance and interference, and it places the burden of moral responsibility on individuals. The difference between John Woodrow's poverty and the relative affluence of Ruby's family is that, in Ruby's words, "my daddy might've simply worked for what we had" (*Virtuous Woman* 36). In *Ellen Foster*, Ellen's rejection of the school psychologist's manipulation is connected with her instinctive dislike of another powerful institution: the bureaucracy of clinical psychology and social "welfare."

With the movement of southern people to urban centers and to industrial and service occupations during the twentieth century, the yeoman class has been transformed socially and economically, but a core of cultural beliefs is still operative, even among those who have little knowledge of the agrarian lives of their ancestors. The yeoman class lived by a traditional system of morality based on Protestant religious beliefs and within an ethical culture passed down from their English and Scottish ancestors. Gibbons's cultural rhetoric argues for the "validity" of these people and of the moral values that are embodied in their behavior. Her subject is the overlooked white working class of the South: in her mind, they are the "doers," the moral "good" people possessed of an authentic traditional culture and ethical civilization as opposed to the insubstantial and increasingly "virtual" culture of corporate and urban middle-class America—the hegemonic culture that finds little of value in lives such as Ellen's and Ruby's.

Gibbons stresses the traditional morality of the southern working class. Ruby's parents, who raised her in a "careful" and perhaps too protective manner, were well-to-do farmers, but they earned their economic position rather than inheriting it and were stable, responsible, self-respecting people. Ruby and Jack themselves both possess a highly developed sense of ethics. Their judgment of John Woodrow's "sorriness," for example, is based on the knowledge that, despite whatever prejudices and social environment they have inherited, human beings must still be held responsible for their behavior. Their own marriage rests on a moral basis rather than on romantic illusions: in every gesture, they acknowledge the obligation to take care of each other.

One of Gibbons's intentions is to distinguish between the culture of southern plain folk and that of the poor whites represented by John Woodrow and the migrant workers who visit the farm belonging to Ruby's family. After the migrants trash the farm, Ruby comments: "We saw what people who don't care can do to people who do care about things…" (*Virtuous Woman* 35). This yeoman stewardship of property is frequently stressed in Gibbons's fiction. From the point of view of those who, not far removed from the frontier or from immigration from an impoverished life in the Old World, have had to struggle to make a decent life, the rights of property are sacrosanct. Stealing, cheating, wasting, or destroying another's or one's own property is immoral. To fail to care for property or even to speak lightly of its value is a form of "sorriness" that is not easily overlooked.

The story of Burr's marriage to Tiny Fran, as narrated by Jack, hinges on the importance of stewardship. Like Jack's, Burr's family has worked the Hoover's land as tenants through many generations. Jack tells us that Burr's children would never have had a chance to rise in the world if Burr hadn't accepted Lonnie's offer to marry his erstwhile pregnant daughter, Tiny Fran, in exchange for a section of good land. Thus, in Jack's mind, Burr's decision to exchange personal happiness for economic security (for himself and for his descendents) makes sense. (Again, it is an action that reminds us of *Pamela* and that helps us to comprehend Ellen Foster's unabashed admission of her own "greediness.") Given Burr's and his own family history, Jack admits he might have seized the opportunity himself if offered: "You need something of your own," Jack says, "and you need it young…" (*Virtuous Woman* 62). Burr's case also helps to explain Jack's bitterness toward Lonnie for not bequeathing land to him in his will: given the labor that Jack and his ancestors have expended on the land, it is unjust for Lonnie not to leave a portion of it to Jack, especially since Jack feels a spiritual attachment to the land of his forebears. Jack's attachment to the Hoover land is so great that he decides to remain on the land after his father's death rather than seek greater opportunities in "town," and he refuses to accept Ruby's offer of the land that she inherits from her parents in another part of the state. At the end of the novel, Jack accepts Burr's gift of a portion of the land that Burr himself acquired from Lonnie Hoover.

In reality, however, the acquisition of property for its monetary value is not important to Jack and Ruby: it is the ability to distinguish what is valuable and to set priorities based on an appreciation of the frailty of life and the virtue of goodness. Despite her professed agnosticism, Ruby's ethical system rests in part upon beliefs that many readers may see as "religious." She and Jack possess a sense of awe at the created world, and Ruby believes firmly in an afterlife: she feels the spirits of her parents hovering about her, and she knows that *her* spirit will abide with her husband after her death. Because of their own humanity and reverence for creation, Ruby and Jack are offended by the hypocritical religiosity of Cecil Spangler from Ephesus Free Will Baptist Church, and their profession of agnosticism is a protest against the endless travesty of religion within the heedless religious institutions of their community. Evangelists such as Cecil are seen as busybodies and fanatics: in contrast with Cecil's dogmatic but superficial belief system, Ruby and Jack recognize their own faith in each other and in goodness as a better guide to life.

In *Ellen Foster* and *A Virtuous Woman*, Kaye Gibbons has written moral fables concerning the obligation of taking responsibility for one-self and others. The ethical perspective of these novels, which closely reflects the moral vision of a large class of ordinary southern people and of working-class people in other regions of America as well, recognizes the limiting effects of a colonized history of economic and cultural ex-clusion but insists on the potential of human beings to transcend the legacies of dispossession. In opposition to the culture of absence that has pervaded Western civilization since the 1960s, Kaye Gibbons conceives of the possibilities of families and communities sustained by the positive actions of responsible human beings. Her characters are for the most part poor southerners who have been excluded from full participation in the national culture, but their response to this exclusion is sometimes to dis-cover within themselves and within their traditional culture a code of ethical behavior that is coherent and nurturing. In fiction that envisions a basis for integrity and virtue in the lives of the dispossessed, Kaye Gib-bons achieves a new vision of the South that moves beyond the legacies of the past.

Note

1. In her insightful reading of *A Cure for Dreams*, Tonita Branan focuses on the figure of Lottie Davies as a matriarchal figure within "a community whose talk is largely represented through and controlled by women" (91). In Branan's reading, Lottie Davies is a woman whose use of language, by its assertiveness and unconfined imagination, essentially "rewrites" the condi-tions under which women live. Especially in the way that she addresses men such as Herman Randolph (her daughter Betty's beau), "Mrs. Davies as-sumes a condescending tone" that "denies Herman Randolph any dignity" (Branan 94). Branan notes that Lottie Davies "at times purposefully tampers with meaning" and "lies if truth becomes an inconvenience or obstacle" (96–97)—in many respects almost flaunting her freedom from the narrow expectations of her patriarchal community and garnering particular satisfac-tion from her ability to outwit and contest males such as Herman or Sheriff Carroll. In her interpretation of Mrs. Davies as "the matriarch" of Milk Farm Road (95), however, Branan offers only a partial reading of a charac-ter who, like Ruby in *A Virtuous Woman*, is, within the context of the South during the Great Depression, a matriarch by default more than by design. Her correction of Herman and her outwitting of Sheriff Carroll are not the

result of her female gender per se and thus possessed, as Branan (glossing Patricia Yaeger's *Honey-Mad Women: Emancipatory Strategies in Women's Writing*) implies, of special "aptitude" and "tools" for linguistic self-assertion. Rather, Mrs. Davies corrects Randolph and Carroll simply because they are foolish, just as she defends the reputation of her deceased husband Charles because, despite his economic insecurity, he was decent. The problem with a gendered reading in this case is that in its exclusive focus on one aspect of Gibbons's work, it precludes other crucial elements in the fiction. Surely the fact that Lottie Davies "intimidate[s]" Herman Randolph in a letter that she revises for her daughter Betty and the fact that she sometimes "lies" (Branan 94, 97) do not establish her as a consummate figure of virtue, and certainly it would be incorrect to suggest that she is aligned against men or obtains satisfaction in refuting them. What seems more crucial is Mrs. Davies's ability to make accurate judgments of character (Herman is rebuked because he is heedless in joining the navy without consulting his devoted girlfriend) and her capacity to arrive at a clear sense of right and wrong (the justice of protecting Sade Duplin from prosecution for the murder of her brutal husband). To inject a feminist reading would seem to focus too exclusively on the issue of gender contestation at the expense of broader narrative meanings.

12

Language and Cultural Authority in
Toni Morrison's Jazz

Language is the primary instrument of colonial authority, according to Ngugi wa Thiong'o in *Decolonising the Mind: The Politics of Language in African Literature*. As Ngugi writes, "The choice of language and the use to which language is put is central to a people's definition of themselves in relation to their natural and social environment, indeed in relation to the entire universe" (4). In African American writing, the liberation of the vernacular plays a similar and crucial role in the definition of the culture and consciousness of a people. Conversely, the destructive effects of continuing to accept the conditions of speaking imposed by a colonial system, in which both linguistic and economic authority is retained by a powerful elite apart from the people, include a crippling alienation of self from the sources of identity and creativity. On the social level, the perpetuation of colonized language alienates an educated elite from the general population out of which they have "risen." Since, as Ngugi points out, language "is both a means of communication and a carrier of culture" (13), the cultural effect of suppressing a native or vernacular language is to block the transmission of culture, limiting the full development of identity for groups and for individuals.

In Toni Morrison's fiction, the control of language is the centerpiece of her narrative. The questions of who is enabled to speak, of what may be spoken, and of how the language of the past may be "rewritten" are central in all of her works, but nowhere more so than in *Jazz*, her novel of the ordeals of southern African American immigrants to the northern city. Given the colonial position of southern African Americans within the American economy, it is not surprising that Morrison should be concerned with reclaiming language as a first step toward cultural assertion. With "standard" American speech defined in every respect as "other" than theirs, African Americans arriving in Harlem from the rural South are automatically excluded within a prestige system in which urban speech is taken to be more "cosmopolitan" than rural, white is "better" than black, northern speech is "superior" to southern, and male is "privileged" over female. Within Harlem itself, the culture of the new arrivals is judged inferior by other black residents who have established middle-class credentials of "respectability." Morrison uses every means to mock this prestige system. Simply put, she implies that the "superiority" of the prestige group is derived from a colonizing misuse of power. The "refinement" of middle-class speech is a technique of cultural control intended to restrict access for those outside the controlling social, regional, and ethnic groups. Linguistic "correctness" reflects and supports economic power, and it operates in multiple ways, with systems of education and publishing reflecting similar bases of economic and cultural hegemony.

At the base of this social and linguistic pyramid is Violet Trace. Violet's silence suggests the mythic figure of Philomela, whose protests against rape by her brother-in-law Tereus resulted in her tongue being removed. Madonne M. Miner summarizes the myth in which Philomela is "[d]eprived of speech and lodged in 'walls of stone'" where she "weaves the tale of her plight into a piece of fabric" that reveals the rape to her sister Procne (177). While Miner connects the myth to Nel in *The Bluest Eye*, it is alluded to in the figure of Violet as well. The incoherence and gradual silencing of Violet's voice may result in part from the censorship of truth that her colonial environment has exerted, but her difficult speech serves also as a form of resistance and articulation. As Barbara Rigney notes, the secretive nature of women's communal speech presumes a shared feminine knowledge beyond the conventional reach of men; it is knowledge of the unconscious and of the reality of preoedipal feminine desire and creativity (16–17). As Rigney suggests in a reading of *Sula* and *The Bluest Eye*, Morrison's writing is often about "absence" rather than "presence," an absence connected, as Henry Louis Gates, Jr., believes, with the metaphorical absence of "blackness." (One recalls that Joe's choice of the name "Trace" also refers to absence: after hearing that his mother disappeared "without a trace," Joe believes *he* is the "trace" left behind, as indeed he is.) Like Sula and Nel, Violet finds "life and its choices are defined more by what they are *not* than by what they are" (Rigney 23), yet in the extreme forms imagined in Morrison's narrative, such absences become the foundation for an artful expression. As Rigney goes on to suggest, they are also "political," as narrative silence must be taken to designate historical and cultural structures that enforce silence.

Because of Violet's exclusion and silence, a sympathetic relationship exists between Morrison's narrative voice and Violet. In the absence of her character's power, the narrator brings to her support a powerful satiric control of language. Morrison's narrator not only satirizes Violet's oppressors within the novel, she mocks the reader's (and at times her own) complacency as well. As if to give voice to Violet's inarticulate feelings, the narrator's voice is by turn fanciful, sarcastic, overbearing, self-possessed, subtle, and fluid, slipping in and out of dialect in an effort to authorize the vernacular. Implicitly the narrator identifies her own speech with Violet's. "Words connected only to themself pierced an otherwise normal comment" (Morrison, *Jazz* 23), she says of Violet, but the narrator's own expression claims the same right of free association. Like Morrison herself as an artist, perhaps like "everybody" with "a renegade tongue yearning to be on its own" (24), Violet is constructing an individual voice that at once has everything and nothing to do with her race, gender, and class. Clearly, as Gurleen Grewal insists, "the trauma that is Violet's is not hers alone: it is part of the troubled zeitgeist of the times, the music of the age" (127).

The forms of healing that the narrator claims for her—an ascension to the conditions of privileged expression but a paradoxical dismemberment of hierarchy as well—also intertwine Violet's private condition of silence with an addressing of public or historical traumas, as Violet's "piercing" of normal codes of expression, much like the impact of jazz music upon American culture, forces itself upon the complacent correctness of accepted conduct. The functioning of the narrator within the novel, as more than a few critics have noted, also suggests the improvisational quality of jazz music and, further, as Jill Matus shows, reveals an "ethics of a fiction that represents traumatic history—the problematic implications of writing a history of pain" (122). The articulation of the narrative voice repeats the question that James Agee raised at the beginning of *Let Us Now Praise Famous Men*—the danger of infringement and opportunism inherent in any representation of victimization.

The novel's central action, Violet's "scandalous" knife attack on the corpse at Dorcas's funeral, dramatizes the novel's theme of self-assertion. The attack represents Violet's *public* expression of conflicts that she has silently meditated for a long time. Unlike Joe Trace, who "chose" his own name and who, fleeing work in the fields in Vesper County, Virginia, believes he has been empowered by his association with "a million others" migrating to Harlem, Violet has chosen neither name, speech, nor employment: she has only chosen Joe, from whom she becomes alienated in the course of their marriage. Violet's choices in fact have been circumscribed by her definition within society as a "domestic" woman, but not one whose domesticity implies protection (like Alice or Dorcas Manfred). Even within her domestic setting, however, Violet conjures significance out of her hidden existence, as she arranges the house in a style that is intended for "use" and "comfort," not for conspicuous show.

In her reading of Morrison's earlier novels, Barbara Christian stresses "the integral relationship between the destructive limits imposed on Black women and the inversions of truth in ... society" (179). Certainly the relegation of Violet to the domestic can be discussed as a signifier of society's destructiveness and dishonesty. Her sense of alienation climaxes during her husband's affair with Dorcas, as she, her body wasting away (despite her commitment to "hip development") and her emotions fraught, literally splits into two identities—her disempowered present self and "*that* Violet," the younger and physically desirable woman of thirty years ago. Like Eva Peace in *Sula*, who "converts her very body into a dismembered instrument of defiance" (Houston Baker 141), Violet's silencing of her tongue is a form of defiance of those, including her husband Joe, who would have her speak the normalized language of colonialism. However, if Violet's silence results from her continuing sense of oppression, its effect is also to separate her from Joe, who explains to Malvonne that he is "driven to" an affair by his wife's coldness. The emotional release of stabbing Dorcas's corpse—her knife glancing off Dorcas's ear, that other organ of communication—releases Violet's tongue and reunites her split selves.

The figure of Violet is a particularly subtle reworking in Morrison's fiction of the pattern of women who struggle toward a "sense of owning themselves" (de Weever 32). However, unlike the character of Jadine in *Tar Baby*, who "rejects the maternal role and adopts a more active, aggressive stance" (de Weever 33)—a stance that results in denial not only of maternal but of marital roles—Violet manages to enact her assertion of selfhood within the intimate communion of marriage. Violet's predicament draws attention to the gender conflicts that alienate women and men, an aspect of Morrison's fiction that Barbara Smith has explored. In *Sula*, for instance, Smith notes "Morrison's consistently critical stance toward the heterosexual institutions of male-female relationships, marriage, and the family" (165). Clearly Violet's mute isolation is associated with authoritative mythologies of gender and race under which she has lived. As Miner notes of Pecola Breedlove in *The Bluest Eye*, "men, potential rapists, assume presence, language, and reason as their particular province. Women, potential victims, fall prey to absence, silence, and madness" (181). The same critique of gendered language and culture informs *Jazz*, and the same potential for madness and death exist in the case of Violet as in that of Pecola and Sula, yet the resolution of this novel challenges Smith's and Miner's readings of the degree of criticism of heterosexual institutions in Morrison's writing. In *Jazz* the marriage of Violet and Joe is lovingly restored, and the supportive potential of married life is affirmed.

At the same time that Morrison sets her fiction against racial, class, and gender mythologies, she undermines the confidence of the machine age in its "advanced" civilization. Set in the Jazz Age in New York, the preeminent American city of the modernist period, *Jazz* pokes fun at the modern's naive confidence in science and technology. Nonetheless, the northern city is an appealing destination, especially for African Americans who have migrated from the rural and small-town South. In contrast with the past, Harlem seems to new arrivals in the first decades of the century a near paradise of racial freedom and economic opportunity. Like a million others, Joe participates in the freedom of Harlem in the 1920s as one who "treated language like the same intricate, malleable toy designed for their play" (Morrison, *Jazz* 33). In their love of the city, these new arrivals quickly forget, or attempt to forget, their rural past in the South. For these immigrants, the northern city promises freedom not only from racial oppression but also from the conservatism of their own culture, in which religious fundamentalism and class consciousness are important elements.

Upon arrival in the North, however, recent immigrants find that they are not always welcomed by their own race, for, as the novel reveals, African American middle-class culture may serve as an extension of the colonial system. Elliott Butler-Evans has analyzed the extent to which middle-class education and the aspiration to "respectability" have "suppressed desire" in Morrison's characters (70–71). In *Jazz*, fifty-year-old Alice Manfred is the product of middle-class "training" that is largely negative in its teaching of how to avoid the "pitfalls" of one's native language and culture. In creating the character of Alice Manfred, Morrison cites literary models of Victorian respectability as they began to be widely critiqued in the context of social revolt during the Jazz Age. The familiar figure of the Victorian spinster suffering from crazed repression references an entire modern canon of warped antagonists, including several characters in Sherwood Anderson's *Winesburg, Ohio* and William Faulkner's Joanna Burden in *Light in August*. Like her predecessors, Alice is secretly fascinated by the new sensuality of the 1920s, even as, like her closest friends, the God-haunted Miller sisters, she is disturbed by the quality of "appetite" in the contemporary popular music. Serving as it does as an expressive medium that transcends the divisive cultural hierarchies embedded in language, popular music becomes a source not only of disturbance but of healing, a life-sustaining art similar to Morrison's own forms of expression. As Rigney notes, music is not merely a "motif" in Morrison's novels but a mode of writing as well: "One of the freedoms Morrison claims in her novels is to move beyond language, even while working *through* it, to incorporate significance beyond the denotation of words, to render experience and emotion, for example, as musicians do" (7).

One of the few characters in *Jazz* who resists the seductive power of music, Alice Manfred is portrayed as a woman of "independent means," a person not only of economic status but of cultural authority. Unlike most other middle-class figures in her circle, however, Alice Manfred is black—a fact that, despite her wealth and culture, connects her more with Violet Trace than with the white middle class, and a number of facts suggest that Alice's mask of separateness from her race and her class pretensions are damaging illusions. As Julia V. Emberley notes of Morrison's bourgeois figures in *Tar Baby*, "they use correct eating habits to thinly veil family violence" (408). Similarly, Alice's careful manner of reserved correctness dissimulates by concealing her personal history of violence and her continuing motives of repression. Not only is Alice snubbed by white middle-class women, her sister and brother-in-law have been killed in the East St. Louis race riots of 1917, and their daughter, whom Alice has adopted, is attracted to the "[street]life below the sash" (Morrison, *Jazz* 60) rather than to the protective upbringing she receives.

Alice's dilemma, in fact, reflects what Missy Dehn Kubitschek sees as the "incompatibility between middle-class life and historical memory which [from a middle-class perspective] can only be conceived of as embarrassing, limiting" (129). It also illustrates the error of the former colonial in identifying more with the imperial culture than with one's native culture, an error that results in alienation from one's historical culture and language. As Ngugi writes, "colonial alienation takes two interlinked forms: an active (or passive) distancing of oneself from the reality around; and an active (or passive) identification with that which is most external to one's environment" (28). In the case of the colonized elite, this process of alienation involves a repression of spoken vernacular and a simultaneous identification with the written language. Alice Manfred's focus on "respectable" speech and "proper" reading, and her quite literal closing out of the local environment—closing her windows to the music and speech of the street—illustrates Ngugi's point. Alice's alienated obsession with contemporary mass culture is shared by her adopted daughter Dorcas, and even by Morrison's sympathetic narrator, who, commenting on Dorcas's unbearable adolescence, writes: "when I think about it, I know just how she felt" (63). The limited options of her life are suggested by Dorcas's feeling that by age seventeen sex and romance are everything: "there is no other thing to do" (63). In Dorcas's affair with Joe Trace, the consequence is, in the language of her mother's circle, "pregnancy without marriageability" (76).

If a young girl's life in this environment centers on romance, such as Dorcas's adventure of sneaking out to a forbidden dance party or her love of "foxy" clothing and makeup, the forms of expression generally available to young African American men are limited as well. The spectacle of youths dancing, provocative as "young roosters" (70), is succeeded by a lifetime of relationships with women in which men are seen as alluring but unworthy of respect. The club women who automatically adopt a flirting manner toward Joe Trace communicate this disrespect: "they thought men were ridiculous and delicious and terrible, taking every opportunity to let them know that they were" (70–71).

In order to "rewrite" this colonized past, that is, to revise the very language in which the past makes ethical choice available to the present, Morrison returns to Violet's and Joe's family histories. We learn that True Belle, Violet's grandmother, had accompanied Vera Louise Gray, the daughter of Virginia planter Col. Wordsworth Gray, to Baltimore after Vera becomes pregnant with the child of a black servant named Henry Lestroy. Morrison's tale of miscegenation artistically retraces a literary tradition that includes novels such as *Light in August* and *Absalom, Absalom!* in which William Faulkner represented the consciousness of the "tragic mulatto," with the difference that Morrison intends to heal rather than agonize the mulatto's fate. Morrison's parody of Faulknerian language retraces, and by retracing exhausts, the cultural myth of the tragic mulatto, and by this deconstructive technique makes possible a new language for the figure's presentation. Even specific images and concepts are repeated from Faulkner, as for example the mulatto's focus on the supposed fecundity and associated "corruption" of the black female body, the emphasis on blood in connection with the menstrual cycle and with the birth process, and the metaphorical comparison of miscegenation with contagion.

Like the Faulknerian narrator—Quentin Compson in *Absalom, Absalom!* imaginatively constructing the consciousness of Thomas Sutpen and Charles Bon or the nameless voices piecing a collective memory of the lynching of Joe Christmas in *Light in August*—Morrison's first-person narrator enters the text to suggest versions, correct and incorrect, of Golden Gray, the child of Henry Lestroy and Vera Louise Gray. In narrating the incident of Golden's discovery and "rescue" of a nude pregnant black woman while he is en route to find and kill his black father, Morrison's narrator presents a "hateful" version of Gray, the arrogant and racist "white gentleman," disgusted by the woman he calls "Wild," but honor-bound to rescue her. In arriving at Golden's real pain as he grieves for a father he has never known, however, Morrison's narrator alters her telling, having now worked through different versions of his character, from initial dislike to liking or loving, and even beyond love to an imagining that "alter[s] things" (161). The language in which Gray is imagined will put at his disposal "a kind of confident, enabling, serene power" (161).

The enabling power that the narrative language extends to Golden Gray is also extended to Violet and Alice, whose limits of expression are the legacy of national divisions of race and class that also produced Golden Gray's distorted selfhood. As Matus writes, "the Golden Gray fable works economically ... to suggest the psychic freight that Joe and Violet bring to the City" (137). In their friendship after Dorcas's death, the dialogue between Violet and Alice admits only "clarity." The relentless clarity of Violet's questioning elicits Alice's memories of her own secret violence in her desire to kill the woman who claimed her childhood lover in St. Louis thirty years ago. Alice in turn helps Violet to understand that she needs to "make life," not to fear Dorcas or others who are also victims of the same environment. In the process of talking, or simply in the silent communion of sewing and ironing in Alice's company, Violet explores her own repression of her maternal instinct, stemming from her determination not to repeat her mother's brutal existence. Violet's craving for children grows as she nears menopause, which she believes demarcates the point after which she can never be loved for her own sake. Confronting her fear of aging is as important for Violet as confronting the fear of having been denied choice is for Joe.

In her reexamination of consciousness and language, Violet realizes that both she and Joe had imagined "golden" lovers and were each, in the other's mind, "substitutes" for the other's perfect dream. Controlled by illusions based on ideologies of race and class, Violet and Joe are incapable at this point of attaining "an understanding of and empathy with the other" that Axel Nissen views as "essential to an ethical position" (276). As Morrison's narrative retraces the historical origins of Violet's and Joe's searches for the golden beloved, it attempts gradually to heal their pain. In the story of Violet's mother and grandmother, and in the events of Joe Trace's childhood, Morrison uncovers sources of their present motives. In 1888, Violet's mother, Rose Dear, with her five children, were dispossessed by a paper signed by her husband, who temporarily disappeared (only to reappear periodically with "gifts and stories" [100]). Four years later Rose Dear committed suicide and her mother, True Belle, was left to raise the family. In this retracing of family history, Morrison establishes the relationship of historical and ancestral abuse to the marital problems of Violet and Joe, as Violet's "love" for Joe, whose "talking" alleviates her pain, is founded not so much on affection as on her desire to escape memories of her mother's suicide.

In a narrative that moves between present and past, and from the present to the future, Morrison overcomes a difficult artistic problem of representing the possibilities for the sort of change that exist outside the colonized value system within which her characters exist. How, in other words, does the artist convey *change* for both black and white characters who, from within their limited cultural roles, are themselves unable to imagine such change? Morrison conceives of the artist's role as central in promoting such change, but, as the novel makes clear in the presentation of the improvisational narrator, the artist herself does not operate autonomously outside her culture but draws instead on mass culture—the popular music, everyday speech, dance, costume, and storytelling of the popular and folk culture—to suggest points of "opening" within the experience of a people. To promote change, Morrison explores the ambiguities, connotations, and associations of language, so that language will not merely replicate conventional consciousness but open the past to imaginative "rewriting." If a colonized language often replicates the attitudes of colonization, it can also be used to oppose colonial attitudes.

The relationship of the artist to the culture, and the way in which the culture itself can be used to promote change, is suggested in Morrison's figuration of "the City" in *Jazz*, since the city itself is a kind of artist, transforming those who migrate to it. The vitality of city life is expressive, especially in spring when "the range of what an artful City can do" (118) becomes more apparent. Although its power is not always benevolent, the city forces change and maturity on its residents. The transforming power of urban life is suggested by the speed with which new residents are transformed, seemingly to the extreme of forgetting their past lives entirely. Whereas a majority of Harlem residents have roots in the rural South, they quickly forget that they are "country people" and fall in love with the city: "There, in a city, they are not so much new as themselves: their stronger, riskier selves" (33).

Joe Trace, for example, is said to be on a "track ... spun by the City" that carries him back to a hunger for "young loving" (120). Joe describes the "loving" that he seeks as a "loneliness," and he comes to understand that it is related to his problem of never having "chosen" to love. In reality, Morrison is not so much suggesting the superiority of urban over rural experience as the necessity for change within any environment. The false lesson that Joe had learned from the "hunter's hunter," Frank Lestroy, involved survival as a colonial: "the secret of kindness from white people—they had to pity a thing before they could like it" (125). This lesson is associated with the rural South, in which a system of racial and class patronage continued to exist well into the twentieth century, but the lessons of the city can involve a more subtle perpetuation of colonial legacies. Violet's and Joe's migration to the city removes them from the manipulation of their former slave masters, but the urban environment by itself does not remake consciousness: it only provides a neutral space in which the immediate conditions of past colonialism have been transcended.

What makes a rewarding life possible for African American migrants to the city, in Morrison's view, is "the presence of the ancestor, the person who connects past and present and embodies a sense of historical continuity and communal wisdom" (Scruggs 174). For the city to become fully livable, an imaginative return to ancestral origins is mandated in order to image an "erasure" of the colonial culture and to revise the language in which it is passed down. By circling back to their childhood and imagining the lives of their ancestors, Violet and Joe open a path for new lives. Although only implicit in this novel, the figure of the wise ancestor "imagined as surviving in the village but not in the city" (Morrison, quoted in Houston Baker 136) is always invoked in Morrison's writing in connection with an imaginative return to ancestral times, although in *Jazz* it would be difficult to attribute wisdom to any specific ancestor. Baker is accurate in stating that "Morrison's narrative is ... marked by the motion of return, of reclamation" (137).

The manner in which a retracing of the past may lead to a changing of consciousness is illustrated in the case of Joe's reliance on his early training as a hunter. The metaphor of hunting by which Joe interprets his life continues to determine his actions, but, paradoxically, it may lead him to a maturity in which he understands the limits of "pursuit" and "prey." In his jealous pursuit of Dorcas, Joe relies on his tracking skills, as he imagines, to discover Dorcas's affairs with his rivals. Joe Trace is not easily adept at change, although he convinces himself that he has changed "seven times" by the time he settles in New York. Morrison in fact suggests that Joe, who had mastered the rural art of hunting and loved the woods, would have stayed in the South, where he held on for eighteen years, had he not been driven off his farm by swindlers. It is economic necessity, as well as the allure of the city, that carries him forward.

In part because of Joe's resistance to change, his transformation into a mature and emotionally sensitive man is a crucial action in the novel, and his ultimate ability to change makes him one of Morrison's more significant male characters—a character who departs from de Weever's generalization that "[i]n Morrison's novels, it is not the men who develop a feeling, feminine side, but the women who develop male attributes" (31). In de Weever's use of the figure, Joe Trace becomes an androgynous hero whose "heroic deeds" consist of resisting his masculine training and gaining "wholeness" and humanity. The track that leads him to fall in love with but finally murder Dorcas also involves the lesson of how to "choose," for in falling in love with Dorcas, Joe feels that he has "chosen" love for the first time—not "falling" (as he had from the walnut tree into Violet's presence) but "rising" in love. As an "orphan" abandoned by his mother "Wild," Joe resembles all the major characters in the novel, for all have been abandoned by the supportive communal environment that might have promoted integral selfhood. The entire past, however filled with memories of assault and loss, is integral to the present and must be understood as such before it can be transcended. Despite the impetus for Joe and the other migrants to "forget" their country manners, their very forgetting of the rural past, by its repression of necessary knowledge, hinders the present. Paradoxically, the uncovering of secrets of family history frees one from the past. The "pattern of departure, initiation, and return" that de Weever defines as the classic myth of the hero, and that she traces in Morrison's earlier novels, is apparent in *Jazz* as well, as both Violet and Joe undertake their heroic quests. When Joe goes "hunting" for Dorcas, his mind returns to the simultaneous memory of "hunting" his mother in Virginia. When Joe "accidentally" shoots Dorcas, he is deluded by the powerful memory of his firing an unloaded gun at his mother (the "indecent speechless lurking insanity" [Morrison, *Jazz* 179]—a figuration of woman repeated in Violet) whose absence nonetheless tormented him. By revisiting the wound of his abandonment, Joe begins the process of relieving the control that repressed memory exerts over him.

In her fiction, Morrison investigates the ways in which a colonial system alienates persons from their language and culture. Without self-determination, Violet and Joe grow unaccustomed to moral choice and are increasingly alienated from their own "appetites" and will. While each discovers tactics of surviving in the absence of social equality (Violet compensates for having to cut hair without a license by improving her art and accommodating her customers to the point that her labor is appreciated; Joe charms his female customers by playing an alluring and at the same time boyish role), the long-term effect of subordination is to silence their voices and dull if not nullify their wills. In a destructive dialectic, colonial alienation displaces the wound of powerlessness into other forms of control: for example, Joe's "maniacal" labor after he attempts to kill his mother, Dorcas's obsession with getting and holding onto Acton, Violet's silent rejection of Joe. In place of the self-determination denied within the colonial system, Morrison's characters substitute forms of control over personal relationships, as for instance in the illusory "power" of young women over young men at a train stop: "The red lips and the silk flash power. A power they will exchange for the right to be overcome, penetrated" (181–82).

The social freedom of the city works to subvert this repression, but its freedom is dangerous as well as promising. The urban environment can remove some of the traditional controls that exist in the rural and small-town culture, but it is up to Violet and Joe to "make" life. After

Joe's murder of Dorcas, he and Violet begin, with the help of others, to remake their lives together. When Dorcas's friend Felice visits them to retrieve her opal ring, she is attracted to Violet and Joe, in part because they seem to substitute for her own absent parents. The opal ring itself, stolen by Felice's mother "to get back at the whiteman who thought she was stealing even when she wasn't" (215), embodies the defensive inheritance passed down to Felice. She is rescued from this colonial posture by Joe, whose concerned gaze makes her feel "interesting" and by Violet, who tells her to make the world "something more than what it is" (208). As he repeats her name, Joe understands the true meaning of the name "Felice"—the "happiness" that one makes for oneself in the world.

Just as Felice is saved from repeating the mistakes of her parents' generation, Violet, Joe, and even Alice seem determined to salvage what happiness remains. Violet realizes that she has lived most of her life fascinated by the "little blond child" of her grandmother's stories, and Joe admits that he shot Dorcas because he was "scared" and "didn't know how to love anybody" (213). Repeating the novel's musical motif, Alice, possibly the most damaged character in the novel, admits the wastefulness of her own life. Like Violet and Joe, she had been controlled by the memory of past injuries: "the past was an abused record with no choice but to repeat itself at the crack and no power on earth could lift the arm that held the needle" (220). With this realization at least, Alice is able to return to St. Louis, where she will revisit the locality of her own controlling fictions.

From the perspective of an ethics of literature, it is important to consider carefully the implications of Morrison's treatment of characters such as Joe and Violet Trace. As Jan Furman writes (perhaps overstating the case to some extent), "crime and punishment do not concern Morrison…. Morrison does not brand Joe Trace as an immoral man. He and Violent are good people whose circumstances shape their bizarre behavior" (86). As Furman adds, "Morrison suggests, as she always does of deranged episodes in otherwise rational lives, that no definitive, easy-to-grasp explanation exists for the exception. Some experiences are paradoxical and irreconcilable" (88). Unlike the fiction of Ernest J. Gaines, which seeks for *both* an understanding of the historical circumstances that produce "irreconcilable" behavior *and* for a recovery of traditional norms of conduct based on shared ethical assumptions, Morrison's writing insists that "huge allowances must be made for the variances of conduct" (Furman 90). In ways similar to Martha C. Nussbaum's ethical theory, in which "perception ... the ability to discern, acutely and responsibly, the salient features of one's particular situation" (37) is given priority, the ethics implied in Morrison's *Jazz* is open-ended in its recognition of the nonrepeatability of ethical cases. As Morrison explained, the formal structure of *Jazz* resembles jazz music in its qualities of improvization and tentativeness. The novel itself "has to listen to the characters it has invented, and then learn something from them" (quoted in Furman 102). If Joe Trace is in a strict sense a morally ambiguous character, the implication of his presentation in the novel is that all lives are equally unpredictable and thus unjudgable. In writing of Aristotle and Henry James, Nussbaum stresses that "one point of the emphasis on perception is to show the ethical crudeness of moralities based exclusively on general rules" (37). Much the same could be said of Morrison's fiction, in which at a fundamental level there appears to be less urgency to restore ethical boundaries and communal moral identities than to protect a conception of indeterminacy and personal freedom against inflexible ethical judgment and definition. Some critics have suggested that the postponement of identity in Morrison's narrative is infinite: as Julia V. Emberley writes, "the identity politics of the 1980s, a politics of representation, searched for a ground of truth in an original identity.... Morrison dissimulate[s] the desire for identity in a labyrinthine play of difference and repetition" (422).

As in the fiction of James and Proust, however, the ethical difficulty of this "dissimulation" lies in its inability to delineate a collective basis for ethical action. The conclusion of *Jazz* may be satisfying in narrative terms, offering as it does a sense of an "earned" redemption from the alienating pressure of historical legacies, but the ethical "solutions" of Violet and Joe's reconciliation, and of the psychological healing of Alice Manfred, and even of Dorcas (through the appearance of the substitute daughter-figure of Felice), appear to some readers as overly sentimental and personal solutions. Clearly, an ethics of fiction that is figured *only* in terms of "ethical listening" (Grewal 120) could not easily intervene in a public discourse of what constitutes a just society or of how to evaluate standards of responsibility within society, yet the ending of *Jazz*, as Michael Nowlin writes, affords a solution to "the erotic impasses in [Violet's and Joe's] lives" even as it makes possible for the narrator a recovery of "her connection to the community she represents with such affection" (160).

The ethical implications of the particular ways in which Morrison's narrative functions, in terms of a recovery or "re-memory" through revisiting the sites of repressed grief and violence, need to be clearly understood. In the case of *Jazz* and in other novels, it would be misleading to characterize Morrison's approach as a preservation or restoration of traditional ethical structures or assumptions. Re-memory does not lead Violet and Joe to a recovery of general rules of conduct, even less to a recovery of weakened institutions of law, family, or religion that surely governed at some point in their ancestral history: it points instead to a freedom to improvise a modern or postmodern ethics. There is no restoration of the authority of elders or of traditional wisdom; Violet and Joe, and the novel's implied reader as well, are impelled to reshape ethical knowledge and structures, not to recover them. As in the case of Morrison's redefinition of "kinship" in *Beloved*, "decontextualized units of signification" are used in "piecing together of a language with which to affirm kinship bonds" (Heller 111).

In its ending Morrison's narrative strives paradoxically to suggest *both* the nonrepeatability of the ethical case of Violet and Joe *and* the relevance of their ethical case for the broader community. For Violet and Joe, there exists the more hopeful possibility of love restored in a narrative conclusion that appears to embody "the ideals of wholeness, completeness, self-presence, and self-ownership" involved in Morrison's conception of retracing race-consciousness (Nowlin 159). At the end of *Jazz*, they lie under the covers of an old quilt—the emblematic but now banal objectification of African American heritage—that they plan to replace (like the patchwork of past abuses and the discourse of ancestral heritage) with a new comforter, and like lovers they are "whispering, old-time love" (228). They now think of their life as chosen; they lie "in a bed they chose together and kept together" (228), but the significance of their restored love extends beyond the privacy of their domestic relationship. As Scruggs points out in a discussion of Sethe and Paul D in *Beloved*, the restoration of intimacy between two persons can have meaning for an entire community, as their lives become the subject of public comment and a matter of "collective understanding" (199). Paradoxically, the first-person narrator, who reenters the text in the last paragraphs, speaks of her "envy" for their "public love." Unlike Violet and Joe, she has not quite arrived, as a narrative voice can never fully arrive, at the *embodiment* of love that Violet and Joe convey in every "public" gesture. Perhaps only the reader can duplicate their recovery of love, as the narrator implies in the novel's final words: "You are free to do it and I am free to let you because look, look. Look where your hands are. Now" (229).

Bibliography

Addison, Gayle, Jr. *The Way of the New World: The Black Novel in America*. Garden City, NY: Anchor, 1975.

Agee, James. *Agee on Film*. Vol. 1. New York: McDowell, Obolensky, 1958.
———. *The Collected Poems of James Agee*. Ed. Robert Fitzgerald. Boston: Houghton Mifflin, 1962.
———. *A Death in the Family*. New York: Vintage, 1998.
———. *The Letters of James Agee to Father Flye*. New York: Braziller, 1962.
———. *The Morning Watch*. Boston: Houghton Mifflin, 1950.

Agee, James, and Walker Evans. *Let Us Now Praise Famous Men*. Boston: Houghton Mifflin, 1941.

Anderson, Sherwood. *Winesburg, Ohio*. New York: Penguin, 1992.

Andrews, William L. "'We Ain't Going Back There': The Idea of Progress in *The Autobiography of Miss Jane Pittman*." *Black American Literary Forum* 11 (1977): 146–49.

Ashdown, Paul. "Prophet from Highland Avenue: Agee's Visionary Journalism." *James Agee: Reconsiderations*. Ed. Michael A. Lofaro. Knoxville: U of Tennessee P, 1992. 59–81.

Aubert, Alvin. "Ernest J. Gaines's Truly Tragic Mulatto." *Callaloo* 1 (May 1978): 68–75.

Ayers, Edward C. *The Promise of the New South: Life After Reconstruction*. New York: Oxford UP, 1992.

Babb, Valerie. *Ernest Gaines*. Boston: Twayne, 1991.

Bacon, Jon Lance. *Flannery O'Connor and Cold War Culture*. Cambridge: Cambridge UP, 1993.

Baker, Houston A., Jr. *Workings of the Spirit: The Poetics of Afro-American Women's Writing*. Chicago: U of Chicago P, 1991.

Baker, Lewis. *The Percys of Mississippi: Politics and Literature in the New South*. Baton Rouge: Louisiana State UP, 1983.

Baldwin, James. "Everybody's Protest Novel." *Notes of a Native Son*. 9–17.
———. *Nobody Knows My Name: More Notes of a Native Son*. New York: Dell, 1963.
———. *Notes of a Native Son*. New York: Bantam, 1955.
———. "Notes of a Native Son." *Notes of a Native Son*. 71–95.
———. "Stranger in the Village." *Notes of a Native Son*. 135–49.

Barson, Alfred. *A Way of Seeing: A Critical Study of James Agee*. Amherst: U of Massachusetts P, 1968.

Barthes, Roland. *Writing Degree Zero*. Trans. Annette Lavers and Colin Smith. New York: Hill and Wang, 1968.

Bergreen, Laurence. *James Agee: A Life*. New York: Dutton, 1984.

Booth, Wayne C. *The Company We Keep: An Ethics of Fiction*. Berkeley: U of California P, 1988.

Bradbury, Malcolm. *The Modern American Novel*. New Edition. Oxford: Oxford UP, 1992.

Branan, Tonita. "Women and 'The Gift for Gab': Revisionary Strategies in *A Cure for Dreams*." *Southern Literary Journal* 26.2 (1994): 91–103.

Brignano, Russell Carl. *Richard Wright: An Introduction to the Man and His Works*. Pittsburgh: U of Pittsburgh P, 1970.

Brinkmeyer, Robert H., Jr. *The Art & Vision of Flannery O'Connor*. Baton Rouge: Louisiana State UP, 1989.

Broughton, Panthea Reid. "Walker Percy and the Myth of the Innocent Eye." *Literary Romanticism in America*. Ed. William L. Andrews. Baton Rouge: Louisiana State UP, 1981. 94–108.

Bryant, Jerry H. "Ernest J. Gaines: Change, Growth, and History." *Southern Review* 10 (1984): 851–64.

Buell, Lawrence. "Introduction: In Pursuit of Ethics." *PMLA* 114.1 (1999): 7–19.

Butler-Evans, Elliott. *Race, Gender, and Desire: Narrative Strategies in the Fiction of Toni Cade Bambara, Toni Morrison, and Alice Walker*. Philadelphia: Temple UP, 1989.

Caldwell, Erskine. *Tobacco Road*. Athens: U of Georgia P, 1995.

Chambers, Whitaker. "Agee." *Remembering James Agee*. Ed. David Madden. Baton Rouge: Louisiana State UP, 1974. 150–52.

Christian, Barbara. *Black Women Novelists*. Westport, CT: Greenwood, 1980.

Cobb, Nina Kressner. "Richard Wright and the Third World." *Critical Essays on Richard Wright*. Ed. Yoshinobu Hakutani. Boston: Hall, 1982. 228–39.

Coles, Robert. *Irony in the Mind's Life: Essays on Novels by James Agee, Elizabeth Bowen, and George Eliot*. Charlottesville: U of Virginia P, 1974.

da Ponte, Durant. "James Agee: The Quest for Identity." *Tennessee Studies in Literature* 8 (1963): 25–37.

Davis, Mary Kemp. "William Styron's Nat Turner as an Archetypal Hero." *Southern Literary Journal* 28.1 (1995): 67–84.

Davis, Thadious. "Headlands and Quarters: Louisiana in *Catherine Carmier*." *Callaloo* 7.2 (1984): 1–13.

de Man, Paul. *Allegories of Reading*. New Haven, CT: Yale UP, 1986.

de Weever, Jacqueline. *Mythmaking and Metaphor in Black Women's Fiction*. London: Macmillan, 1991.

Delbanco, Andrew. "An American Hunger." *Critical Essays on Richard Wright's* Native Son. Ed. Keneth Kinnamon. New York: Twayne, 1997. 138–46.
———. *The Death of Satan: How Americans Have Lost the Sense of Evil*. New York: Farrar, Straus & Giroux, 1995.

Derrida, Jacques. *The Gift of Death*. Trans. David Wills. Chicago: U of Chicago P, 1996.

Dickey, James. *Deliverance*. Boston: Houghton Mifflin, 1970.

Dissanayake, Wimal. "Richard Wright: A View from the Third World." *Callaloo* 9.3 (1986): 481–91.

Doty, Mark A. *Tell Me Who I Am: James Agee's Search for Selfhood*. Baton Rouge: Louisiana State UP, 1981.

Doyle, Mary Ellen. "Ernest Gaines' Materials: Place, People, Author." *MELUS* 15.3 (1988): 75–93.

Dupuy, Edward J. *Autobiography in Walker Percy*. Baton Rouge: Louisiana State UP, 1995.
———. "The Confessions of an Ex-Suicide: Relenting and Recovering in Richard Ford's *The Sportswriter*." *Southern Literary Journal* 23.1 (1990): 93–103.

Ellis, John M. *Literature Lost: Social Agendas and the Corruption of the Humanities*. New Haven and London: Yale UP, 1997.

Emberley, Julia V. "A Historical Transposition: Toni Morrison's *Tar Baby* and Frantz Fanon's Post-Enlightenment Phantasms." *Modern Fiction Studies* 45.2 (1999): 403–31.

Eyster, Warren. "Conversations with James Agee." *Southern Review* 17.2 (1981): 346–57.

Fabre, Michel. "Bayonne or the Yoknapatawpha of Ernest Gaines." *Callaloo* 1 (May 1978): 110–24.
———. "Wright's Exile." *Richard Wright: Impressions and Perspectives*. Ed. David Ray and Robert T. Farnsworth. Ann Arbor: U of Michigan P, 1973. 121–39.

Faulkner, William. *Absalom, Absalom!* New York: Random, 1964.
———. *Go Down, Moses*. New York: Vintage, 1973.
———. *Light in August*. New York: Random, 1972.
———. *The Sound and the Fury*. New York: Vintage, 1954.

Felgar, Robert. *Richard Wright*. Boston: Hall, 1980.

Ferraro, Thomas J. "Ethnicity and the Marketplace." *The Columbia History of the American Novel*. Ed. Emory Elliott. New York: Columbia UP, 1991. 380–406.

Fitzgerald, Robert. "A Memoir." *Remembering James Agee*. Ed. David Madden. Baton Rouge: Louisiana State UP, 1974. 35–94.

Ford, Richard. *Independence Day*. New York: Vintage, 1995.
———. "An Interview with Richard Ford." By Kay Bonetti. *Missouri Review* 10 (1987): 71–96.
———. *The Sportswriter*. New York: Vintage, 1986.
———. "The Three Kings." *Esquire* 100 (1983): 577–87.
———. "Walker Percy: Not Just Whistling Dixie." *National Review* 29 (13 May 1977): 558–64.

Furman, Jan. *Toni Morrison's Fiction*. Columbia: U of South Carolina P, 1996.

Gaines, Ernest J. *The Autobiography of Miss Jane Pittman*. New York: Bantam, 1972.
———. *Catherine Carmier*. New York: Atheneum, 1964.
———. "Ernest J. Gaines Talks to Bernard Magnier." Interview by Bernard Magnier. *UNESCO Courier* 4 (Apr. 1995): 7.
———. *A Gathering of Old Men*. New York: Knopf, 1987.
———. *In My Father's House*. New York: Vintage, 1992.
———. *A Lesson Before Dying*. New York: Vintage, 1994.
———. "'This Louisiana Thing That Drives Me': An Interview with Ernest J. Gaines." By Charles H. Rowell. *Callaloo* 1 (May 1978): 39–51.
———. "Miss Jane and I." *Callaloo* 1.3 (1978): 23–38.
———. *Of Love and Dust*. New York: Dial, 1967.
———. "A Very Big Order: Reconstructing Identity." *Southern Review* 26.2 (1990): 245–53.

Gardner, John. *On Moral Fiction*. New York: Basic Books, 1978.

Gates, Henry Louis. *Figures in Black: Words, Signs, and the Racial Self*. New York: Oxford UP, 1989.

Gaudet, Marica, and Carl Wooton. *Porch Talk with Ernest Gaines: Conversations on the Writer's Craft*. Baton Rouge: Louisiana State UP, 1992.

Genovese, Eugene. *Roll Jordan, Roll: The World the Slaves Made*. New York: Random House, 1976.

Gentry, Marshall Bruce. *Flannery O'Connor's Religion of the Grotesque*. Jackson: U of Mississippi P, 1986.

Giannone, Richard. *Flannery O'Connor and the Mystery of Love*. New York: Fordham UP, 1999.

Gibbons, Kaye. *A Cure for Dreams*. Chapel Hill: Algonquin, 1991.
———. *Ellen Foster*. New York: Vintage, 1990.
———. *A Virtuous Woman*. New York: Vintage, 1990.

Ginsberg, Lesley. "Slavery and the Gothic Horror of Poe's 'The Black Cat.'" *American Gothic: New Interventions in a National Narrative*. Ed. Robert K. Martin and Eric Savoy. Iowa City: U of Iowa P, 1997. 99–127.

Gold, Michael. *Jews Without Money*. New York: Carroll and Graf, 1996.

Grewal, Gurleen. *Circles of Sorrow, Lines of Struggle: The Novels of Toni Morrison*. Baton Rouge: Louisiana State UP, 1998.

Hakutani, Yoshinobu. "*Native Son, Pudd'nhead Wilson*, and Racial Discourse." *Critical Essays on Richard Wright's* Native Son. Ed. Keneth Kinnamon. New York: Twayne, 1997. 183–95.

Harpham, Geoffrey Galt. *Getting It Right: Language, Literature, and Ethics*. Chicago: U of Chicago P, 1992.

Harris, Trudier. "Native Sons and Foreign Daughters." *New Essays on* Native Son. Ed. Keneth Kinnamon. Cambridge: Cambridge UP, 1990. 63–84.

Heller, Dana. "Reconstructing Kin: Family, History, and Narrative in Toni Morrison's *Beloved*." *College Literature* 21.2 (1994): 105–17.

Hobson, Fred. *But Now I See: The White Southern Racial Conversion Narrative*. Baton Rouge: Louisiana State UP, 1999.
———. *The Southern Writer in the Postmodern World*. Athens: U of Georgia P, 1991.
———. *Tell About the South: The Southern Rage to Explain*. Baton Rouge: Louisiana State UP, 1998.

Holder, Alan. "Encounter in Alabama: Agee and the Tenant Farmer." *Virginia Quarterly Review* 39 (1966): 189–206.

Howland, Mary Deems. *The Gift of the Other: Gabriel Marcel's Concept of Intersubjectivity in Walker Percy's Novels*. Pittsburgh: Duquesne UP, 1990.

Kahin, George. *The Asian-African Conference*. Ithaca, NY: Cornell UP, 1956.

Kazin, Alfred. "Introduction." *Call It Sleep*. By Henry Roth. New York: Noonday, 1991. ix–xx. "The Art of *Call It Sleep*." *New York Review of Books* 38 (1991): 15–18.

Keneally, Thomas. *The Chant of Jimmie Blacksmith*. Collins Australia: Fontana, 1978.
———. *Confederates*. Athens: U of Georgia P, 2000.
———. *The Great Shame, and the Triumph of the Irish in the English-Speaking World*. New York Doubleday, 1999.
———. *A River Town*. New York: Plume, 1996.
———. *Schindler's List*. New York: Simon and Schuster, 1994.

Kennedy, J. Gerald. "The Sundered Self and the Riven World: *Love in the Ruins*." *The Art of Walker Percy*. Ed. Panthea Reid Broughton. Baton Rouge: Louisiana State UP, 1979. 115–36.

Kessler, Edward. *Flannery O'Connor and the Language of Apocalypse*. Princeton: Princeton UP, 1986.

King, Richard H. *A Southern Renaissance: The Cultural Awakening of the American South, 1930–1955*. Oxford: Oxford UP, 1980.

Kramer, Victor. "Urban and Rural Balance in *A Death in the Family*." *James Agee: Reconsiderations*. Ed. Michael A. Lofaro. Knoxville: U of Tennessee P, 1992. 104–18.

Kronenberger, Louis. "A Real Bohemian." *Remembering James Agee*. Ed. David Madden. Baton Rouge: Louisiana State UP, 1974. 108–13.

Kubitschek, Missy Dehn. *Claiming the Heritage: African-American Women Novelists and History*. Oxford: UP of Mississippi, 1991.

Lesser, Wayne. "A Narrative's Revolutionary Energy: The Example of Henry Roth's *Call It Sleep*." *Criticism* 23 (1981): 155–76.

Lewis, C. S. *Surprised by Joy: The Shape of My Early Life*. New York: Harcourt Brace, 1955.

Lewis, Sinclair. *Main Street*. New York: Bantam, 1996.

Lukács, Georg. *The Historical Novel*. Lincoln: U of Nebraska P, 1990.
———. "The Ideology of Modernism." *20th Century Literary Criticism: A Reader*. Ed. David Lodge. London: Longman, 1972. 474–88.

Lyons, Bonnie. *Henry Roth: The Man and His Work*. New York: Cooper, 1977.

MacIntyre, Alasdair. *After Virtue: A Study in Moral Theory*. 2nd Edition. London: Duckworth, 1985.

Madden, David. "The Test of a First-Rate Intelligence: Agee and the Cruel Radiance of What Is." *James Agee: Reconsiderations*. Ed. Michael A. Lofaro. Knoxville: U of Tennessee P, 1992. 32–43.

Makowsky, Veronica. "'The Only Hard Part Was the Food': Recipes for Self-Nurture in Kaye Gibbons's Novels." *Southern Quarterly* 30.2 (1992): 103–12.

Marcel, Gabriel. *The Mystery of Being*. 2 vols. Trans. R. Hague. London, 1951.

Maryles, Daisy. "Behind the Bestsellers." *Publishers Weekly* (22 Sept. 1997): 21.

Matus, Jill. *Toni Morrison*. Manchester and New York: Manchester UP, 1998.

McCombs, Phil. "Century of Thanatos: Walker Percy and His Subversive Message." *Southern Review* 24 (1988): 808–24.

Mencken, H. L. *Notes on Democracy*. New York: Knopf, 1926.
———. *Treatise on the Gods*. New York: Knopf, 1930.
———. *Treatise on Right and Wrong*. New York: Knopf, 1934.

Milner, Joseph O. "Autonomy and Communion in *A Death in the Family*." *Tennessee Studies in Literature* 21 (1976): 105–13.

Miner, Madonne M. "Lady No Longer Sings the Blues: Rape, Madness, and Silence in *The Bluest Eye*." *Conjuring: Black Women, Fiction, and Literary Tradition*. Ed. Marjorie Pryse and Hortense J. Spillers. Bloomington: Indiana UP. 176–91.

Moore, Jack B. "*Black Power* Revisited: In Search of Richard Wright." *Missis-sippi Quarterly* 41 (1988): 161–86.

———. "Richard Wright's Dream of Africa." *Journal of African Studies* 2 (1975): 231–46.

Morrison, Toni. *Beloved*. New York: Knopf, 1998.

———. *The Bluest Eye*. New York: Knopf, 2000.

———. *Jazz*. New York: Knopf, 1992.

———. *Sula*. New York: Knopf, 1973.

———. *Tar Baby*. New York: Knopf, 1981.

Neumann, Erich. *The Origins and History of Consciousness*. Trans. R. F. C. Hull. Princeton: Princeton UP, 1995.

Newman, Charles. *The Postmodern Aura: The Act of Fiction in an Age of Infla-tion*. Evanston: Northwestern UP, 1985.

Ngugi wa Thiong'o. *Decolonising the Mind: The Politics of Language in Afri-can Literature*. London: Currey, 1986.

Nissen, Axel. "Form Matters: Toni Morrison's *Sula* and the Ethics of Narrative." *Contemporary Literature* 40.2 (1999): 263–85.

Nowlin, Michael. "Toni Morrison's *Jazz* and the Racial Dreams of the American Writer." *American Literature* 71.1 (1999): 151–74.

Nussbaum, Martha C. *Love's Knowledge: Essays on Philosophy and Literature*. New York: Oxford UP, 1990.

O'Brien, John. *Interviews with Black Writers*. New York: Liveright, 1973.

O'Connor, Flannery. *Collected Works*. New York: Library of America, 1988.

———. *Conversations with Flannery O'Connor*. Ed. Rosemary Magee. Jack-son: UP of Mississippi, 1987.

———. *Everything That Rises Must Converge*. New York: Farrar, Straus & Gi-roux, 1965.

———. *The Habit of Being*. Ed. Sally Fitzgerald. New York: Farrar, Straus & Giroux, 1979.

———. "Introduction." *A Memoir of Mary Ann*. Ed. Flannery O'Connor. New York: Farrar, Straus & Giroux, 1962.

———. *Mystery and Manners*. Ed. Sally Fitzgerald and Robert Fitzgerald. New York: Farrar, Straus & Giroux, 1962.

————. *The Violent Bear It Away*. In *Three by Flannery O'Connor*. 2nd ed. New York: Signet, 1983.

————. *Wise Blood*. In *Three by Flannery O'Connor*. 2nd ed. New York: Signet, 1983.

Ochshorn, Kathleen. "The Community of *Native Son*." *Mississippi Quarterly* 42 (1989): 387–92.

Paulson, Suzanne Morrow. *Flannery O'Connor: A Study of the Short Fiction*. Boston: Twayne, 1988.

Percy, Walker. *Lancelot*. New York: Farrar, Straus & Giroux, 1977.

————. *The Last Gentleman*. New York: Farrar, Straus & Giroux, 1966.

————. *Love in the Ruins*. New York: Farrar, Straus & Giroux, 1971.

————. *The Message in the Bottle*. New York: Farrar, Straus & Giroux, 1975.

————. "Mississippi: The Fallen Paradise." *Signposts in a Strange Land*. 39–52.

————. *The Moviegoer*. New York: Avon, 1980.

————. "The Reentry Option: An Interview with Walker Percy." By Jo Gulledge. *Southern Review* 20 (1984): 93–115.

————. *The Second Coming*. New York: Picador, 1999.

————. *Signposts in a Strange Land*. Ed. Patrick Samway. New York: Farrar, Straus & Giroux, 1991.

————. "A Talk with Walker Percy." By Zoltan Abadi-Nagy. *Southern Literary Journal* 6 (Fall 1973): 3–19.

————. *The Thanatos Syndrome*. New York: Farrar, Straus & Giroux, 1988.

————. "Walker Percy: An Interview." By Ben Forkner and J. Gerald Kennedy. *Delta* 13 (Nov. 1981): 1–20.

Percy, William Alexander. *Lanterns on the Levee: Recollections of a Planter's Son*. New York: Knopf, 1941.

Reilly, John M., ed. *Richard Wright: The Critical Reception*. New York: Franklin, 1978.

"Review of *A Lesson Before Dying*." *Black Scholar* 25 (Spring 1995): 66.

The Revolutionary Flame of Bandung. Jakarta: The Executive Command, n.d.

Rewak, William J. "James Agee's *Let Us Now Praise Famous Men*: The Shadow Over America." *Tennessee Studies in Literature* 21 (1976): 91–104.

Rideout, Walter B. *The Radical Novel in the United States. 1900–1954*. New York: Columbia UP, 1956.

Rigney, Barbara Hill. *The Voices of Toni Morrison*. Columbus: Ohio State UP, 1991.

Romulo, Carlos. *The Meaning of Bandung*. Chapel Hill: U of North Carolina P, 1956.

Roth, Henry. *Call It Sleep*. 1934. New York: Noonday, 1991.
———. *A Diving Rock on the Hudson*. New York: St. Martin's, 1995.
———. *From Bondage*. New York: St. Martin's, 1996.
———. *Mercy of a Rude Stream: A Star Shines over Mt. Morris Park*. New York: St. Martin's, 1994.
———. *Requiem for Harlem*. New York: St. Martin's, 1998.
———. *Shifting Landscape*. New York: St. Martin's, 1994.

Rowell, Charles H. "The Quarters: Ernest Gaines and the Sense of Place." *Southern Review* 21.3 (1985): 733–50.

Rubin, Louis D., Jr, and Robert D. Jacobs. *Southern Renascence: The Literature of the Modern South*. Baltimore: Johns Hopkins UP, 1953.

Said, Edward. *Culture and Imperialism*. New York: Vintage, 1994.

Savoy, Eric. "The Face of the Tenant: A Theory of American Gothic." *American Gothic: New Interventions in a National Narrative*. Ed. Robert K. Martin and Eric Savoy. Iowa City: U of Iowa P, 1997. 3–19.

Schenker, Daniel. "Walker Percy and the Problem of Cultural Criticism." *South Atlantic Review* 53.1 (1988): 83–97.

Schoenfeld, Bernard C. "Aiken, Agee, and Sandburg: A Memoir." *Virginia Quarterly Review* 59.2 (1983): 299–315.

Scruggs, Charles. *Sweet Home: Invisible Cities in the Afro-American Novel*. Baltimore: Johns Hopkins UP, 1993.

Shloss, Carol. "The Privilege of Perception." *Virginia Quarterly Review* 56 (1980): 596–611.

Smith, Barbara. "Toward a Black Feminist Criticism." *All the Women Are White, All the Blacks Are Men, But Some of Us Are Brave: Black Women's Studies*. Old Westbury, NY: The Feminist Press, 1982. 157–75.

Smith, Valerie. "Alienation and Creativity in *Native Son*." *Bigger Thomas*. Ed. Harold Bloom. New York: Chelsea House, 1990. 143–50.

Sommer, Doris. "Textual Conquests: On Readerly Competence and 'Minority' Literature." *Modern Language Quarterly* 54 (1993): 141–53.

Spivak, Gayatri. "Translator's Preface." *Imaginary Maps*. By Mahasweta Devi. Trans. and ed. Gayatri Spivak. New York: Routledge, 1995. xxiii–xxix.

Stampp, Kenneth M. *The Peculiar Institution: Slavery in the Ante-Bellum South*. New York: Vintage, 1956.

Staub, Michael. "As Close as You Can Get: Torment, Speech, and Listening in *Let Us Now Praise Famous Men*." *Mississippi Quarterly* 41.2 (1988): 147–60.

Steiner, George. *George Steiner: A Reader*. New York: Oxford UP, 1984.

Sturma, Lee. "Flannery O'Connor, Simone Weil, and the Virtue of Necessity." *Studies in the Literary Imagination* 20.2 (1987): 109–21.

Styron, William. *The Confessions of Nat Turner*. New York: Signet, 1968.
———. *Sophie's Choice*. New York: Modern Library, 1999.

Tate, Mary Barbara. "Flannery O'Connor at Home in Milledgeville." *Studies in the Literary Imagination* 20.2 (1987): 31–36.

Taylor, Clyde. "Black Writing as Immanent Humanism." *Southern Review* 21 (1985): 790–99.

Taylor, Gordon. *Chapters of Experience*. New York: St. Martin's, 1983.

Todorov, Tzvetan. *The Discovery of America*. New York: Harper and Row, 1984.

Tolson, Jay. *Pilgrim in the Ruins: A Life of Walker Percy*. New York: Simon and Schuster, 1992.

Vancil, David E. "Redemption According to Ernest Gaines." *African American Review* 28 (Fall 1994): 490.

Vinson, Audrey L. "The Deliverers: Ernest J. Gaines's Sacrificial Lambs." *Obsidian II* 2.1 (1987): 34–47.

Wagner-Martin, Linda. *"Let Us Now Praise Famous Men*—and Women: Agee's Absorption in the Sexual." *James Agee: Reconsiderations*. Ed. Michael A. Lofaro. Knoxville: U of Tennessee P, 1992. 44–58.

Walker, Margaret. *Richard Wright, Daemonic Genius: A Portrait of the Man; A Critical Look at His Work*. New York: Warner, 1988.

Weiss, M. Lynn. *Gertrude Stein and Richard Wright: The Poetics and Politics of Modernism*. Oxford: UP of Mississippi, 1998.

Werner, Craig. "Bigger's Blues: *Native Son* and the Articulation of Afro-American Modernism." *New Essays on* Native Son. Ed. Keneth Kinnamon. Cambridge: Cambridge UP, 1990. 117–52.

Westarp, Karl-Heinz. "Teilhard de Chardin's Impact on Flannery O'Connor: A Reading of 'Parker's Back.'" *The Flannery O'Connor Bulletin* 12 (Autumn 1983): 93–113.

White, Hayden. *Tropics of Discourse*. Baltimore: Johns Hopkins UP, 1985.

Wideman, John Edgar. "Preface." *Breaking Ice: An Anthology of Contemporary African-American Fiction*. Ed. Terry McMillan. New York: Penguin, 1990.

Wirth-Nesher, Hana. "Afterword." *Call It Sleep*. By Henry Roth. New York: Noonday, 1991. 443–62.

Wright, Richard. *Black Boy*. In *Later Works*. 1–365.
———. *Black Power*. New York: Harper, 1954.
———. *The Color Curtain: A Report on the Bandung Conference*. Cleveland: World, 1956.
———. *Later Works*. New York: Library of America, 1991.
———. *Native Son*. Restored Ed. New York: Harper Perennial, 1993.
———. *The Outsider*. In *Later Works*. 367–841.
———. *Pagan Spain*. 1956. London: Bodley Head, 1960.
———. *12 Million Black Voices*. 1941. New York: Arno, 1969.

Wyatt, David. *Prodigal Sons*. Baltimore: Johns Hopkins UP, 1980.

Wydeven, Joseph J. "Photography and Privacy: The Protests of Wright Morris and James Agee." *Midwest Quarterly* 23.1 (1981): 103–15.

Yaeger, Patricia. *Honey-Mad Women: Emancipatory Strategies in Women's Writing*. New York: Columbia UP, 1988.

Zhang Yan. "I Wish I Had Met Richard Wright at Bandung in 1955 (Reflections on a Conference Attended by Both Wright and the Author)." *Mississippi Quarterly* 50 (Spring 1997): 277–87.

Index

MODERN AMERICAN LITERATURE
New Approaches

Yoshinobu Hakutani, General Editor

The books in this series deal with many of the major writers known as American realists, modernists, and post-modernists from 1880 to the present. This category of writers will also include less known ethnic and minority writers, a majority of whom are African American, some are Native American, Mexican American, Japanese American, Chinese American, and others. The series might also include studies on well-known contemporary writers, such as James Dickey, Allen Ginsberg, Gary Snyder, John Barth, John Updike, and Joyce Carol Oates. In general, the series will reflect new critical approaches such as deconstructionism, new historicism, psychoanalytical criticism, gender criticism/feminism, and cultural criticism.

For additional information about this series or for the submission of manuscripts, please contact:

Peter Lang Publishing
Acquisitions Department
516 N. Charles St., 2nd Floor
Baltimore, MD 21201

To order other books in this series, please contact our Customer Service Department at:

800-770-LANG (within the U.S.)
(212) 647-7706 (outside the U.S.)
(212) 647-7707 FAX

Or browse online by series at:

www.peterlang.com